OSCAR WILDE was born in Dublin, Ireland, on October 16, 1854. He was an outstanding student of classics at Trinity College and, in 1874, entered Magdalen College, Oxford, where he won the Newdigate Prize with his poem "Ravenna" (1878). An early leader of the Aesthetic Movement, which advanced the concept of "art for art's sake," Wilde became a prominent personality in literary and social circles. His volume of fairy tales, *The Happy Prince and Other Tales* (1888), was followed by *The Picture of Dorian Gray* (1891) and *The House of Pomegranates* (1892). However, it was not until his play *Lady Windermere's Fan* (1892) was presented to the public that he became widely famous. *A Woman of No Importance* (1893), *An Ideal Husband* (1895), and *The Importance of Being Earnest* (1895) confirmed his stature as a dramatist. In 1895 he brought libel action against the Marquis of Queensbury, who had accused him of the crime of sodomy. He lost, however, and was sentenced under the Criminal Law Amendment Act to two years' imprisonment with hard labor. Upon his release in 1897, he settled in France, where he wrote his most powerful and enduring poem, "The Ballad of Reading Gaol" (1898). Wilde never returned to England; he died in Paris on November 30, 1900.

GARY SCHMIDC_____ ranger
*Wilde: Interpret_____ d His
Friends*. He live_____

D0980944

TWO PLAYS
BY OSCAR WILDE

An Ideal Husband
AND
*A Woman of No
Importance*

*With an Introduction by
Gary Schmidgall*

A SIGNET CLASSIC

SIGNET CLASSIC
Published by the Penguin Group
Penguin Books USA Inc., 375 Hudson Street,
New York, New York 10014, U.S.A.
Penguin Books Ltd, 27 Wrights Lane,
London W8 5TZ, England
Penguin Books Australia Ltd, Ringwood,
Victoria, Australia
Penguin Books Canada Ltd, 10 Alcorn Avenue,
Toronto, Ontario, Canada M4V 3B2
Penguin Books (N.Z.) Ltd, 182–190 Wairau Road,
Auckland 10, New Zealand

Penguin Books Ltd, Registered Offices:
Harmondsworth, Middlesex, England

Published by Signet Classic, an imprint of Dutton Signet,
a division of Penguin Books USA Inc.

First Signet Classic Printing, June, 1997
10 9 8 7 6 5 4 3 2 1

Introduction copyright © Gary Schmidgall, 1997
All rights reserved

 REGISTERED TRADEMARK—MARCA REGISTRADA

Library of Congress Catalog Card Number: 96–72085

Printed in the United States of America

Contents

Contents

Introduction

by Gary Schmidgall

When the box office manager came to write his memoir of fifty years at one of London's most venerable theaters, the Theatre Royal, Haymarket, he recalled, "The most difficult first-night allotment at which I ever assisted was that of Oscar Wilde's play, *A Woman of No Importance*." Wilde, it seems, had requested from the redoubtable Haymarket manager, Herbert Beerbohm Tree, forty of the best seats in the house for his entourage. He was, of course, willing to pay for them. Tree, who was also assuming the plum role of Lord Illingworth (Wilde's thinly disguised alter ego) in the production, did not like the smell of this. He insisted on knowing the names of those who would be attending the gala opening on April 19, 1893.

Wilde, by this time a London celebrity, was still riding the crest of a smashing success with the first of his four society comedies, *Lady Windermere's Fan*, which had run for an impressive six months the previous year. Tree's demand made him furious. "Do you think, my dear Tree, that I'm going to submit the names of my friends for your approval?" Tree pretended that he merely thought some of these forty friends might already have tickets set aside for them, but his suspicions were darker. Being accustomed to holding tyrannic sway in his own theater, he held firm. Further heated argument, deadlock, and Wilde fumed out ticketless. Later, the ticket manager tells us, "a better temper prevailed on both sides, and the matter was amicably compromised. The play was a great success."

Tree was not alone in his nervousness about Oscar and his kind. Much of respectable London, not to mention Victorian England, found something curiously repellent and subversive in Wilde's writings and in his behavior in society, which were to an astonishing degree reverse sides of the same coin. Lady Colin Campbell famously captured this animus when she called the notorious social butterfly a "great white caterpillar." Why the haughty resentment of Lady Campbell and the suspicions of Tree in 1893, at the midpoint of the mere half-dozen years or so in which Wilde wrote all his superb fictions, plays, and criticism?

Perhaps the best answer to this question lies in a brilliantly perceptive profile of Wilde that appeared in the *Anglo-American Times* on March 25, less than a month before the altercation in Tree's office. Its author was described merely as "An American," but it was in fact Tree's half brother, Max Beerbohm. As far as is known, this was the very first published work of Beerbohm's long and witty life, and one cannot imagine a more auspicious beginning.

Beerbohm, who was personally familiar with Wilde and his circle, begins cheekily by describing Wilde's "half-fatuous but wholly charming smile," his penchant for being "most exquisitely overdressed" and sporting a "bunch of Parma violets in his buttonhole," and his being fat in the fashion of "some huge overgrown schoolboy." But there are sly allusions to more profound unorthodoxy about this frightfully, not to say frighteningly, clever schoolboy. Beerbohm says Wilde's face and form are "excellently in accord with the strange, exotic reputation which is his." Mention is also made of the "admiring cohort of young men" who so disconcerted Tree. We also learn that, most un–Victorianly, Wilde is "indolent by nature, writing seldom and never save when the fancy seizes him."

He is also, most irksomely to a society so rigid and stultified as that of late Victorian England, simply *himself*. "He has passed through as many phases as Proteus," writes Beerbohm, "yet never surrendered one tittle of his personality." Wilde, in other words, was succeeding splendidly at being true to a lifelong credo, which he had most succinctly expressed in his 1891 essay, "The Soul of Man Under Socialism." It is not selfish to live as one wishes to live, he believed; true selfishness is "asking others to live as one wishes to live."

But it is when Beerbohm insists on taking Wilde seriously that he pierces home. He discerns beneath Wilde's inimitable paradoxes and epigrams a courageous personality possessed of a genuine philosophy. Anticipating the droll pun in the title of Wilde's most famous play, Beerbohm warns, "to say that Mr. Wilde is not in earnest is manifestly false. . . . No writer is more enamoured of purpose than he." And what is this purpose? The same one, Beerbohm shrewdly saw, that motivated the ancient gadfly of Athens: "If Wilde had lived in the days of Socrates he would surely have been impeached on a charge not only of 'making the worse cause appear the better'—for paradox as a method is never acceptable to the many—but also of 'corrupting the youth'; he would have been condemned, and would have drunk the hemlock under protest." And Beerbohm adds, "the harm that Mr. Wilde has done within a certain radius is incalculable."

"Literature always anticipates life," Wilde had observed several years before, and in his little essay Beerbohm was certainly anticipating Wilde's theatrical career—and his life. He was anticipating the glorious paradoxing dialogue of Lord Illingworth and Mrs. Allonby in *A Woman* and of Lord Goring, Mrs. Cheveley, and Mabel Chiltern in *An Ideal Husband.* He was prophesying Wilde's virtuoso dexterity, displayed in these two plays, of making the "worse" cause seem thrilling. On Wilde's topsy-turvy stage, narcissistic self-regard was preferable to "public charities," apolitical sloth superior to the "high moral tone" of Parliamentary debate, and risky philandering outshines "the beauty of our English home-life."

In casting Wilde as an intimidating though utterly charming philosopher, Beerbohm was also auguring well the exquisitely overdressed Lord Goring in *An Ideal Husband.* In one of the play's many fanciful stage directions, we learn about its most obvious "Oscar" character: "His are all the delicate fopperies of Fashion. One sees that he stands in immediate relation to modern life, makes it indeed, and so masters it. He is the first well-dressed philosopher in the history of thought."

And Beerbohm was, of course, anticipating the judicial catastrophe that fell upon Wilde exactly three months after the January 3, 1895, premiere of *An Ideal Husband.* For the "incalculable" harm he had wreaked upon Victorian complacencies and laws, he was not obliged to take a poison so quick-acting as the hemlock given to Socrates. Hemlock, however, might have been a blessing for Wilde. Having utterly lost his joy in life—as well as his fortune, fame, family, and creative powers—in cell C.3.3 of Reading Prison, he was, for the few years he survived after his release, a dead man walking.

The other deeply subversive and philosophical

Irishman loose on the English theatrical scene of the early 1890s, by the way, was Bernard Shaw, who was Wilde's almost exact contemporary. Though they were utterly incompatible in their styles and poses, they were mutual admirers of each other's stagecraft. Wilde even joked in a letter to Shaw about their constituting "the great Celtic School" in drama. They also saw eye to eye on the peculiarly Irish ruse of using laughter to incite serious thought. Shaw sensed this immediately in what they agreed was Opus 1 of the Celtic School: "My most serious and blunt statements sometimes raise a laugh and create an impression that I am intentionally jesting. I admit that some Irishmen do take advantage of the public in this way. Wilde, unquestionably the ablest of our dramatists, has done so in *Lady Windermere's Fan*."

Wilde would later play with precisely this paradox when he describes Lord Goring, in *An Ideal Husband*, as "fond of being misunderstood. It gives him a post of vantage." Later, he has Goring observe, "I usually say what I really think. A great mistake nowadays. It makes one so liable to be misunderstood." Small wonder, as we shall see later, that Shaw thought *Husband* the greatest of Wilde's plays.

Lady Campbell attended Opus 3 of the great Celtic School, *A Woman of No Importance* (Opus 2 was Shaw's *Widowers' Houses*). She aired her disgust in the manner of one of Wilde's stuffy old stage battle-axes, and Shaw leapt to Wilde's defense in a letter to her. "You are wrong to rail thus at Oscar. . . . There are only two literary schools in England today: the Norwegian school [of Ibsen, Strindberg] and the Irish school. Our school is the Irish school, and Wilde is doing us good service in teaching the theatrical public that 'a play' may be a playing with ideas instead of a feast of sham emotions compounded from dog's eared prescriptions. Compare his epigrams with the platitudes of the rest—and this is taking him beyond all bounds in his praise. No, let us be just to the great white caterpillar: he is no blockhead and he finishes his work, which puts him high above his rivals here in London."

Had Shaw seen the play? Well, no. His duties as a music critic had kept him away, but with characteristic impertinence he did not let this small matter get in the way of his jousting. Besides, he was right. Shaw was always right, as he often boasted at the top of his voice. On the other hand, William Archer—the eminent drama critic, translator and knight in armor for Ibsen in England—did attend the opening of *A Woman*, and he published a glowing notice in the *World* that exactly echoed Shaw. "The one essential fact about Mr. Oscar Wilde's dramatic work is that it must be taken on the very highest plane of modern English drama, and furthermore, that it stands alone on that plane. In intellectual calibre, artistic competence—ay, and in dramatic instinct to boot—Mr. Wilde has no rival among his fellow-workers for the stage."

So charmed by the review was Wilde that he could not resist thanking Archer for "your luminous, brilliant criticism of my play." Wilde's taste for rave reviews never left him. Shortly after *An Ideal Husband* premiered, an interviewer for the *St. James's Gazette* asked his definition of ideal dramatic criticism. He replied, "As far as my work is concerned, unqualified appreciation."

Both Shaw and Archer were strenuous and ubiquitous cultural revolutionaries, though. Any siege machine useful to their project of dismantling the grievously stolid Victorian establishment was bound to appeal to them. Wilde's comedies—the product of a mind both Falstaffian and Hamlet-like, carefree and corrosive—suited their purposes admirably. By no means as radical theatrically as Ibsen's plays or Strindberg's, Wilde's comedies boasted so many well-placed petards for hoisting English hypocrisies and pieties that Shaw and Archer were willing to overlook some of their hoary stage business, melodramatic devices, and a difficulty with plotting which Wilde at first fussed over and later had the good sense to revel in.

Punch, the venerable humor magazine of the establishment, turned a more jaundiced eye upon the Haymarket stage. Its review, under the headline "A Work of—Some Importance," begins with a quotation from the *"Uncommonplace Book* of Mr. O. Wilde": "Let who will give me a plot, *I* will write their dialogue." Mr. Punch was irked that for the first two acts of *A Woman* "Mr. Wilde's *dramatis personae* are all gathered together, with nothing to do and plenty to say." At a loss for a plot, the author "cannot keep melodrama out of his play, and what ought to have been a comedy pure and simple (or the reverse) drops suddenly into old-fashioned theatrical melodrama."

Also condemned are some "wearisome tirades," like the young American girl's withering attack on English society as "shallow, selfish, foolish" and the country as lying like "a leper in purple." Such a speech, dripping with Shavian venom, it must be admitted, does almost topple the comedy. (Wilde also wrote a lengthy, teeth-baring attack on the "Puritan spirit" as the "real enemy of modern life," to be spoken by Illingworth to Gerald at the beginning of act three. In it "this England of ours" is said to behave like Caliban, Shakespeare's monster of ignorance, for nine months of the year and Molière's hypocritical Tartuffe for the other three. Tree succeeded in convincing the playwright to delete this Swiftian outburst entirely.)

What saved the day, *Punch* makes clear, was the "Christy-Minstrel epigrammatic dialogue" and "the first-rate acting all round." Singled out for praise was the drollery of Rose Leclercq playing old Lady Hunstanton in "the Mrs. Nickleby vein." Leclercq would two years afterward assure herself a place in the comic pantheon as the first Lady Bracknell in *Earnest*. Even more impressive, *Punch* reported, was the husband-and-wife team at the top of the bill: "It would be difficult, if not impossible, to find fault with Mr. Tree's Lord Illingworth. Mrs. Tree, as Mrs. Allonby, is a very charming battledore in the game of repartee-shuttlecock."

The review closes with a satirical recipe for playmaking extrapolated from *A Woman of No Importance.* It is ill-meant but, one must grant, pretty well on target: "First catch your epigrams: preserve them for use: serve with *sauce piquante un peu risquée* distributed impartially among a variety of non-essential *dramatis personae,* invented for the purpose. Provide fine old crusted copybook moral sentiments to suit *bourgeois* palate: throw in the safe situation of someone concealed, behind door or window, listening to a private conversation. Add one well-tried effective dramatic situation to bring down curtain on penultimate Act, and there's a stage-dish to set before the appreciative B.P., if only it can be presented to them effectively garnished by a clever and popular Manager at a first-class theatre."

His play *was* thus garnished, and the British Public indeed appreciative, in spite of most reviewers turning in dismissive notices. The few good reviews counted, however. The Prince of Wales came the second night and was most complimentary backstage afterward. The London *Times* must have sold tickets when, aping Wilde's penchant for alliteration, it reported on his "passion for paradox, persiflage, and proverbial perversity." Royalties of about £100 a week began to flow in, easing somewhat the strained finances at the Wilde family household in Tite Street, Chelsea, where Oscar and his wife Constance were raising two boys, seven-year-old Cyril and six-year-old Vyvyan. *A Woman* ran for four months, closing on August 16. The following December it opened in New York City, and in October 1894, a few days before Wilde's fortieth birthday, it appeared in book form. The dedication was to the beautiful, fashionable (and philandering) society hostess, Gladys Countess de Grey.

As Wilde was putting the finishing touches on the play, an actor inquired whether there was a part in it for him. He replied, "In my new play there are very few men's parts—it is a woman's play." This is largely true. The sole character with credible access to emotion is Mrs. Arbuthnot, and Wilde had originally planned *Mrs. Arbuthnot* as the play's title. Mrs. Allonby makes a feisty Beatrice to Lord Illingworth's Benedick in the "merry war" scenes which are one of the best things in *A Woman*. Juicy, too, are the smaller caricature roles at which Wilde was so good: the terminally blasé Lady Hunstanton, for whom "the secret of life is to take things very, very easily"; the terminally literal-minded Lady Caroline, who opines, "Femininity is the quality I admire most in women"; and Hester, the pert young American with the tendency to lecture. "All Americans lecture," says Illingworth, "I suppose it is something in their climate."

The irresistibly paradoxing Illingworth aside, the play's men do come up short, but always with comic rewards. Young Gerald's ingenue status will strike most in the audience as overdone, and Lady Caroline's husband exists solely to submit meekly to her orders. Kelvil, the Member of Parliament who thinks

Purity is "the one subject of really national importance," is a mere excuse (and an effective one) for Wilde's many epigrams skewering politicians and their awful wake of platitudes. Even Archdeacon Daubeny's wife, whose ailments multiply alarmingly as the play unfolds, upstages her husband—and she never even appears.

Superficially, then, one can agree with Wilde about women being of considerable importance in this play. Examined more carefully, however, *A Woman of No Importance* is most decidedly a man's play—or rather *one* man's play. The most important member of its *dramatis personae*, like the Archdeacon's wife, never appears on stage: Wilde himself. Beerbohm ended his *Anglo-American* essay with this wise admonition: "it is not by his works alone that we must judge him, but by the personality of which his works are a part." Wilde's personality and intellect are everywhere at work in the play, and they are what make *A Woman* not merely a charming comedy but also a substantial one even a century after its premiere.

Wilde's "presence" in *A Woman* is multifaceted, as it was in all his 1890s plays. Most obviously, with Lord Illingworth he deployed his real-life pose as a flawlessly witty and distinctively dressed London dandy. He had done the same thing with Lord Henry Wotton in his notorious novel *The Picture of Dorian Gray* and with Lord Darlington in *Lady Windermere's Fan*. He would do so again with Lord Goring in *An Ideal Husband* and Algernon Moncrieff in *The Importance of Being Earnest*.

As almost always in Wilde's writings, details large and small from his own life abound. A remark about Lady Caroline's black sheep brother, Lord Henry Weston, having "a hideous smile and a hideous past" glances blatantly to *Dorian Gray*. Giving Mrs. Allonby's tedious husband (who never appears) the name of Ernest was probably Wilde's private joke to delight his dear friend Ada Leverson; her much older husband Ernest was well known to be a bland City of London fellow. Lord Alfred smokes gold-tipped cigarettes, which everyone in the first-night audience would have delighted to recognize as an "Oscar" touch.

Other autobiographical moments are striking and poignant. In act two comes a wicked exchange. Lord Illingworth: "All women become like their mothers. That is their tragedy." Mrs. Allonby: "No man does. That is his." But Wilde *did* become like his flamboyantly bohemian mother, Lady Wilde, who liked to style herself Speranza. She lived nearby in Chelsea, and Wilde was deeply devoted to her. His relations with his philandering father, Sir William Wilde, were distant, which perhaps helps to explain why fathers have such a bad time of it in *A Woman* and *An Ideal Husband*. Wilde doted so much on this exchange, by the way, that he recycled it verbatim in *Earnest*.

Illingworth's praise of youth at the opening of the third act also touches on a central fact of Wilde's life: "There is nothing like youth. The middle-aged are mortgaged to Life. The old are in life's lumber-room. But youth is the lord of life." Wilde, however, not only adored youth but also youths—male youths. The friendly appeal of twenty-something Gerald for forty-ish Lord Illingworth, in fact, delicately reflects the intense relationship Wilde had been having with Lord Alfred ("Bosie") Douglas while *A Woman* was being written. The play, in fact, was created partly in a rented farmhouse in Norfolk, while Wilde's wife and children were vacationing far away in Devon. Bosie, then aged twenty-two, stayed with him there for ten days during this time. A few months later Wilde wrote the famous youth-adoring letter to Bosie that would do such damage at his trial for what the

English law called "gross indecency": "My Own Boy, Your sonnet is quite lovely, and it is a marvel that those red rose-leaf lips of yours should have been made no less for music of song than for madness of kisses." Wilde completed his "woman's play" in Devon, with not only his sons but also Bosie and a Cambridge tutor on hand to amuse him.

Constance was safely distant in Europe at the time. The fact that Wilde's marriage had for several years been turning into a sad one of convenience gives a keen edge to *A Woman*'s sometimes hilarious, sometimes brutal attacks on marriage and its sarcastic debate about the Ideal Husband. "My husband is a sort of promissory note," says Mrs. Allonby, "I'm tired of meeting him." Lord Illingworth remarks, more chillingly, "Men marry because they are tired; women because they are curious. Both are disappointed." Exactly at the time Wilde was composing such bon mots, he was boldly increasing his activities in London's homosexual underground, and his circle of friends there was widening. Rumors of this were bound to spread; clearly, they had reached the ears of Bosie's furious father, the Marquess of Queensberry, and the manager's office at the Haymarket, not to mention the Tite Street hearth. Constance's thoughts could not have been cheerful when, at the premiere of *A Woman*, she heard the unhappily married Mrs. Allonby say that husbands are "always trying to escape from us"—or Lady Stutfield boast that she can tell a man with "home claims upon his life" by "a very, very sad expression in his eyes."

Eerily, there is even something of Wilde's own *future* in the play, literature once again anticipating life. As he sat in prison, the happiness of his two boys destroyed forever, he perhaps recalled his Lord Illingworth's caustic remark, "Children begin by loving their parents. After a time they judge them. Rarely, if ever, do they forgive them."

Finally, though, the most important product of Wilde's presence in *A Woman* is the rich vein of serious fun that runs through the action. Of course, the silly fun is not to be sniffed at either: Lady Caroline calling M.P. Kelvil "Mr. Kettle" in spite of constant corrections, for example. Or the repeated displays of Lady Hunstanton's appallingly bad memory: when Lady Belton left her husband for another man, she recalls, "poor Lord Belton died three days afterwards of joy, or gout. I forget which." But it is the serious or, as Beerbohm dared to say, earnest fun in the play that gives it continuing theatrical life.

For Wilde had a very serious side that was not entirely disguised by his flippant sense of the ridiculous. He was, in short, a deep and deeply subversive thinker. Lady Hunstanton might be speaking for the obtuse British Public when she remarks, "Now I am quite out of my depth. I usually am when Lord Illingworth says anything." And Lord Illingworth might, as he nearly always does, be speaking for his creator when he comments on the "vulgar habit . . . people have nowadays of asking one, after one has given them an idea, whether one is serious or not."

Wilde gave his audiences ideas, serious ones, but they came cleverly disguised by laughter. Wilde himself boasted of this technique to Tree after a preliminary reading of *A Woman*: "I have given them what they like, so that they may learn to appreciate what I like to give them." And what he liked to give them was his view that late-Victorian society and culture were a ghastly botch—or, as Mrs. Allonby says flatly of the Ideal Husband, "The institution is wrong." "England is the land of intellectual fogs," Wilde wrote to Shaw as he was completing *A Woman*, and his efforts to lift that fog are evident throughout the play.

Delivering such criticism could not be done by hectoring, as Hester, the truth-saying American, does in act two. Deftness and dizzying paradox were infinitely preferable, and Wilde gives us the perfect image for this in his play. Lord Illingworth says to Mrs. Allonby of her sharp tongue, "You fence divinely. But the button has come off your foil." Wilde himself rarely let his button fall from his rapier, at least in his four comedies. He thrust home constantly, but no blood was let. He may have had something of Hamlet's dark cast of mind and his eye for the rottenness around him, but not Shakespeare's taste for carnage on stage.

And so Wilde made a joyous and ingratiating dismantler. He worked upon his audience precisely as Lord Illingworth works on Lady Hunstanton: "I don't know how it is . . . but everything you have said today seems to me excessively immoral. It has been most interesting, listening to you." If one serious idea underlies all of Wilde's charming satire, it is the idea of freedom. A desire for freedom from Victorian morality causes Illingworth to admire an orchid "as beautiful as the seven deadly sins" in Lady Hunstanton's conservatory ("I will certainly speak to the gardener," she says). A desire for freedom from politicians' cant causes him to assert that "the human being becomes a bore" who begins to take sides on political issues. Wilde also wanted freedom from the Victorian ideal of manliness. That is why he allows hopelessly stuffy Lady Stutfield to announce, "I think a man should look very, very strong, and that his chin should be quite, quite square." Wilde's chin was far from square . . . and he did not look strong. His fleshy form was designed, rather, for "lolling on a sofa," as Wilde instructs Lord Illingworth to do at the beginning of act three.

He wanted freedom, as Beerbohm observed, to be himself. In his life, as in his theatrical drawing rooms, the word *selfish* is by no means pejorative. "Self-culture is the true ideal of man," Wilde wrote in his essay "The Critic as Artist," and this animating principle lies behind all his comedies. It would lie, too, behind his personal tragedy.

Wilde also despised the tyranny of do-gooders, whose notion of "good" is usually of their, rather than one's own, devising. In all his plays Wilde is relentless in his attack on philanthropists and seekers after good-conduct prizes. Like Illingworth, he is excessively proud of his "bad qualities," and Lady Hunstanton's compliment to him in act three perfectly captures the Wildean method: "You always find that one's most glaring fault is one's most important virtue."

The play's many allusions to the tyranny of marriage have already been noticed. Almost as constant are Wilde's satirical barbs aimed at liberation from the tyranny of "society" and "fashion" and any form of education that is not *self*-education. Lady Hunstanton's notion that too much care taken with education "shuts one out from so much" is typically Wildean wisdom. And Kelvil is a typical Wilde stage idiot; he assumes that temptation exists to be resisted.

Finally, and most Wildean of all, is the praise in *A Woman* for running toward danger or, as Lady Caroline says, "playing with fire." The autobiographical element (the prophetic element, too) again emerges when Mrs. Allonby asserts the joys of bad conduct. She says women have a much better time than men because "there are far more things forbidden to us than are forbidden to them." She is sorry that "danger has become so rare in modern life," a view, we have seen, that Wilde was recklessly acting upon in his own adulterous marauding.

Lady Hunstanton tells Illingworth she has the dim idea that he is "always on the side of the sinners."

His creator certainly was. He had written in his superb essay "The Critic as Artist" (1890), "What is termed Sin is an essential element of progress. Without it the world would stagnate." He would doubtless had been delighted at the conclusion of James Joyce, some years later, that sin in fact is "the pulse of Wilde's art." This supremely bad quality of his is the main reason Wilde's spectacular fall from grace was greeted with such pleasure and relief by most Englishmen.

It is also why, when he died in 1900, the London *Times* obituary summed up his comedies by saying their two most prominent qualities were "a paradoxical humour and a perverted outlook on life." Wilde's imprisonment five years before was the occasion for a young Willa Cather, sounding very much like the browbeating American girl in *A Woman*, to condemn Wilde more colorfully: "He used the holiest things for ends the basest. He made the ark of the covenant a trick box, the anointed spear a harlequin's wand; he took the tapers from the altar for festival lights and brandished them in the wild melee of a carnival night." A few years before the doors of Reading Prison shut upon him, Wilde would have professed himself thrilled by such "praise."

Cather also wrote dolefully, "Civilization shudders at his name." She was half right. Victorian civilization did shudder at Wilde, but during the early 1890s it was mainly from laughter. Richard Le Gallienne made just this point marvelously—and underscored Wilde's subversive brilliance—when he observed, long after his old friend was dead, "Oscar made dying Victorianism laugh at itself, and it may be said to have died of the laughter."

Soon after the premiere of *A Woman*, Shaw left London's concert halls and opera houses to become a drama critic. Though rambunctious dudgeon was still his chief pose, when he attended Wilde's next play, *An Ideal Husband*, he was thoroughly smitten. Congratulating the playwright on the "subtle and pervading levity" of the evening, Shaw summarized, "Mr. Wilde is to me our only thorough playwright. He plays with everything: with wit, with philosophy, with drama, with actors and audience, with the whole theatre." Then Wilde's fellow Irishman adds, intent on irritating his English readers: "Such a feat scandalizes the Englishman, who can no more play with wit and philosophy than he can with a football or cricket bat."

The immortal *Importance of Being Earnest*, by contrast, Shaw reviewed six weeks later and said it left him feeling he had wasted an evening. The second act left him "out of sorts," the third "out of temper." "Though extremely funny . . . essentially hateful." *An Ideal Husband* is a superb play indeed, one must think, if it could put Algernon Moncrieff's hilarious disappearing muffins and Miss Prism's infamous handbag in the shade.

I paused at length over *A Woman of No Importance* out of an instinct to side with the underdog, which it certainly has been among Wilde connoisseurs. H. Montgomery Hyde thought it the only one of the four that had dated, and Wilde's biographer Richard Ellmann called it the "weakest." Lord Alfred Douglas, in spite of his being "in" the play shadowing the character of Gerald, wrote nearly a half century later that it was the "least good"—though he did add that "it is redeemed by its delightful dialogue and its firework display of sparkling wit." Finally, though, one must grant that the ground for superlatives is much firmer when we turn to *An Ideal Husband*.

Bosie certainly felt this way. Though he counted *Windermere* and *Earnest* superior plays, he ventured

that *An Ideal Husband* "is better than any other plays
(except perhaps for two of Mr. Shaw's) that have
been staged since Wilde's death. I firmly believe that
in time to come these four plays will be as regularly
produced as the plays of Sheridan . . . and that they
will in the long run outlive all the English plays of
the epoch extending from the 'Nineties to the present
day." Bosie published his view in 1940, making this
a particularly impressive compliment. The play has
indeed been regularly revived, most recently in the
vicinity of the 1995 centennials of its premiere and
the trials at the Old Bailey. In 1996 *The New Yorker*
said of the Broadway revival directed by Peter Hall
that "the evening flies by in a flash of epigrammatic splendor."

    To be sure, *An Ideal Husband* and *A Woman* have
very much in common. Their comic routines, for example: Lady Hunstanton's bad memory is passed on
to Lady Markby: "She ultimately was so broken-
hearted that she went into a convent, or on the operatic stage, I forget which." Further delectable variations
are spun on former themes: neckties and youth are
again praised, the "utterly tedious amusements" of
country-house life again ridiculed. Old bones of
comic contention are fretted, most notably marriage
and the Ideal Husband, producing such drollery as
Lady Markby's "Ah, I forgot, your husband is an
exception. Mine is the general rule, and nothing ages
a woman so rapidly as having married the general
rule." Also, Wilde was not above tinkering with and
recycling a good line. Mrs. Allonby's adoring London
dinner parties because "the clever people never listen, and the stupid people never talk" becomes Mrs.
Cheveley's bon mot, "If one could only teach the
English how to talk, and the Irish how to listen, society here would be quite civilized."

    But most obviously, the two plays (indeed, all four

of the comedies) could easily be played by about the same company of actors. A fine Mrs. Allonby would find tart-tongued Mrs. Cheveley fits like a glove, and likewise for the roles of the devilishly clever Lords Illingworth and Goring, the pathetically suffering Mrs. Arbuthnot and Lady Chiltern, the Lady Bracknell-like Ladies Hunstanton and Markby, and the utterly pert Hester Worsley and Mabel Chiltern. And the actor doing the butler Farquhar in *A Woman* would be thrilled at the increased opportunity for scene stealing that Wilde gave to the butler Phipps in *Husband*.

And yet . . . *An Ideal Husband* does stand somewhat apart from the other three Wilde comedies. For one thing, it has grander proportions. Like *Hamlet*, it is its author's lengthiest theater piece, nearly half again as long as each of the other comedies. Also, like *Hamlet*, there is an extraordinary philosophical resonance to this play, a more tantalizing interpenetration of the serious and the comic. Then there is the title character, for whom there is no real equivalent in *A Woman* or any other Wilde play. Though Sir Robert Chiltern is like Lord Illingworth in having a dark secret from a distant past, he has little of that lord's mercurial wit. He has instead, and takes very seriously (as does his wife, with a vengeance), something unheard of in Wilde's plays: a moral dilemma. To be or not to be honest and own up to his crime and, even worse, his hypocrisy—that is the play's question. The pompous twit Kelvil in *A Woman* and Sir Robert are both Wildean attacks upon the cant of politicians, but the latter represents a huge advance in Wilde's interest in creating and then exploring the interior of a character. But as we shall see, he had very good reason to be interested in Sir Robert.

What enabled this leap forward was, of all things, a plot. The day after *An Ideal Husband* opened, Wilde gave an interview to *The Sketch* about his play-writing technique (this brilliant performance is included in this edition). Here he loftily confronted the complaint that his plays lacked action. "I wrote the first act of *A Woman of No Importance* in answer to the critics who said that *Lady Windermere's Fan* lacked action. In the act in question there was absolutely no action at all. It was a perfect act." In his new play there were still scenes of superb standing and talking, but there was also an "action," about which Wilde proceeded to lecture the *Sketch* interviewer—Irishmen also lecture sometimes. "English critics always confuse the action of a play with the incidents of a melodrama," Wilde points out, and what makes *Husband* a special play in his oeuvre is that, beyond the incidents of a missing brooch and purloined letter, it has a cogent, focused action. It is centered upon Mrs. Cheveley's devastating assault on what Lord Caversham, in the last act, calls Chiltern's "high character, high moral tone, high principles."

All of Wilde's own assaults upon the same targets in Victorian society, elsewhere in the play, reflect off this central action, like light beamed at a revolving glass ball. It was doubtless because Wilde was, as Mrs. Marchmont says of Lord Goring, "in the camp of the enemy, as usual," that *Husband* so tickled Shaw. Shaw doted on the grace with which the demolition was achieved, praising "the imperturbable good sense and good manners with which Mr. Wilde makes his wit pleasant to his comparatively stupid audience."

Wilde was a born devil's advocate, and he had the very good fortune to be born in an age of false saints. What makes *Husband* still very much worth attending is that his devilishly clever good sense is still needed: it is, a century later, still an astonishingly timely play. The case of insider trading and the founding of a successful political career on prior corruption could scarcely be more apropos. Nearly every daily newspaper brings us new reason to agree with Mrs. Cheveley's caustic appraisal: "Nowadays, with our modern mania for morality, everyone has to pose as a paragon of purity, incorruptibility, and all the other seven deadly virtues—and what is the result? You all go over like ninepins—one after the other. Not a year passes in England without somebody disappearing." On both sides of the Atlantic, and many places else, this is still true. Embarrassing "disappearances"—sometimes into prison—are commonplace among our leaders of commerce and government.

Much else about our public life has changed little in a hundred years. The banalities uttered by our elected leaders are perfectly squelched by Mrs. Cheveley, varying Shakespeare's phrase: "In modern life nothing produces such an effect as a good platitude. It makes the whole world kin." Lord Goring's view of politics still holds true, too: "a man who can't talk morality twice a week to a large, popular, immoral audience is quite over as a serious politician." Politicians, being mostly lawyers, are still a pretty dull race, and so Lord Goring's rejection of his father's idea of entering Parliament could apply to the U.S. Congress as well: "only people who look dull ever get into the House of Commons, and only people who are dull ever succeed there."

Members of the moral majority still hector the citizenry, and *An Ideal Husband* continues Wilde's unremitting attack upon these tyrants of propriety so eager to impose their notions of "good" and "evil" on innocent bystanders. "Morality is simply the attitude we adopt towards people whom we personally dislike," says Mrs. Cheveley to Lady Chiltern. Another familiar part of the play's background is the "loathsome joy," mentioned by Mrs. Cheveley, of journalists and newspaper publishers in dragging public figures into the mire. As Sir Robert himself observes, "spies are of no use nowadays. Their profession is over. The newspapers do their work instead." A *Husband* set in our own *fin de siècle* would of course add "television" too.

Wilde was, in his flourishing years, always a trenchant observer of the profound emptiness and falsity of the so-called fashionable life, to which (be it also said) he was utterly devoted. Most of his observations about Society have lost none of their pungency. It is still filled with "beautiful idiots and brilliant lunatics," as twenty-something Mabel Chiltern proudly asserts. Getting to know such people can still be unwise: "as a rule, everybody turns out to be somebody else," says Lady Markby. The round of merry fast-lane parties still tempts us to lose our way: "Horribly tedious! Never know why I go. Never know why I go anywhere," says Lady Basildon. Old fogeys still gripe like Lord Caversham about the antics of generation-Xers: "The thing has gone to the dogs, a lot of damned nobodies talking about nothing." Or they try to pass on good advice—the *only* thing to do with good advice, says Lord Goring. This from Lady Markby to young Mabel certainly remains true today for fashion's slaves: "Nothing is so dangerous as being too modern. One is apt to grow old-fashioned quite suddenly."

Finally, however, as with *A Woman*, the main fascination of *An Ideal Husband* lies in the author's presence within and behind the action. "Enter invisible," Shakespeare's famous stage direction for Ariel in *The Tempest*, perfectly describes what Wilde so often does in his play. What is more, he was unduly proud of the fact. Two weeks after the premiere, the *St. James's Gazette* published a dashingly arrogant Wilde interview, which is also included in this edition. The interviewer, though unnamed, was very likely Robert Ross, his most devoted friend and eventual literary executor (also, some think, his first male lover). Wilde is asked at one point, "Have you heard it said that all the characters in your play talk as you do?" His reply is candid and revealing:

> Rumours of that kind have reached me from time to time. . . . The fact is that it is only in the last few years that the dramatic critic has had the opportunity of seeing plays written by any one who has a mastery of style. In the case of a dramatist also an artist, it is impossible not to feel that the work of art, to be a work of art, must be dominated by the artist. Every play of Shakespeare is dominated by Shakespeare. Ibsen and Dumas dominate their works. My works are dominated by myself.

Some of the characters who helped Wilde to dominate his play must have been obvious to everyone in the opening-night audience. He had given his alter ego in *Dorian Gray*, Lord Henry, the nickname of Prince Paradox, and the skillful paradoxing heard in the voices of Mrs. Cheveley and Lord Goring is vintage Wilde. Of course, one need not even hear Lord Goring to know Wilde typecast him as himself, for he decks the dandy out, in one of the play's many precious stage directions, with a buttonhole, silk hat, Inverness cape, white gloves, and a Louis Seize cane—a perfect Oscarian costume.

Elsewhere, Wilde's delighted partisanship for selfishness, especially that of the youthful kind, is charmingly disseminated through Mabel Chiltern, who says the only charity that interests her is "in aid of the Undeserving." In the end, she makes a perfect mate for Lord Goring, who believes, "To love oneself is the beginning of a lifelong romance." Wilde's drawling contralto is also distinctly heard in venerable Lady Markby's brief but hilarious scenes, notably when she bemoans the degeneration of her husband through service in the House of Commons or country society being "honeycombed" with curates. "It is most irreligious," she says.

The charm and interest of all these characters derived from the transparent ways they mimicked Wilde's public persona. He dominates other characters in *An Ideal Husband* in more subtly concealed ways—ways its first audiences could not possibly have appreciated. Only his intimates and a few shrewd observers at the Haymarket would have caught the comic, poignant, sometimes even searing allusions to his private life woven through the play. As our knowledge of Wilde's personal life during the writing of the play has been filled out in subsequent decades, the play's autobiographical ironies—as opposed to the stage irony that Wilde loved too well—have added enormously to the play's interest.

Entering into the autobiographical "play within the play," so to speak, requires some detective work, and it never hurts to begin an investigation with the butler. As it happens, Wilde leaves a perfect self-sketch in his stage direction introducing Lord Goring's butler in act three: "the distinction of Phipps is his impassivity. He has been termed by enthusiasts the Ideal Butler. The Sphinx is not so uncommunicable. He is a mask with a manner. Of his intellectual or emotional life, history knows nothing." As regarded his own emotional life, at least, Wilde had very good reason for wearing a mask and seeming to the public impassive.

In order to write the play and pursue his secret homosexual life more vigorously, in fact, Wilde had from October 1893 rented rooms in Piccadilly, a safe distance from the Tite Street house. His two occupations at this time are clearly revealed in a letter he wrote to a young admirer the next February: "Will you come and see me? I am writing a play, and go to St. James's Place, number 10, where I have rooms, every day at 11.30. Come on Tuesday about 12.30, will you? But perhaps you are busy? Still, we can meet, surely, some day. Your handwriting fascinates me, your praise charms me." A short time later Wilde actually sent a typescript of *An Ideal Husband* to another idolatrous young admirer, one who apparently had written confessionally. In reply, Wilde confessed too—and told of doing what Sir Robert Chiltern must do through most of the play: hide a dark secret behind a mask. "To the world I seem, by intention on my part, a dilettante and dandy merely—it is not wise to show one's heart to the world. . . . In so vulgar an age as this we all need masks." And Wilde adds sadly, "Write to me about yourself; tell me your life and loves, and all that keeps you wondering. Who are you? (what a difficult question for any of us to answer!)."

Moments of genuine emotional force are not common in Wilde's plays, but Chiltern's heartbreaking outburst in act two is certainly one of them: "I would to God I had been able to tell the truth . . . to live the truth. Ah! that is the great thing in life, to live the truth." This eruption is made all the more poignant by our knowledge of letters such as those just quoted and of the sham Wilde's life had become by the time he created Sir Robert. For different reasons, neither the character nor its creator could safely reveal who he was and what he had done.

Our knowledge of Wilde's private life also helps us to enjoy the relationship between insouciant Lord Goring and his blithering father. Doubtless this plot thread owed something to the constant fighting that took place between Lord Alfred Douglas and his father, the fiery, boorish Marquess of Queensberry, during the play's composition. In April 1893 the father had threatened to disown Bosie if he did not cease his association with Wilde. Bosie telegraphed in reply, "What a funny little man you are," and was soon planning a secret May meeting with Wilde in Florence. In June Queensberry burst into Tite Street to make a similar demand of Wilde, who later described him as "waving his small hands in the air in epileptic fury" and "uttering every foul word his foul mind could think of." Queensberry's awareness that he was being caricatured in Lord Caversham probably egged him on, a few weeks after *Husband*'s premiere, to plan a disturbance of the premiere of *Earnest* with a bouquet of vegetables (he was recognized and refused entrance).

Far more daring was the extent to which Wilde put himself and his wife, Constance, into the characters of Sir Robert and Lady Chiltern. Wilde could have looked in a mirror for many of the details of his description of Sir Robert in a first-act stage direction: a man of forty, clean-shaven, not popular but "intensely admired by the few," possessed of a manner of "perfect distinction, with a touch of pride," and one whose "thought and emotion were each isolated in its own sphere."

It is now impossible to experience *An Ideal Husband* as innocently as its first audience did, for the Wildes' marital tragedy, its denouement just weeks away, haunts many of its scenes—Chiltern, for instance, lecturing his wife before she learns his secret, "public and private life are different things. They have different laws, and move on different lines." Many of Wilde's friends, like Ross, More Adey, or Frank Harris, must have warned Wilde often as Mrs. Cheveley warns Chiltern, "You know you are standing on the edge of a precipice." And Lady Chiltern pleads with her husband, "I know that there are men with horrible secrets in their lives—men who have done some shameful thing, and who in some critical moment have to pay for it. . . . Robert, is there in your life any secret dishonour or disgrace?"

Constance, however, was fully aware of her husband's horrible secret—had probably been gallantly living with it for several years—by the time this play about their marriage appeared. There must have been a scene or two in Tite Street in which she chided her husband as Lady Chiltern does: "Oh! What a mask you have been wearing all these years! A horrible painted mask!" And how chagrined Constance must have been to hear Lord Goring say on the Haymarket stage that "no man should have a secret from his own wife. She invariably finds it out. Women have a wonderful instinct about things. They can discover everything except the obvious." This wife, however, had a keen grasp of the obvious.

Constance may even have been aware that, like Sir Robert, her husband had been subject to a blackmail attempt over compromising correspondence that had been stolen. In February 1893, Wilde met a seventeen-year-old named Alfred Wood, an acquaintance of Bosie's, and had a brief liaison with him, including assignations at the Tite Street house when his family was away. Wilde's love letters to Bosie came into Wood's hands, and he appeared one day at the Haymarket during rehearsals for A Woman to make an extortionate offer. He was only half-successful. For £30 Wilde got back all but the one letter that eventually found its way into court, and Wood was packed off to America for a year.

The way Wilde and his wife lived their lives is also faithfully reflected in the play. At Lady Chiltern's core, one might even say, is Constance Mary

Lloyd, whom Wilde married in 1883. Gertrude Chiltern is a gallingly ideal and conventional spouse. "She stands apart as good women do," says her husband sullenly, "pitiless in her perfection." Mrs. Cheveley professes to see her moral rectitude even in her handwriting—"The ten commandments in every stroke of the pen." Of their school days together, she says snidely, "I have a distinct recollection of Lady Chiltern always getting the good conduct prize!" She is the kind of "thoroughly sensible wife" that Lord Goring thinks would reduce him to idiocy in six months.

It is impossible to avoid seeing all this as shamefully ungallant exaggeration of Constance's performance as a wife throughout their marriage. She had been ideal in all the respectable Victorian ways—devoted mother, well-dressed beauty, conscientious keeper of a well-known "house beautiful" (she was interviewed in the papers about it), and a forward-thinking participant in many of the worthy causes that Wilde loved to ridicule. She was a member of the Rational Dress Society, edited its *Gazette*, belonged to the Chelsea Women's Liberal Association, and was a protégée of the Dowager Baroness Sandhurst, a pillar of English church work. And she seems to have managed with poise the hard duty of living with a famous genius. For, as Mabel Chiltern notes, geniuses "are always thinking about themselves, when I want them to be thinking about me."

Constance got little thought from her genius in their last years together, it is clear. Tellingly, she was not present when, after the premiere of *An Ideal Husband*, Wilde dined at the Albemarle Club with Bosie, Tree, and Beerbohm. Telling, too, that she appears to have developed in the preceding months something of a crush, revealed in letters, for her husband's publisher, Arthur Humphreys. Being an ideal wife, she had even undertaken in 1894 a small anthology of Oscar's witticisms titled *Oscariana*, to be published by Humphreys. Imagine her thoughts at having to cull such gems inscribing her own life as "Women are a decorative sex. They never have anything to say, but say it charmingly" or "How marriage ruins a man! It is as demoralizing as cigarettes, and far more expensive." When Wilde saw her handiwork, he wrote privately to Humphreys to say how badly Constance had botched it, quoting too much or too little of his witticisms. "My wife does not understand my art," Wilde later wrote to Ross from prison, and this appears to have been the case.

Wilde, for his part, was carrying on the dangerous life of succumbing to temptation praised by Sir Robert in act two: "I tell you there are terrible temptations that it requires strength, strength and courage, to yield to. To stake all one's life on a single moment, to risk everything on one throw, whether the stake be power or pleasure, I care not—there is no weakness in that." Two weeks later, he was staking all on pleasure once again, traveling for ten days to North Africa with Bosie amid rehearsals for *Earnest*. Two months later he would stake all on a throw in court and lose everything.

There is thus perhaps no more poignant and ironic speech in *Husband*, or anything else Wilde ever wrote, than Sir Robert's lament, heartfelt by the character and the author, near the final curtain: "Loveless marriages are horrible. But there is one thing worse than an absolutely loveless marriage. A marriage in which there is love, but on one side only; faith, but on one side only; devotion, but on one side only, and in which of the two hearts one is sure to be broken."

All of this personal history makes the denouement Wilde wrought for *An Ideal Husband* fascinating indeed. He works something of a miracle in the last act, with the far-fetched help of a stolen brooch with the concealed lock and perhaps the most odious speech he ever penned. This is the one in which Lord Goring becomes a "philosopher" and urges Lady Chiltern to embrace her grievously tainted husband: "Women are not meant to judge us, but to forgive us. . . . A man's life is of more value than a woman's. . . . A woman who can keep a man's love, and love him in return, has done all the world wants of women." Like Kate's famous speech of abasement to her husband, Petruchio, at the end of Shakespeare's *Taming of the Shrew*, Goring's ghastly performance is hard to stomach and demands more finesse than anything else in the play. A director today would probably urge his actress to put on a caustic edge when, a few moments later, Lady Chiltern, having decided to "do the right thing," repeats verbatim Lord Goring's assertion about a man's life being of more value than a woman's.

With heavy irony Wilde decorates the octagon room of Chiltern's Grosvenor Square mansion with a tapestry depicting "The Triumph of Love." In the end, however, he achieves the theatrical coup of saving the loveless marriage through Lady Chiltern's charity. When Sir Robert asks if love or pity motivates her, true to her "ennobling" character, she replies, "Love, and only love. For both of us a new life is beginning."

Here, for once and stunningly, Wilde's literature did *not* anticipate his life. On February 18, Queensberry left at Wilde's club the infamous calling card branding him a sodomite, and Wilde initiated the libel suit that would end disastrously and result in his arrest. Before that, on March 7, Constance did behave briefly like Lady Chiltern; in a show of wifely solidarity, she consented to the ignominy of attending a performance of *Earnest* in the company of

Oscar and Bosie, who later recalled she had tears in her eyes all through the evening. Wilde repaid her gallantry by disappearing with Bosie for a week in Monte Carlo later in the month.

After the conviction, there were some who took Lord Goring's approach with her. "I will make her stand by her husband. That is the only thing for her to do. That is the only thing for any woman to do." Constance mentions such advice in a letter written from Italy just before Oscar's release from prison: "I have again had pressure put upon me to persuade me to go back to Oscar, but . . . that is impossible. I am told that I would save a human soul, but I have no influence over Oscar. I have had none, and though I think he is affectionate I see no reason for believing that I should be able now to perform a miracle." There was to be no stagy miracle of reconciliation or new life here.

As between the love or pity Sir Robert inquires about at play's end, Constance chose pity: "My poor misguided husband, who is weak rather than wicked, repents most bitterly all his past madness and I cannot refuse to him the forgiveness that he has asked." But when she was importuned by go-betweens about Oscar's difficult straits after prison, she wrote witheringly, on March 10, 1898, "I don't care to be written as though it were my fault. He says he loved me too much and that that is better than hate! This is true abstractedly, but his was an unnatural love, a madness that I think is worse than hate. I have no hatred for him, but I confess that I am afraid of him."

Less than a month later Constance was lying in the Protestant Cemetery in Genoa. She had died from complications of a spinal injury suffered when, her children off at school and her husband perhaps on one of his trips with Bosie, she was alone in Tite Street and fell down a flight of stairs. Her gravestone read, "CONSTANCE MARY/DAUGHTER OF HORACE LLOYD, Q.C." Wilde visited the grave soon after and wrote touchingly to Ross, who had been very close to his wife: "It was very tragic seeing her name carved on a tomb—her surname, my name not mentioned of course. . . . I brought some flowers. I was deeply affected. . . . Life is a very terrible thing." But to another London friend he wrote, not even mentioning the cemetery, "On my way I stopped at Genoa, where I met a beautiful young actor, a Florentine, whom I wildly loved. He has the strange name of Didaco. He had the look of Romeo, without Romeo's sadness: a face chiseled for high romance. We spent three days together." That "wildly" is the saddest pun Oscar ever invented.

André Gide was at first very severe in his criticism of Wilde's plays. The two plays printed here, in particular, he initially regarded merely as "dramatic entertainment which was itself 'of no importance.'" Much later he admitted that he had taken his cue from fashion and the playwright himself: "The English as well as the French led me to do this, and Wilde himself at times showed an amusing disdain for his comedies, by which I allowed myself to be taken in." But then he began to see them as more substantial. When Arthur Ransome published his early Wilde biography in 1912, Gide chided him in his journal for not seeing how "revelatory—I was going to say confidential" are *A Woman of No Importance* and *An Ideal Husband*. Gide summed up, "To be sure I have not come to consider these plays perfect; but they appear to me, now that I know them better, as among the most curious, the most significant and, whatever may have been said about them, the newest things in the contemporary theater."

One can no longer say these plays are new; they

were not even that on the days they premiered. But otherwise Gide's summary is fair. They are not perfect. Wilde's taste for moments of heavy stage irony is excessive—as for example when Lord Caversham goes on about Sir Robert's "probity" and "high moral tone" long after the audience knows the worst about him. Other moments are impossibly stagy—Mrs. Arbuthnot's first entrance, for example, upon Hester's self-righteous announcement, "Let all women who have sinned be punished." The stage directions in *Husband* are self-indulgent (Mabel Chiltern is "like a Tanagra statuette, and would be rather annoyed if she were told so") and sometimes unintentionally funny, as when Lady Chiltern collapses at the end of act two: "Pale with anguish, bewildered, helpless, she sways like a plant in the water. Her hands, outstretched, seem to tremble in the air like blossoms in the wind." And once too often Wilde asks his actors to do what actors should never, *ever* be asked to do: bite their lip to convey consternation.

What saves these plays, as Gide wrote and I hope I have suggested in the preceding pages, is that they are "significant" and "curious"—significant in the philosophical depth concealed beneath their charming surface and curious in the personality that produced their brilliantly individual style. There is no better witness to Wilde's philosophical depth than Shaw, and in the sole essay he devoted to Wilde (oddly enough, it appeared only in German in a Viennese newspaper in 1905), there is a splendid summary that can serve as a conclusion. Wilde's "originality lay in his superiority to the delusive morality of our time," Shaw wrote. "Wilde's claim to greatness rests on the fact that our morality could not fool him, and the moralists of his time could neither break him nor dishonor him. He held fast to his pose to the very last, because it was an honest pose." How Wilde and Mrs. Cheveley would have liked that paradox! Shaw then ends his essay, "For that very reason it has been unspeakably annoying to English morality which, too, is a pose, but without benefit of the excuse of being an honest one."

For a witness to offer a summary about the curious infusion of personality (and personal life) in the Wilde style, one might turn to his generous, loyal, and boisterous friend Frank Harris, to whom *An Ideal Husband* was so gratefully dedicated when Wilde published it in 1899. Harris's 1916 Wilde biography may not be factually reliable, but few have conveyed his personality more vividly. Instead, however, let us cross the Atlantic Ocean and give the task of summing up Wilde—I hope he would appreciate the irony—to an American even more harshly judgmental and inclined to lecture than Miss Worsley in *A Woman*: H. L. Mencken. When Harris's book appeared, Mencken reviewed it for the *Smart Set* and, being Mencken, bluntly called Wilde many terrible names: "a fop and a snob, a toady and a social pusher, a coward and an ingrate, a glutton and a grafter, a plagiarist and a mountebank." One wonders whimsically if Wilde, like Lord Illingworth, would have considered himself flattered by this long list of "bad qualities."

All the more powerful and moving, then, is the climax of the review, in which Mencken eloquently praises the double-helix relationship of style and personality in Wilde. In his oeuvre, Mencken says, there are

rare and precious things—the best wit that England has produced since the Restoration, three or four incomparably amusing plays, the noblest ballad in English [*The Ballad of Reading Gaol*], some essays that have left their mark, a story or two of the first rank, an endless stream of good writing. Wilde, beyond all things was a stylist, and perhaps the greatest of his time. . . . The charm of his style is in the very least of his writings, his squibs, the speeches in his plays, his letters to the newspapers. He could no more put words together without making music than he could face a temptation without yielding to it. Our depressing Puritan philosophy is against such men. It distrusts the artist with a great distrust; it sees in him a prophet of that innocent gusto, that pagan joy in life, which is its chief abomination; it is always ecstatically eager to discover him a criminal, and to fall upon him with the utmost rigors of its savage justice. Wilde was in the wrong country and the wrong time.

Or, one might say, exactly the right country at the right time.

Mencken concludes that the Harris biography "is a grim and unsentimentalized record, but there is shot through it the enchantment of a personality that, after all, must have had something fine and inspiring in it." Readers of *A Woman of No Importance* and *An Ideal Husband* will find them similarly shot through with Wilde's enchanting personality.

An Ideal Husband

An Ideal Husband was first performed at the Theatre Royal, Haymarket on 3rd January, 1895, with the following cast:

THE EARL OF CAVERSHAM, K.G.	Mr. Alfred Bishop
LORD GORING (his son)	Mr. Charles H. Hawtrey
SIR ROBERT CHILTERN (Under-Secretary for Foreign Affairs)	Mr. Lewis Waller
VICOMTE DE NANJAC (Attaché at the French Embassy in London)	Mr. Cosmo Stuart
MR. MONTFORD	Mr. Henry Stanford
PHIPPS (Lord Goring's servant)	Mr. C. H. Brookfield
MASON (Butler to Sir Robert Chiltern)	Mr. H. Deane
FOOTMAN (at Lord Goring's)	Mr. Charles Meyrick

FOOTMAN (at Sir Robert Chiltern's)	Mr. Goodhart
LADY CHILTERN	Miss Julia Neilson
LADY MARKBY	Miss Fanny Brough
LADY BASILDON	Miss Vane Featherston
MRS. MARCHMONT	Miss Helen Forsyth
MISS MABEL CHILTERN (Sir Robert's sister)	Miss Maude Millett
MRS. CHEVELEY	Miss Florence West

Stage Manager: Mr. Shelton
Musical Director: Mr. Carl Armbruster

THE SCENES OF THE PLAY

The action of the play is completed within twenty-four hours.

First Act

SCENE

The octagon room at Sir Robert Chiltern's house in Grosvenor Square.

The room is brilliantly lighted and full of guests. At the top of the staircase stands LADY CHILTERN, *a woman of grave Greek beauty, about twenty-seven years of age. She receives the guests as they come up. Over the well of the staircase hangs a great chandelier with wax lights, which illumine a large eighteenth-century French tapestry—representing the Triumph of Love, from a design by Boucher—that is stretched on the staircase well. On the right is the entrance to the music-room. The sound of a string quartette is faintly heard. The entrance on the left leads to other reception-rooms.* MRS. MARCHMONT *and* LADY BASILDON, *two very pretty women, are seated together on a Louis Seize sofa. They are types of exquisite fragility. Their affectation of manner has a delicate charm. Watteau would have loved to paint them.*

MRS. MARCHMONT. Going on to the Hartlocks' to-night, Margaret?

9

LADY BASILDON. I suppose so. Are you?

MRS. MARCHMONT. Yes. Horribly tedious parties they give, don't they?

LADY BASILDON. Horribly tedious! Never know why I go. Never know why I go anywhere.

MRS. MARCHMONT. I come here to be educated.

LADY BASILDON. Ah! I hate being educated!

MRS. MARCHMONT. So do I. It puts one almost on a level with the commercial classes, doesn't it? But dear Gertrude Chiltern is always telling me that I should have some serious purpose in life. So I come here to try to find one.

LADY BASILDON (*looking round through her lorgnette*). I don't see anybody here tonight whom one could possibly call a serious purpose. The man who took me in to dinner talked to me about his wife the whole time.

MRS. MARCHMONT. How very trivial of him!

LADY BASILDON. Terribly trivial! What did your man talk about?

MRS. MARCHMONT. About myself.

LADY BASILDON (*languidly*). And were you interested?

MRS. MARCHMONT (*shaking her head*). Not in the smallest degree.

LADY BASILDON. What martyrs we are, dear Margaret!

MRS. MARCHMONT (*rising*). And how well it becomes us, Olivia!

They rise and go towards the music-room. The VI-COMTE DE NANJAC, a young attaché known for his

10

*neckties and his Anglomania, approaches with a low
bow, and enters into conversation.*

MASON (*announcing guests from the top of the staircase*). Mr. and Lady Jane Barford. Lord Caversham.

Enter LORD CAVERSHAM, *an old gentleman of seventy, wearing the riband and star of the Garter. A
fine Whig type. Rather like a portrait by Lawrence.*

LORD CAVERSHAM. Good evening, Lady Chiltern!
Has my good-for-nothing young son been here?

LADY CHILTERN (*smiling*). I don't think Lord Goring
has arrived yet.

MABEL CHILTERN (*coming up to* LORD CAVERSHAM).
Why do you call Lord Goring good-for-nothing?

MABEL CHILTERN *is a perfect example of the English
type of prettiness, the apple-blossom type. She has
all the fragrance and freedom of a flower. There is
ripple after ripple of sunlight in her hair, and the
little mouth, with its parted lips, is expectant, like
the mouth of a child. She has the fascinating tyranny
of youth, and the astonishing courage of innocence.
To sane people she is not reminiscent of any work
of art. But she is really like a Tanagra statuette, and
would be rather annoyed if she were told so.*

LORD CAVERSHAM. Because he leads such an idle
life.

MABEL CHILTERN. How can you say such a thing?
Why, he rides in the Row at ten o'clock in the
morning, goes to the Opera three times a week,
changes his clothes at least five times a day, and

dines out every night of the season. You don't call that leading an idle life, do you?

LORD CAVERSHAM (*looking at her with a kindly twinkle in his eye*). You are a very charming young lady!

MABEL CHILTERN. How sweet of you to say that, Lord Caversham! Do come to us more often. You know we are always at home on Wednesdays, and you look so well with your star!

LORD CAVERSHAM. Never go anywhere now. Sick of London Society. Shouldn't mind being introduced to my own tailor; he always votes on the right side. But object strongly to being sent down to dinner with my wife's milliner. Never could stand Lady Caversham's bonnets.

MABEL CHILTERN. Oh, I love London Society! I think it has immensely improved. It is entirely composed now of beautiful idiots and brilliant lunatics. Just what Society should be.

LORD CAVERSHAM. Hum! Which is Goring? Beautiful idiot, or the other thing?

MABEL CHILTERN (*gravely*). I have been obliged for the present to put Lord Goring into a class quite by himself. But he is developing charmingly!

LORD CAVERSHAM. Into what?

MABEL CHILTERN (*with a little curtsey*). I hope to let you know very soon, Lord Caversham!

MASON (*announcing guests*). Lady Markby. Mrs. Cheveley.

Enter LADY MARKBY *and* MRS. CHEVELEY. LADY MARKBY *is a pleasant, kindly, popular woman, with grey hair à la marquise and good lace.* MRS. CHEVE-

LEY, *who accompanies her, is tall and rather slight. Lips very thin and highly-coloured, a line of scarlet on a pallid face. Venetian red hair, aquiline nose, and long throat. Rouge accentuates the natural paleness of her complexion. Grey-green eyes that move restlessly. She is in heliotrope, with diamonds. She looks rather like an orchid, and makes great demands on one's curiosity. In all her movements she is extremely graceful. A work of art, on the whole, but showing the influence of too many schools.*

LADY MARKBY. Good evening, dear Gertrude! So kind of you to let me bring my friend, Mrs. Cheveley. Two such charming women should know each other!

LADY CHILTERN (*advances toward* MRS. CHEVELEY *with a sweet smile. Then suddenly stops, and bows rather distantly*). I think Mrs. Cheveley and I have met before. I did not know she had married a second time.

LADY MARKBY (*genially*). Ah, nowadays people marry as often as they can, don't they? It is most fashionable. (*To* DUCHESS OF MARYBOROUGH.) Dear Duchess, and how is the Duke? Brain still weak, I suppose? Well, that is only to be expected, is it not? His good father was just the same. There is nothing like race, is there?

MRS. CHEVELEY (*playing with her fan*). But have we really met before, Lady Chiltern? I can't remember where. I have been out of England for so long.

13

LADY CHILTERN. We were at school together, Mrs. Cheveley.

MRS. CHEVELEY (*superciliously*). Indeed? I have forgotten all about my schooldays. I have a vague impression that they were detestable.

LADY CHILTERN (*coldly*). I am not surprised!

MRS. CHEVELEY (*in her sweetest manner*). Do you know, I am quite looking forward to meeting your clever husband, Lady Chiltern. Since he has been at the Foreign Office, he has been so much talked of in Vienna. They actually succeed in spelling his name right in the newspapers. That in itself is fame, on the continent.

LADY CHILTERN. I hardly think there will be much in common between you and my husband, Mrs. Cheveley! (*Moves away.*)

VICOMTE DE NANJAC. Ah! chère Madame, quelle surprise! I have not seen you since Berlin!

MRS. CHEVELEY. Not since Berlin, Vicomte. Five years ago!

VICOMTE DE NANJAC. And you are younger and more beautiful than ever. How do you manage it?

MRS. CHEVELEY. By making it a rule only to talk to perfectly charming people like yourself.

VICOMTE DE NANJAC. Ah! you flatter me. You butter me, as they say here.

MRS. CHEVELEY. Do they say that here? How dreadful of them!

VICOMTE DE NANJAC. Yes, they have a wonderful language. It should be more widely known.

SIR ROBERT CHILTERN *enters. A man of forty, but looking somewhat younger. Clean-shaven, with finely-cut features, dark-haired and dark-eyed. A personality of mark. Not popular—few personalities are. But intensely admired by the few, and deeply respected by the many. The note of his manner is that of perfect distinction, with a slight touch of pride. One feels that he is conscious of the success he has made in life. A nervous temperament, with a tired look. The firmly-chiselled mouth and chin contrast strikingly with the romantic expression in the deep-set eyes. The variance is suggestive of an almost complete separation of passion and intellect, as though thought and emotion were each isolated in its own sphere through some violence of will-power. There is nervousness in the nostrils, and in the pale, thin, painted hands. It would be inaccurate to call him picturesque. Picturesqueness cannot survive the House of Commons. But Vandyck would have liked to have painted his head.*

SIR ROBERT CHILTERN. Good evening, Lady Markby! I hope you have brought Sir John with you?

LADY MARKBY. Oh! I have brought a much more charming person than Sir John. Sir John's temper since he has taken seriously to politics has become quite unbearable. Really, now that the House of Commons is trying to become useful, it does a great deal of harm.

SIR ROBERT CHILTERN. I hope not, Lady Markby. At any rate we do our best to waste the public time, don't we? But who is this charming person you have been kind enough to bring to us?

LADY MARKBY. Her name is Mrs. Cheveley. One of the Dorsetshire Cheveleys, I suppose. But I really don't know. Families are so mixed nowadays. Indeed, as a rule, everybody turns out to be somebody else.

SIR ROBERT CHILTERN. Mrs. Cheveley? I seem to know the name.

LADY MARKBY. She has just arrived from Vienna.

SIR ROBERT CHILTERN. Ah! yes. I think I know whom you mean.

LADY MARKBY. Oh! she goes everywhere there, and has such pleasant scandals about all her friends. I really must go to Vienna next winter. I hope there is a good chef at the Embassy.

SIR ROBERT CHILTERN. If there is not, the Ambassador will certainly have to be recalled. Pray point out Mrs. Cheveley to me. I should like to see her.

LADY MARKBY. Let me introduce you. (*To* MRS. CHEVELEY.) My dear, Sir Robert Chiltern is dying to know you!

SIR ROBERT CHILTERN (*bowing*). Every one is dying to know the brilliant Mrs. Cheveley. Our attachés at Vienna write to us about nothing else.

MRS. CHEVELEY. Thank you, Sir Robert. An acquaintance that begins with a compliment is sure to develop into a real friendship. It starts in the right manner. And I find that I know Lady Chiltern already.

SIR ROBERT CHILTERN. Really?

MRS. CHEVELEY. Yes. She has just reminded me that we were at school together. I remember it perfectly now. She always got the good conduct prize. I have a distinct recollection of Lady Chiltern always getting the good conduct prize!

SIR ROBERT CHILTERN (*smiling*). And what prizes did you get, Mrs. Cheveley?

MRS. CHEVELEY. My prizes came a little later on in life. I don't think any of them were for good conduct. I forget!

SIR ROBERT CHILTERN. I am sure they were for something charming!

MRS. CHEVELEY. I don't know that women are always rewarded for being charming. I think they are usually punished for it! Certainly, more women grow old nowadays through the faithfulness of their admirers than through anything else! At least that is the only way I can account for the terribly haggard look of most of your pretty women in London!

SIR ROBERT CHILTERN. What an appalling philosophy that sounds! To attempt to classify you, Mrs. Cheveley, would be an impertinence. But may I ask, at heart, are you an optimist or a pessimist? Those seem to be the only two fashionable religious left to us nowadays.

MRS. CHEVELEY. Oh, I'm neither. Optimism begins in a broad grin, and Pessimism ends with blue spectacles. Besides, they are both of them merely poses.

SIR ROBERT CHILTERN. You prefer to be natural?

MRS. CHEVELEY. Sometimes. But it is such a very difficult pose to keep up.

SIR ROBERT CHILTERN. What would those modern psychological novelists, of whom we hear so much, say to such a theory as that?

MRS. CHEVELEY. Ah! the strength of women comes from the fact that psychology cannot explain us. Men can be analysed, women . . . merely adored.

SIR ROBERT CHILTERN. You think science cannot grapple with the problem of women?

MRS. CHEVELEY. Science can never grapple with the irrational. That is why it has no future before it, in this world.

SIR ROBERT CHILTERN. And women represent the irrational.

MRS. CHEVELEY. Well-dressed women do.

SIR ROBERT CHILTERN (*with a polite bow*). I fear I could hardly agree with you there. But do sit down. And now tell me, what makes you leave your brilliant Vienna for our gloomy London—or perhaps the question is indiscreet?

MRS. CHEVELEY. Questions are never indiscreet. Answers sometimes are.

SIR ROBERT CHILTERN. Well, at any rate, may I know if it is politics or pleasure?

MRS. CHEVELEY. Politics are my only pleasure. You see nowadays it is not fashionable to flirt till one is forty, or to be romantic till one is forty-five, so we poor women who are under thirty, or say we are, have nothing open to us but politics or philanthropy. And philanthropy seems to me to have become simply the refuge of people who wish to annoy their fellow-creatures. I prefer politics. I think they are more . . . becoming!

SIR ROBERT CHILTERN. A political life is a noble career!

MRS. CHEVELEY. Sometimes. And sometimes it is a clever game, Sir Robert. And sometimes it is a great nuisance.

SIR ROBERT CHILTERN. Which do you find it?

MRS. CHEVELEY. I? A combination of all three. (*Drops her fan.*)

SIR ROBERT CHILTERN (*picks up fan*). Allow me!

MRS. CHEVELEY. Thanks.

SIR ROBERT CHILTERN. But you have not told me yet what makes you honour London so suddenly. Our season is almost over.

MRS. CHEVELEY. Oh! I don't care about the London season! It is too matrimonial. People are either hunting for husbands, or hiding from them. I wanted to meet you. It is quite true. You know what a woman's curiosity is. Almost as great as a man's! I wanted immensely to meet you, and . . . to ask you to do something for me.

SIR ROBERT CHILTERN. I hope it is not a little thing, Mrs. Cheveley. I find that little things are so very difficult to do.

MRS. CHEVELEY (*after a moment's reflection*). No, I don't think it is quite a little thing.

SIR ROBERT CHILTERN. I am so glad. Do tell me what it is.

MRS. CHEVELEY. Later on. (*Rises.*) And now may I walk through your beautiful house? I hear your pictures are charming. Poor Baron Arnheim—you remember the Baron—used to tell me you had some wonderful Corots.

SIR ROBERT CHILTERN (*with an almost imperceptible start*). Did you know Baron Arnheim well?

MRS. CHEVELEY (*smiling*). Intimately. Did you?

SIR ROBERT CHILTERN. At one time.

MRS. CHEVELEY. Wonderful man, wasn't he?

SIR ROBERT CHILTERN (*after a pause*). He was very remarkable, in many ways.

MRS. CHEVELEY. I often think it such a pity he never wrote his memoirs. They would have been most interesting.

SIR ROBERT CHILTERN. Yes: he knew men and cities well, like the old Greek.

MRS. CHEVELEY. Without the dreadful disadvantage of having a Penelope waiting at home for him.

MASON. Lord Goring.

Enter LORD GORING. *Thirty-four, but always says he is younger. A well-bred, expressionless face. He is clever, but would not like to be thought so. A flawless dandy, he would be annoyed if he were considered romantic. He plays with life, and is on perfectly good terms with the world. He is fond of being misunderstood. It gives him a post of vantage.*

SIR ROBERT CHILTERN. Good evening, my dear Arthur! Mrs. Cheveley, allow me to introduce to you Lord Goring, the idlest man in London.

MRS. CHEVELEY. I have met Lord Goring before.

LORD GORING (*bowing*). I did not think you would remember me, Mrs. Cheveley.

MRS. CHEVELEY. My memory is under admirable control. And are you still a bachelor?

LORD GORING. I . . . believe so.

MRS. CHEVELEY. How very romantic!

LORD GORING. Oh! I am not at all romantic. I am not old enough. I leave romance to my seniors.

SIR ROBERT CHILTERN. Lord Goring is the result of Boodle's Club, Mrs. Cheveley.

MRS. CHEVELEY. He reflects every credit on the institution.

LORD GORING. May I ask are you staying in London long?

MRS. CHEVELEY. That depends partly on the weather, partly on the cooking, and partly on Sir Robert.

SIR ROBERT CHILTERN. You are not going to plunge us into a European war, I hope?

MRS. CHEVELEY. There is no danger, at present!

She nods to LORD GORING, *with a look of amusement in her eyes, and goes out with* SIR ROBERT CHILTERN. LORD GORING *saunters over to* MABEL CHILTERN.

MABEL CHILTERN. You are very late!

LORD GORING. Have you missed me?

MABEL CHILTERN. Awfully!

LORD GORING. Then I am sorry I did not stay away longer. I like being missed.

MABEL CHILTERN. How very selfish of you!

LORD GORING. I am very selfish.

MABEL CHILTERN. You are always telling me of your bad qualities, Lord Goring.

LORD GORING. I have only told you half of them as yet, Miss Mabel!

MABEL CHILTERN. Are the others very bad?

LORD GORING. Quite dreadful! When I think of them at night I go to sleep at once.

MABEL CHILTERN. Well, I delight in your bad qualities. I wouldn't have you part with one of them.

LORD GORING. How very nice of you! But then you are always nice. By the way, I want to ask you a question, Miss Mabel. Who brought Mrs. Cheveley here? That woman in heliotrope, who has just gone out of the room with your brother?

MABEL CHILTERN. Oh, I think Lady Markby brought her. Why do you ask?

LORD GORING. I haven't seen her for years, that is all.

MABEL CHILTERN. What an absurd reason!

LORD GORING. All reasons are absurd.

MABEL CHILTERN. What sort of a woman is she?

LORD GORING. Oh! a genius in the daytime and a beauty at night!

MABEL CHILTERN. I dislike her already.

LORD GORING. That shows your admirable good taste.

VICOMTE DE NANJAC (*approaching*). Ah, the English young lady is the dragon of good taste, is she not? Quite the dragon of good taste.

LORD GORING. So the newspapers are always telling us.

VICOMTE DE NANJAC. I read all your English newspapers, I find them so amusing.

LORD GORING. Then, my dear Nanjac, you must certainly read between the lines.

VICOMTE DE NANJAC. I should like to, but my profes-
sor objects. (*To* MABEL CHILTERN.) May I have the
pleasure of escorting you to the music-room,
Mademoiselle?

MABEL CHILTERN (*looking very disappointed*). Delighted, Vicomte, quite delighted! (*Turning to*
LORD GORING.) Aren't you coming to the music-
room?

LORD GORING. Not if there is any music going on,
Miss Mabel.

MABEL CHILTERN (*severely*). The music is in German.
You would not understand it.

Goes out with the VICOMTE DE NANJAC. LORD CAVER-
SHAM *comes up to his son.*

LORD CAVERSHAM. Well, sir! what are you doing
here? Wasting your life as usual! You should be
in bed, sir. You keep too late hours! I heard of
you the other night at Lady Rufford's dancing
till four o'clock in the morning!

LORD GORING. Only a quarter to four, father.

LORD CAVERSHAM. Can't make out how you stand
London Society. The thing has gone to the dogs,
a lot of damned nobodies talking about nothing.

LORD GORING. I love talking about nothing, father.
It is the only thing I know anything about.

23

LORD CAVERSHAM. You seem to me to be living entirely for pleasure.

LORD GORING. What else is there to live for, father? Nothing ages like happiness.

LORD CAVERSHAM. You are heartless, sir, very heartless!

LORD GORING. I hope not, father. Good evening, Lady Basildon!

LADY BASILDON (*arching two pretty eyebrows*). Are you here? I had no idea you ever came to political parties!

LORD GORING. I adore political parties. They are the only place left to us where people don't talk politics.

LADY BASILDON. I delight in talking politics. I talk them all day long. But I can't bear listening to them. I don't know how the unfortunate men in the House stand these long debates.

LORD GORING. By never listening.

LADY BASILDON. Really?

LORD GORING (*in his most serious manner*). Of course. You see, it is a very dangerous thing to listen. If one listens one may be convinced; and a man who allows himself to be convinced by an argument is a thoroughly unreasonable person.

LADY BASILDON. Ah! that accounts for so much in men that I have never understood, and so much in women that their husbands never appreciate in them!

MRS. MARCHMONT (*with a sigh*). Our husbands never appreciate anything in us. We have to go to others for that!

LADY BASILDON (*emphatically*). Yes, always to others, have we not?

LORD GORING (*smiling*). And those are the views of the two ladies who are known to have the most admirable husbands in London.

MRS. MARCHMONT. That is exactly what we can't stand. My Reginald is quite hopelessly faultless. He is really unendurably so, at times! There is not the smallest element of excitement in knowing him.

LORD GORING. How terrible! Really, the thing should be more widely known!

LADY BASILDON. Basildon is quite as bad; he is as domestic as if he was a bachelor.

MRS. MARCHMONT (*pressing* LADY BASILDON'S *hand*). My poor Olivia! We have married perfect husbands, and we are well punished for it.

LORD GORING. I should have thought it was the husbands who were punished.

MRS. MARCHMONT (*drawing herself up*). Oh dear, no! They are as happy as possible! And as for trusting us, it is tragic how much they trust us.

LADY BASILDON. Perfectly tragic!

LORD GORING. Or comic, Lady Basildon?

LADY BASILDON. Certainly not comic, Lord Goring. How unkind of you to suggest such a thing!

MRS. MARCHMONT. I am afraid Lord Goring is in the camp of the enemy, as usual. I saw him talking to that Mrs. Cheveley when he came in.

LORD GORING. Handsome woman, Mrs. Cheveley!

LADY BASILDON (*stiffly*). Please don't praise other

women in our presence. You might wait for us to do that!

LORD GORING. I did wait.

MRS. MARCHMONT. Well, we are not going to praise her. I hear she went to the Opera on Monday night, and told Tommy Rufford at supper that, as far as she could see, London Society was entirely made up of dowdies and dandies.

LORD GORING. She is quite right, too. The men are all dowdies and the women are all dandies, aren't they?

MRS. MARCHMONT (*after a pause*). Oh! do you really think that is what Mrs. Cheveley meant?

LORD GORING. Of course. And a very sensible remark for Mrs. Cheveley to make, too.

Enter MABEL CHILTERN. *She joins the group.*

MABEL CHILTERN. Why are you talking about Mrs. Cheveley? Everybody is talking about Mrs. Cheveley! Lord Goring says—what did you say, Lord Goring, about Mrs. Cheveley? Oh! I remember, that she was a genius in the daytime and a beauty at night.

LADY BASILDON. What a horrid combination! So very unnatural!

MRS. MARCHMONT (*in her most dreamy manner*). I like looking at geniuses, and listening to beautiful people.

LORD GORING. Ah! that is morbid of you, Mrs. Marchmont!

MRS. MARCHMONT (*brightening to a look of real plea-*

sure). I am so glad to hear you say that. Marchmont and I have been married for seven years, and he has never once told me that I was morbid. Men are so painfully unobservant!

LADY BASILDON (*turning to her*). I have always said, dear Margaret, that you were the most morbid person in London.

MRS. MARCHMONT. Ah! but you are always sympathetic, Olivia!

MABEL CHILTERN. Is it morbid to have a desire for food? I have a great desire for food. Lord Goring, will you give me some supper?

LORD GORING. With pleasure, Miss Mabel. (*Moves away with her.*)

MABEL CHILTERN. How horrid you have been! You have never talked to me the whole evening!

LORD GORING. How could I? You went away with the child-diplomatist.

MABEL CHILTERN. You might have followed us. Pursuit would have been only polite. I don't think I like you at all this evening!

LORD GORING. I like you immensely.

MABEL CHILTERN. Well, I wish you'd show it in a more marked way!

They go downstairs.

MRS. MARCHMONT. Olivia, I have a curious feeling of absolute faintness. I think I should like some supper very much. I know I should like some supper.

LADY BASILDON. I am positively dying for supper, Margaret!

MRS. MARCHMONT. Men are so horribly selfish, they never think of these things.

LADY BASILDON. Men are grossly material, grossly material!

The VICOMTE DE NANJAC *enters from the music-room with some other guests. After having carefully examined all the people present, he approaches* LADY BASILDON.

VICOMTE DE NANJAC. May I have the honour of taking you down to supper, Comtesse?

LADY BASILDON (*coldly*). I never take supper, thank you, Vicomte. (*The* VICOMTE *is about to retire.* LADY BASILDON, *seeing this, rises at once and takes his arm.*) But I will come down with you with pleasure.

VICOMTE DE NANJAC. I am so fond of eating! I am very English in all my tastes.

LADY BASILDON. You look quite English, Vicomte, quite English.

They pass out, MR. MONTFORD, *a perfectly groomed young dandy, approaches* MRS. MARCHMONT.

MR. MONTFORD. Like some support, Mrs. Marchmont?

MRS. MARCHMONT (*languidly*). Thank you, Mr. Montford, I never touch supper. (*Rises hastily and takes his arm.*) But I will sit beside you, and watch you.

MR. MONTFORD. I don't know that I like being watched when I am eating!

MRS. MARCHMONT. Then I will watch someone else.

MR. MONTFORD. I don't know that I should like that either.

MRS. MARCHMONT (*severely*). Pray, Mr. Montford, do not make these painful scenes of jealousy in public!

They go downstairs with the other guests, passing SIR ROBERT CHILTERN *and* MRS. CHEVELEY, *who now enter.*

SIR ROBERT CHILTERN. And are you going to any of our country houses before you leave England, Mrs. Cheveley?

MRS. CHEVELEY. Oh, no! I can't stand your English house-parties. In England people actually try to be brilliant at breakfast. That is so dreadful of them! Only dull people are brilliant at breakfast. And then the family skeleton is always reading family prayers. My stay in England really depends on you, Sir Robert. (*Sits down on the sofa.*)

SIR ROBERT CHILTERN (*taking a seat beside her*). Seriously?

MRS. CHEVELEY. Quite seriously. I want to talk to you about a great political and financial scheme, about this Argentine Canal Company, in fact.

SIR ROBERT CHILTERN. What a tedious, practical subject for you to talk about, Mrs. Cheveley!

MRS. CHEVELEY. Oh, I like tedious, practical subjects. What I don't like are tedious, practical people. There is a wide difference. Besides, you are interested, I know, in International Canal schemes. You were Lord Radley's secretary, weren't you, when the Government bought the Suez Canal shares?

SIR ROBERT CHILTERN. Yes. But the Suez Canal was a very great and splendid undertaking. It gave us our direct route to India. It had imperial value. It was necessary that we should have control. This Argentine scheme is a common-place Stock Exchange swindle.

MRS. CHEVELEY. A speculation, Sir Robert! A brilliant, daring speculation.

SIR ROBERT CHILTERN. Believe me, Mrs. Cheveley, it is a swindle. Let us call things by their proper names. It makes matters simpler. We have all the information about it at the Foreign Office. In fact, I sent out a special Commission to inquire into the matter privately, and they report that the works are hardly begun, and as for the money already subscribed, no one seems to know what has become of it. The whole thing is a second Panama, and with not a quarter of the chance of success that miserable affair ever had. I hope you have not invested in it. I am sure you are far too clever to have done that.

MRS. CHEVELEY. I have invested very largely in it.

SIR ROBERT CHILTERN. Who could have advised you to do such a foolish thing?

MRS. CHEVELEY. Your old friend—and mine.

SIR ROBERT CHILTERN. Who?

MRS. CHEVELEY. Baron Arnheim.

SIR ROBERT CHILTERN (*frowning*). Ah! yes. I remember hearing, at the time of his death, that he had been mixed up in the whole affair.

MRS. CHEVELEY. It was his last romance. His last but one, to do him justice.

SIR ROBERT CHILTERN (*rising*). But you have not seen my Corots yet. They are in the music-room. Corots seem to go with music, don't they? May I show them to you?

MRS. CHEVELEY (*shaking her head*). I am not in a mood tonight for silver twilights, or rose-pink dawns. I want to talk business. (*Motions to him with her fan to sit down again beside her.*)

SIR ROBERT CHILTERN. I fear I have no advice to give you, Mrs. Cheveley, except to interest yourself in something less dangerous. The success of the Canal depends, of course, on the attitude of England, and I am going to lay the report of the Commissioners before the House tomorrow night.

MRS. CHEVELEY. That you must not do. In your own interests, Sir Robert, to say nothing of mine, you must not do that.

SIR ROBERT CHILTERN (*looking at her in wonder*). In my own interest? My dear Mrs. Cheveley, what do you mean? (*Sits down beside her.*)

MRS. CHEVELEY. Sir Robert, I will be quite frank with you. I want you to withdraw the report that you had intended to lay before the House, on the ground that you have reasons to believe that the Commissioners have been prejudiced or misinformed, or something. Then I want you to say a few words to the effect that the Government is going to reconsider the question, and that you have reason to believe that the Canal, if completed, will be of great international value. You know the sort of things ministers say in cases of this kind. A few ordinary platitudes will do. In modern life nothing produces such an effect as a good platitude. It makes the whole world kin. Will you do that for me?

SIR ROBERT CHILTERN. Mrs. Cheveley, you cannot be serious in making me such a proposition!

MRS. CHEVELEY. I am quite serious.

SIR ROBERT CHILTERN (*coldly*). Pray allow me to believe that you are not.

MRS. CHEVELEY (*speaking with great deliberation and emphasis*). Ah! but I am. And if you do what I ask you, I . . . will pay you very handsomely!

SIR ROBERT CHILTERN. Pay me!

MRS. CHEVELEY. Yes.

SIR ROBERT CHILTERN. I am afraid I don't understand what you mean.

MRS. CHEVELEY (*leaning back on the sofa and looking at him*). How very disappointing! And I have come all the way from Vienna in order that you should thoroughly understand me.

SIR ROBERT CHILTERN. I fear I don't.

MRS. CHEVELEY (*in her most nonchalant manner*). My dear Sir Robert, you are a man of the world, and you have your price, I suppose. Everybody has nowadays. The drawback is that most people are so dreadfully expensive. I know I am. I hope you will be more reasonable in your terms.

SIR ROBERT CHILTERN (*rises indignantly*). If you will allow me, I will call your carriage for you. You have lived so long abroad, Mrs. Cheveley, that you seem to be unable to realize that you are talking to an English gentleman.

MRS. CHEVELEY (*detains him by touching his arm with her fan, and keeping it there while she is talking*). I realize that I am talking to a man who laid the foundation of his fortune by selling to a Stock Exchange speculator a Cabinet secret.

SIR ROBERT CHILTERN (*biting his lip*). What do you mean?

MRS. CHEVELEY (*rising and facing him*). I mean that I know the real origin of your wealth and your career, and I have got your letter, too.

SIR ROBERT CHILTERN. What letter?

MRS. CHEVELEY (*contemptuously*). The letter you wrote to Baron Arnheim, when you were Lord Radley's secretary, telling the Baron to buy Suez Canal shares—a letter written three days before the Government announced its own purchase.

SIR ROBERT CHILTERN (*hoarsely*). It is not true.

MRS. CHEVELEY. You thought that letter had been destroyed. How foolish of you! It is in my possession.

SIR ROBERT CHILTERN. The affair to which you allude was no more than a speculation. The House of Commons had not yet passed the bill; it might have been rejected.

MRS. CHEVELEY. It was a swindle, Sir Robert. Let us call things by their proper names. It makes everything simpler. And now I am going to sell you that letter, and the price I ask for it is your public support of the Argentine scheme. You made your own fortune out of one canal. You must help me and my friends to make our fortunes out of another!

SIR ROBERT CHILTERN. It is infamous, what you propose—infamous!

MRS. CHEVELEY. Oh, no! This is the game of life as we all have to play it, Sir Robert, sooner or later!

SIR ROBERT CHILTERN. I cannot do what you ask me.

MRS. CHEVELEY. You mean you cannot help doing it. You know you are standing on the edge of a precipice. And it is not for you to make terms. It is for you to accept them. Supposing you refuse—

SIR ROBERT CHILTERN. What then?

MRS. CHEVELEY. My dear Sir Robert, what then? You are ruined, that is all! Remember to what a point your Puritanism in England has brought you. In old days nobody pretended to be a bit better than his neighbours. In fact, to be a bit better than one's neighbour was considered excessively vulgar and middle-class. Nowadays, with our modern mania for morality, everyone has to pose as a paragon of purity, incorruptibility, and all the other seven deadly virtues—and what is the result? You all go over like ninepins—one after the other. Not a year passes in England without somebody disappearing. Scandals used to lend charm, or at least interest, to a man—now they crush him. And yours is a very nasty scandal. You couldn't survive it. If it were known that as a young man, secretary to a great and important minister, you sold a Cabinet secret for a large sum of money, and that that was the origin of your wealth and career, you would be hounded out of public life, you would disappear completely. And after all, Sir Robert, why should you sacrifice your entire future rather than deal diplomatically with your enemy? For the moment I am your enemy. I admit it! And I am much stronger than you are. The big battallions are on my side. You have a splendid position, but it is your splendid position that makes you so vulnerable. You can't defend it! And I am in attack. Of course I have not talked morality to you. You must admit in fairness that I have spared you that. Years ago you did a clever, unscrupulous thing; it turned out a great success. You owe to it your fortune and position. And now you have got to pay for it. Sooner or later we have all to pay for what we do. You have to pay now. Before I leave you tonight, you have got to promise me to suppress your report, and to speak in the House in favour of this scheme.

SIR ROBERT CHILTERN. What you ask is impossible.

MRS. CHEVELEY. You must make it possible. You are going to make it possible. Sir Robert, you know what your English newspapers are like. Suppose that when I leave this house I drive down to some newspaper office, and give them this scandal and the proofs of it! Think of their loathsome joy, of the delight they would have

in dragging you down, of the mud and mire
they would plunge you in. Think of the hypocrite with his greasy smile penning his leading
article, and arranging the foulness of the public placard.

SIR ROBERT CHILTERN. Stop! You want me to withdraw the report and to make a short speech
stating that I believe there are possibilities in
the scheme?

MRS. CHEVELEY (*sitting down on the sofa*). Those are
my terms.

SIR ROBERT CHILTERN (*in a low voice*). I will give you
any sum of money you want.

MRS. CHEVELEY. Even you are not rich enough, Sir
Robert, to buy back your past. No man is.

SIR ROBERT CHILTERN. I will not do what you ask
me. I will not.

MRS. CHEVELEY. You have to. If you don't . . . (*Rises
from the sofa.*)

SIR ROBERT CHILTERN (*bewildered and unnerved*). Wait
a moment! What did you propose? You said
that you would give me back my letter, didn't
you?

MRS. CHEVELEY. Yes. That is agreed. I will be in
the Ladies' Gallery tomorrow night at half-past
eleven. If by that time—and you will have had
heaps of opportunity—you have made an announcement to the House in the terms I wish, I
shall hand you back your letter with the prettiest
thanks, and the best, or at any rate the most suitable, compliment I can think of. I intend to play
quite fairly with you. One should always play

fairly . . . when one has the winning cards. The Baron taught me that . . . among other things.

SIR ROBERT CHILTERN. You must let me have time to consider your proposal.

MRS. CHEVELEY. No; you must settle now!

SIR ROBERT CHILTERN. Give me a week—three days!

MRS. CHEVELEY. Impossible! I have got to telegraph to Vienna tonight.

SIR ROBERT CHILTERN. My God! what brought you into my life?

MRS. CHEVELEY. Circumstances. (*Moves towards the door.*)

SIR ROBERT CHILTERN. Don't go. I consent. The report shall be withdrawn. I will arrange for a question to be put to me on the subject.

MRS. CHEVELEY. Thank you. I knew we should come to an amicable agreement. I understood your nature from the first. I analysed you, though you did not adore me. And now you can get my carriage for me, Sir Robert. I see the people coming up from supper, and English men always get romantic after a meal, and that bores me dreadfully.

Exit SIR ROBERT CHILTERN.

Enter guests, LADY CHILTERN, LADY MARKBY, LORD CAVERSHAM, LADY BASILDON, MRS. MARCHMONT, VI-COMTE DE NANJAC, MR. MONTFORD.

LADY MARKBY. Well, dear Mrs. Cheveley, I hope you have enjoyed yourself. Sir Robert is very entertaining, is he not?

MRS. CHEVELEY. Most entertaining! I have enjoyed my talk with him immensely.

LADY MARKBY. He has had a very interesting and brilliant career. And he has married a most admirable wife. Lady Chiltern is a woman of the very highest principles, I am glad to say. I am a little too old now, myself, to trouble about setting a good example, but I always admire people who do. And Lady Chiltern has a very ennobling effect on life, though her dinner-parties are rather dull sometimes. But one can't have everything, can one? And now I must go, dear. Shall I call for you tomorrow?

MRS. CHEVELEY. Thanks.

LADY MARKBY. We might drive in the Park at five. Everything looks so fresh in the Park now!

MRS. CHEVELEY. Except the people!

LADY MARKBY. Perhaps the people are a little jaded. I have often observed that the Season as it goes on produces a kind of softening of the brain. However, I think anything is better than high intellectual pressure. That is the most unbecoming thing there is. It makes the noses of the young girls so particularly large. And there is nothing so difficult to marry as a large nose; men don't like them. Good night, dear! (*To* LADY CHILTERN.) Good night, Gertrude!

Goes out on LORD CAVERSHAM'S *arm.*

MRS. CHEVELEY. What a charming house you have, Lady Chiltern! I have spent a delightful evening.

It has been so interesting getting to know your husband.

LADY CHILTERN. Why did you wish to meet my husband, Mrs. Cheveley?

MRS. CHEVELEY. Oh, I will tell you. I wanted to interest him in this Argentine Canal scheme, of which I dare say you have heard. And I found him most susceptible, —susceptible to reason, I mean. A rare thing in a man. I converted him in ten minutes. He is going to make a speech in the House tomorrow night in favour of the idea. We must go to the Ladies' Gallery and hear him! It will be a great occasion!

LADY CHILTERN. There must be some mistake. That scheme could never have my husband's support.

MRS. CHEVELEY. Oh, I assure you it's all settled. I don't regret my tedious journey from Vienna now. It has been a great success. But, of course, for the next twenty-four hours the whole thing is a dead secret.

LADY CHILTERN (*gently*). A secret? Between whom?

MRS. CHEVELEY. (*with a flash of amusement in her eyes*). Between your husband and myself.

SIR ROBERT CHILTERN (*entering*). Your carriage is here, Mrs. Cheveley!

MRS. CHEVELEY. Thanks. Good evening, Lady Chiltern! Good night, Lord Goring! I am at Claridge's. Don't you think you might leave a card?

LORD GORING. If you wish, Mrs. Cheveley!

MRS. CHEVELEY. Oh, don't be so solemn about it, or I shall be obliged to leave a card on you. In

England I suppose that would hardly be considered *en grèle*. Abroad, we are more civilized. Will you see me down, Sir Robert? Now that we have both the same interests at heart we shall be great friends, I hope!

Sails out on SIR ROBERT CHILTERN'S *arm.* LADY CHILTERN *goes to the top of the staircase and looks down at them as they descend. Her expression is troubled. After a little time she is joined by some of the guests, and passes with them into another reception-room.*

MABEL CHILTERN. What a horrid woman!

LORD GORING. You should go to bed, Miss Mabel.

MABEL CHILTERN. Lord Goring!

LORD GORING. My father told me to go to bed an hour ago. I don't see why I shouldn't give you the same advice. I always pass on good advice. It is the only thing to do with it. It is never of any use to oneself.

MABEL CHILTERN. Lord Goring, you are always ordering me out of the room. I think it most courageous of you. Especially as I am not going to bed for hours. (*Goes over to the sofa.*) You can come and sit down if you like, and talk about anything in the world, except the Royal Academy, Mrs. Cheveley, or novels in Scotch dialect. They are not improving subjects. (*Catches sight of something that is lying on the sofa half hidden by the cushion.*) What is this? Someone has dropped a diamond brooch! Quite beautiful, isn't it? (*Shows it to him.*) I wish it was mine, but Gertrude won't let me wear anything but pearls, and I am thoroughly sick of pearls. They make one look so plain, so good, and so intellectual. I wonder whom the brooch belongs to.

LORD GORING. I wonder who dropped it.

MABEL CHILTERN. It is a beautiful brooch.

LORD GORING. It is a handsome bracelet.

MABEL CHILTERN. It isn't a bracelet. It's a brooch.

LORD GORING. It can be used as a bracelet.

Takes it from her, and, pulling out a green letter-case, puts the ornament carefully in it, and replaces the whole thing in his breast-pocket with the most perfect sang-froid.

MABEL CHILTERN. What are you doing?

LORD GORING. Miss Mabel, I am going to make a rather strange request to you.

MABEL CHILTERN (*eagerly*). Oh, pray do! I have been waiting for it all the evening.

LORD GORING (*is a little taken aback, but recovers himself*). Don't mention to anybody that I have taken charge of this brooch. Should anyone write and claim it, let me know at once.

MABEL CHILTERN. That is a strange request.

LORD GORING. Well, you see I gave this brooch to somebody once, years ago.

MABEL CHILTERN. You did?

LORD GORING. Yes.

LADY CHILTERN *enters alone. The other guests have gone.*

41

MABEL CHILTERN. Then I shall certainly bid you good night. Good night, Gertrude! (*Exit.*)

LADY CHILTERN. Good night, dear! (*To* LORD GORING.) You saw whom Lady Markby brought here tonight?

LORD GORING. Yes. It was an unpleasant surprise. What did she come here for?

LADY CHILTERN. Apparently to try and lure Robert to uphold some fraudulent scheme in which she is interested. The Argentine Canal, in fact.

LORD GORING. She has mistaken her man, hasn't she?

LADY CHILTERN. She is incapable of understanding an upright nature like my husband's!

LORD GORING. Yes. I should fancy she came to grief if she tried to get Robert into her toils. It is extraordinary what astounding mistakes clever women make.

LADY CHILTERN. I don't call women of that kind clever. I call them stupid!

LORD GORING. Same thing often. Good night, Lady Chiltern!

LADY CHILTERN. Good night!

Enter SIR ROBERT CHILTERN.

SIR ROBERT CHILTERN. My dear Arthur, you are not going? Do stop a little!

LORD GORING. Afraid I can't, thanks. I have promised to look in at the Hartlocks'. I believe they have got a mauve Hungarian band that plays mauve Hungarian music. See you soon. Good-bye! (*Exit.*)

SIR ROBERT CHILTERN. How beautiful you look to-night, Gertrude!

LADY CHILTERN. Robert, it is not true, is it? You are not going to lend your support to this Argentine speculation? You couldn't!

SIR ROBERT CHILTERN (*starting*). Who told you I intended to do so?

LADY CHILTERN. That woman who has just gone out, Mrs. Cheveley, as she calls herself now. She seemed to taunt me with it. Robert, I know this woman. You don't. We were at school together. She was untruthful, dishonest, an evil influence on everyone whose trust or friendship she could win. I hated, I despised her. She stole things, she was a thief. She was sent away for being a thief. Why do you let her influence you?

SIR ROBERT CHILTERN. Gertrude, what you tell me may be true, but it happened many years ago. It is best forgotten! Mrs. Cheveley may have changed since then. No one should be entirely judged by their past.

LADY CHILTERN (*sadly*). One's past is what one is. It is the only way by which people should be judged.

SIR ROBERT CHILTERN. That is a hard saying, Gertrude!

LADY CHILTERN. It is a true saying, Robert. And what did she mean by boasting that she had got you to lend your support, your name, to a thing I have heard you describe as the most dishonest and fraudulent scheme there has ever been in political life?

SIR ROBERT CHILTERN (*biting his lip*). I was mistaken in the view I took. We all may make mistakes.

LADY CHILTERN. But you told me yesterday that you had received the report from the Commission, and that it entirely condemned the whole thing.

SIR ROBERT CHILTERN (*walking up and down*). I have reasons now to believe that the Commission was prejudiced, or, at any rate, misinformed. Besides, Gertrude, public and private life are different things. They have different laws, and move on different lines.

LADY CHILTERN. They should both represent man at his highest. I see no difference between them.

SIR ROBERT CHILTERN (*stopping*). In the present case, on a matter of practical politics, I have changed my mind. That is all.

LADY CHILTERN. All!

SIR ROBERT CHILTERN (*sternly*). Yes!

LADY CHILTERN. Robert! Oh! It is horrible that I should have to ask you such a question—Robert, are you telling me the whole truth?

SIR ROBERT CHILTERN. Why do you ask me such a question?

LADY CHILTERN (*after a pause*). Why do you not answer it?

SIR ROBERT CHILTERN (*sitting down*). Gertrude, truth is a very complex thing, and politics is a very complex business. There are wheels within wheels. One may be under certain obligations to people that one must pay. Sooner or later in political life one has to compromise. Everyone does.

LADY CHILTERN. Compromise? Robert, why do you talk so differently tonight from the way I have always heard you talk? Why are you changed?

SIR ROBERT CHILTERN. I am not changed. But circumstances alter things.

LADY CHILTERN. Circumstances should never alter principles!

SIR ROBERT CHILTERN. But if I told you—

LADY CHILTERN. What?

SIR ROBERT CHILTERN. That it was necessary, vitally necessary?

LADY CHILTERN. It can never be necessary to do what is not honourable. Or if it be necessary, then what is it that I have loved! But it is not, Robert; tell me it is not. Why should it be? What gain would you get? Money? We have no need of that! And money that comes from a tainted source is a degradation. Power? But power is nothing in itself. It is power to do good that is fine—that, and that only. What is it, then? Robert, tell me why you are going to do this dishonourable thing!

SIR ROBERT CHILTERN. Gertrude, you have no right to use that word. I told you it was a question of rational compromise. It is no more than that.

LADY CHILTERN. Robert, that is all very well for other men, for men who treat life simply as a sordid speculation; but not for you, Robert, not for you. You are different. All your life you have stood apart from others. You have never let the world soil you. To the world, as to myself, you have been an ideal always. Oh! be that ideal still. That great inheritance throw not away— that tower of ivory do not destroy. Robert, men can love what is beneath them—things unworthy, stained, dishonoured. We women worship when we love; and when we lose our worship, we lose everything. Oh! don't kill my love for you, don't kill that!

SIR ROBERT CHILTERN. Gertrude!

LADY CHILTERN. I know that there are men with horrible secrets in their lives—men who have done some shameful thing, and who in some critical moment have to pay for it, by doing some other act of shame—oh! don't tell me you are such as they are! Robert, is there in your life any secret dishonour or disgrace? Tell me, tell me at once, that—

SIR ROBERT CHILTERN. That what?

LADY CHILTERN (*speaking very slowly*). That our lives may drift apart.

SIR ROBERT CHILTERN. Drift apart?

LADY CHILTERN. That they may be entirely separate. It would be better for us both.

SIR ROBERT CHILTERN. Gertrude, there is nothing in my past life that you might not know.

LADY CHILTERN. I was sure of it, Robert, I was sure of it. But why did you say those dreadful things, things so unlike your real self? Don't let us ever talk about the subject again. You will write, won't you, to Mrs. Cheveley, and tell her that you cannot support this scandalous scheme of hers? If you have given her any promise you must take it back, that is all!

SIR ROBERT CHILTERN. Must I write and tell her that?

LADY CHILTERN. Surely, Robert! What else is there to do?

SIR ROBERT CHILTERN. I might see her personally. It would be better.

LADY CHILTERN. You must never see her again, Robert. She is not a woman you should ever speak to. She is not worthy to talk to a man like you. No; you must write to her at once, now, this moment, and let your letter show her that your decision is quite irrevocable!

SIR ROBERT CHILTERN. Write this moment!

LADY CHILTERN. Yes.

SIR ROBERT CHILTERN. But it is so late. It is close on twelve.

LADY CHILTERN. That makes no matter. She must know at once that she has been mistaken in you—and that you are not a man to do anything base or underhand or dishonourable. Write here, Robert. Write that you decline to support this scheme of hers, as you hold it to be a dishonest scheme. Yes—write the word dishonest. She knows what that word means. (SIR ROBERT CHILTERN *sits down and writes a letter. His wife takes it up and reads it.*) Yes; that will do. (*Rings bell.*) And now the envelope. (*He writes the envelope slowly. Enter* MASON.) Have this letter sent at once to Claridge's Hotel. There is no answer. (*Exit* MASON. LADY CHILTERN *kneels down beside her husband and puts her arms around him.*) Robert,

47

love gives one an instinct to things. I feel tonight that I have saved you from something that might have been a danger to you, from something that might have made men honour you less than they do. I don't think you realize sufficiently, Robert, that you have brought into the political life of our time a nobler atmosphere, a finer attitude towards life, a freer air of purer aims and higher ideals—I know it, and for that I love you, Robert.

SIR ROBERT CHILTERN. Oh, love me always, Gertrude, love me always!

LADY CHILTERN. I will love you always, because you will always be worthy of love. We needs must love the highest when we see it!

(*Kisses him and rises and goes out.*)

(SIR ROBERT CHILTERN *walks up and down for a moment; then sits down and buries his face in his hands. The Servant enters and begins putting out the lights.* SIR ROBERT CHILTERN *looks up.*)

SIR ROBERT CHILTERN. Put out the lights, Mason, put out the lights!

(*The Servant puts out the lights. The room becomes almost dark. The only light there is comes from the great chandelier that hangs over the staircase and illumines the tapestry of the Triumph of Love.*)

Act Drop

Second Act

SCENE

Morning-room at Sir Robert Chiltern's house.

LORD GORING *dressed in the height of fashion, is lounging in an armchair.* SIR ROBERT CHILTERN *is standing in front of the fireplace. He is evidently in a state of great mental excitement and distress. As the scene progresses he paces nervously up and down the room.*

LORD GORING. My dear Robert, it's a very awkward business, very awkward indeed. You should have told your wife the whole thing. Secrets from other people's wives are a necessary luxury in modern life. So, at least, I am always told at the club by people who are bald enough to know better. But no man should have a secret from his own wife. She invariably finds it out. Women have a wonderful instinct about things. They can discover everything except the obvious.

SIR ROBERT CHILTERN. Arthur, I couldn't tell my wife. When could I have told her? Not last

49

night. It would have made a life-long separation between us, and I would have lost the love of the one woman in the world I worship, of the only woman who has ever stirred love within me. Last night it would have been quite impossible. She would have turned from me in horror . . . in horror and in contempt.

LORD GORING. Is Lady Chiltern as perfect as all that?

SIR ROBERT CHILTERN. Yes, my wife is as perfect as all that.

LORD GORING. (*taking off his left-hand glove*). What a pity! I beg your pardon, my dear fellow, I didn't quite mean that. But if what you tell me is true, I should like to have a serious talk about life with Lady Chiltern.

SIR ROBERT CHILTERN. It would be quite useless.

LORD GORING. May I try?

SIR ROBERT CHILTERN. Yes; but nothing could make her alter her views.

LORD GORING. Well, at the worst it would simply be a psychological experiment.

SIR ROBERT CHILTERN. All such experiments are terribly dangerous.

LORD GORING. Everything is dangerous, my dear fellow. If it wasn't so, life wouldn't be worth living. . . . Well, I am bound to say that I think you should have told her years ago.

SIR ROBERT CHILTERN. When? When we were engaged? Do you think she would have married me if she had known that the origin of my fortune is such as it is, the basis of my career such as it is, and that I had done a thing that I suppose most men would call shameful and dishonourable?

LORD GORING (*slowly*). Yes; most men would call it ugly names. There is no doubt of that.

SIR ROBERT CHILTERN (*bitterly*). Men who every day do something of the same kind themselves. Men who, each one of them, have worse secrets in their own lives.

LORD GORING. That is the reason they are so pleased to find out other people's secrets. It distracts attention from their own.

SIR ROBERT CHILTERN. And, after all, whom did I wrong by what I did? No one.

LORD GORING (*looking at him steadily*). Except yourself, Robert.

SIR ROBERT CHILTERN (*after a pause*). Of course I had private information about a certain transaction contemplated by the Government of the day, and I acted on it. Private information is practically the source of every large modern fortune.

LORD GORING (*tapping his boot with his cane*). And public scandal invariably the result.

SIR ROBERT CHILTERN (*pacing up and down the room*). Arthur, do you think that what I did nearly eighteen years ago should be brought up against me now? Do you think it fair that a man's whole career should be ruined for a fault done in one's boyhood almost? I was twenty-two at the time, and I had the double misfortune of being well-born and poor, two unforgivable things nowadays. Is it fair that the folly, the sin of one's youth, if men choose to call it a sin, should wreck a life like mine, should place me in the pillory, should shatter all that I have worked for, all that I have built up? Is it fair, Arthur?

LORD GORING. Life is never fair, Robert. And perhaps it is a good thing for most of us that it is not.

SIR ROBERT CHILTERN. Every man of ambition has to fight his century with its own weapons. What this century worships is wealth. The god of this century is wealth. To succeed one must have wealth. At all costs one must have wealth.

LORD GORING. You underrate yourself, Robert. Believe me, without wealth you could have succeeded just as well.

SIR ROBERT CHILTERN. When I was old, perhaps. When I had lost my passion for power, or could not use it. When I was tired, worn out, disappointed. I wanted my success when I was young. Youth is the time for success. I couldn't wait.

LORD GORING. Well, you certainly have had your success while you are still young. No one in our day has had such a brilliant success. Under-Secretary for Foreign Affairs at the age of forty—that's good enough for anyone, I should think.

SIR ROBERT CHILTERN. And if it is all taken away from me now? If I lose everything over a horrible scandal? If I am hounded from public life?

LORD GORING. Robert, how could you have sold
yourself for money?

SIR ROBERT CHILTERN (*excitedly*). I did not sell myself
for money. I bought success at a great price.
That is all.

LORD GORING (*gravely*). Yes; you certainly paid a
great price for it. But what first made you think
of doing such a thing?

SIR ROBERT CHILTERN. Baron Arnheim.

LORD GORING. Damned scoundrel!

SIR ROBERT CHILTERN. No; he was a man of most
subtle and refined intellect. A man of culture,
charm, and distinction. One of the most intellectual men I ever met.

LORD GORING. Ah! I prefer a gentlemanly fool any
day. There is more to be said for stupidity than
people imagine. Personally I have a great admi-
ration for stupidity. It is a sort of fellow-feeling,
I suppose. But how did he do it? Tell me the
whole thing.

SIR ROBERT CHILTERN (*throws himself into an armchair
by the writing-table*). One night after dinner at
Lord Radley's the Baron began talking about
success in modern life as something that one
could reduce to an absolutely definite science.
With that wonderfully fascinating quiet voice
of his he expounded to us the most terrible
of all philosophies, the philosophy of power,
preached to us the most marvellous of all gos-
pels, the gospel of gold. I think he saw the effect
he had produced on me, for some days afterwards he wrote and asked me to come and see

him. He was living then in Park Lane, in the house Lord Woolcomb has now. I remember so well how, with a strange smile on his pale, curved lips, he led me through his wonderful picture gallery, showed me his tapestries, his enamels, his jewels, his carved ivories, made me wonder at the strange loveliness of the luxury in which he lived; and then told me that luxury was nothing but a background, a painted scene in a play, and that power, power over other men, power over the world, was the one thing worth having, the one supreme pleasure worth knowing, the one joy one never tired of, and that in our century only the rich possessed it.

LORD GORING (*with great deliberation*). A thoroughly shallow creed.

SIR ROBERT CHILTERN (*rising*). I didn't think so then. I don't think so now. Wealth has given me enormous power. It gave me at the very outset of my life freedom, and freedom is everything. You have never been poor, and never known what ambition is. You cannot understand what a wonderful chance the Baron gave me. Such a chance as few men get.

LORD GORING. Fortunately for them, if one is to judge by results. But tell me definitely, how did the Baron finally persuade you to—well, to do what you did?

SIR ROBERT CHILTERN. When I was going away he said to me that if I ever could give him any private information of real value he would make me a very rich man. I was dazed at the prospect he held out to me, and my ambition and my desire for power were at that time boundless. Six weeks later certain private documents passed through my hands.

LORD GORING (*keeping his eyes steadily fixed on the carpet*). State documents?

SIR ROBERT CHILTERN. Yes.

LORD GORING *sighs, then passes his hand across his forehead and looks up.*

LORD GORING. I had no idea that you, of all men in the world, could have been so weak, Robert, as to yield to such a temptation as Baron Arnheim held out to you.

SIR ROBERT CHILTERN. Weak? Oh, I am sick of hearing that phrase. Sick of using it about others. Weak? Do you really think, Arthur, that it is weakness that yields to temptation? I tell you that there are terrible temptations that it requires strength, strength and courage, to yield to. To stake all one's life on a single moment, to risk everything on one throw, whether the stake be power or pleasure, I care not—there is no weakness in that. There is a horrible, a terrible courage. I had that courage. I sat down the same afternoon and wrote Baron Arnheim the letter this woman now holds. He made three-quarters of a million over the transaction.

LORD GORING. And you?

SIR ROBERT CHILTERN. I received from the Baron £110,000.

LORD GORING. You were worth more, Robert.

SIR ROBERT CHILTERN. No; that money gave me exactly what I wanted, power over others. I went into the House immediately. The Baron advised me in finance from time to time. Before five years I had almost trebled my fortune. Since then everything that I have touched has turned out a success. In all things connected with money I have had a luck so extraordinary that sometimes it has made me almost afraid. I remember having read somewhere, in some strange book, that when the gods wish to punish us they answer our prayers.

LORD GORING. But tell me, Robert, did you ever suffer any regret for what you had done?

SIR ROBERT CHILTERN. No. I felt that I had fought the century with its own weapons, and won.

LORD GORING (*sadly*). You thought you had won.

SIR ROBERT CHILTERN. I thought so. (*After a long pause.*) Arthur, do you despise me for what I have told you?

LORD GORING (*with deep feeling in his voice*). I am very sorry for you, Robert, very sorry indeed.

SIR ROBERT CHILTERN. I don't say that I suffered any remorse. I didn't. Not remorse in the ordinary, rather silly sense of the word. But I have paid conscience money many times. I had a wild hope that I might disarm destiny. The sum Baron Arnheim gave me I have distributed twice over in public charities since then.

LORD GORING (*looking up*). In public charities? Dear

me! what a lot of harm you must have done, Robert!

SIR ROBERT CHILTERN. Oh don't say that, Arthur; don't talk like that!

LORD GORING. Never mind what I say, Robert! I am always saying what I shouldn't say. In fact, I usually say what I really think. A great mistake nowadays. It makes one so liable to be misunderstood. As regards this dreadful business, I will help you in whatever way I can. Of course, you know that.

SIR ROBERT CHILTERN. Thank you, Arthur, thank you. But what is to be done? What can be done?

LORD GORING (*leaning back with his hands in his pockets*). Well, the English can't stand a man who is always saying he is in the right, but they are very fond of a man who admits that he has been in the wrong. It is one of the best things in them. However, in your case, Robert, a confession would not do. The money, if you will allow me to say so, is . . . awkward. Besides, if you did make a clean breast of the whole affair, you would never be able to talk morality again. And in England a man who can't talk morality twice a week to a large, popular, immoral audience is quite over as a serious politician. There would be nothing left for him as a profession except Botany or the Church. A confession would be of no use. It would ruin you.

SIR ROBERT CHILTERN. It would ruin me. Arthur, the only thing for me to do now is to fight the thing out.

LORD GORING (*rising from his chair*). I was waiting for you to say that, Robert. It is the only thing to do now. And you must begin by telling your wife the whole story.

SIR ROBERT CHILTERN. That I will not do.

LORD GORING. Robert, believe me, you are wrong.

SIR ROBERT CHILTERN. I couldn't do it. It would kill her love for me. And now about this woman, this Mrs. Cheveley. How can I defend myself against her? You knew her before, Arthur, apparently.

LORD GORING. Yes.

SIR ROBERT CHILTERN. Did you know her well?

LORD GORING (*arranging his necktie*). So little that I got engaged to be married to her once, when I was staying at the Tenbys'. The affair lasted for three days . . . nearly.

SIR ROBERT CHILTERN. Why was it broken off?

LORD GORING (*airily*). Oh, I forget. At least, it makes no matter. By the way, have you tried her with money? She used to be confoundedly fond of money.

SIR ROBERT CHILTERN. I offered her any sum she wanted. She refused.

LORD GORING. Then the marvellous gospel of gold breaks down sometimes. The rich can't do everything, after all.

SIR ROBERT CHILTERN. Not everything. I suppose you are right. Arthur, I feel that public disgrace is in store for me. I feel certain of it. I never knew what terror was before. I know it now. It is as if a hand of ice were laid upon one's heart. It is as if one's heart were beating itself to death in some empty hollow.

LORD GORING (*striking the table*). Robert, you must fight her. You must fight her.

SIR ROBERT CHILTERN. But how?

LORD GORING. I can't tell you how at present. I have not the smallest idea. But everyone has some weak point. There is some flaw in each one of us. (*Strolls over to the fireplace and looks at himself in the glass.*) My father tells me that even I have faults. Perhaps I have. I don't know.

SIR ROBERT CHILTERN. In defending myself against Mrs. Cheveley, I have a right to use any weapon I can find, have I not?

LORD GORING (*still looking in the glass*). In your place I don't think I should have the smallest scruple in doing so. She is thoroughly well able to take care of herself.

SIR ROBERT CHILTERN (*sits down at the table and takes a pen in his hand*). Well, I shall send a cipher telegram to the Embassy at Vienna to inquire if there is anything known against her. There may be some secret scandal she might be afraid of.

LORD GORING (*settling his buttonhole*). Oh, I should fancy Mrs. Cheveley is one of those very modern women of our time who find a new scandal as becoming as a new bonnet, and air them both in the Park every afternoon at five-thirty. I am sure she adores scandals, and that the sorrow of her life at present is that she can't manage to have enough of them.

SIR ROBERT CHILTERN (*writing*). Why do you say that?

LORD GORING (*turning round*). Well, she wore far too much rouge last night, and not quite enough clothes. That is always a sign of despair in a woman.

SIR ROBERT CHILTERN (*striking a bell*). But it is worth while my wiring to Vienna, is it not?

LORD GORING. It is always worth while asking a question, though it is not always worth while answering one.

Enter MASON.

SIR ROBERT CHILTERN. Is Mr. Trafford in his room?

MASON. Yes, Sir Robert.

SIR ROBERT CHILTERN (*puts what he has written into an envelope, which he then carefully closes*). Tell him to have this sent off in cipher at once. There must not be a moment's delay.

MASON. Yes, Sir Robert.

SIR ROBERT CHILTERN. Oh! Just give that back to me again.

Writes something on the envelope. MASON *then goes out with the letter.*

She must have had some curious hold over Baron Arnheim. I wonder what it was.

LORD GORING (*smiling*). I wonder.

SIR ROBERT CHILTERN. I will fight her to the death, as long as my wife knows nothing.

LORD GORING (*strongly*). Oh, fight in any case—in any case.

SIR ROBERT CHILTERN (*with a gesture of despair*). If my wife found out, there would be little left to fight for. Well, as soon as I hear from Vienna, I shall let you know the result. It is a chance, just a chance, but I believe in it. And as I fought the age with its own weapons, I will fight her with her weapons. It is only fair, and she looks like a woman with a past, doesn't she?

LORD GORING. Most pretty women do. But there is a fashion in pasts just as there is a fashion in frocks. Perhaps Mrs. Cheveley's past is merely a slight *décolleté* one, and they are excessively popular nowadays. Besides, my dear Robert, I should not build too high hopes on frightening Mrs. Cheveley. I should not fancy Mrs. Cheveley is a woman who would be easily frightened. She has survived all her creditors, and she shows wonderful presence of mind.

SIR ROBERT CHILTERN. Oh! I live on hopes now. I clutch at every chance. I feel like a man on a ship that is sinking. The water is round my feet, and the very air is bitter with storm. Hush! I hear my wife's voice.

Enter LADY CHILTERN *in walking dress.*

LADY CHILTERN. Good afternoon, Lord Goring!

LORD GORING. Good afternoon, Lady Chiltern! Have you been in the Park?

LADY CHILTERN. No; I have just come from the

Woman's Liberal Association, where, by the way, Robert, your name was received with loud applause, and now I have come in to have my tea. (*To* LORD GORING.) You will wait and have some tea, won't you?

LORD GORING. I'll wait for a short time, thanks.

LADY CHILTERN. I will be back in a moment. I am only going to take my hat off.

LORD GORING (*in his most earnest manner*). Oh! please don't. It is so pretty. One of the prettiest hats I ever saw. I hope the Woman's Liberal Association received it with loud applause.

LADY CHILTERN (*with a smile*). We have much more important work to do than look at each other's bonnets, Lord Goring.

LORD GORING. Really? What sort of work?

LADY CHILTERN. Oh! dull, useful, delightful things, Factory Acts, Female Inspectors, the Eight Hours' Bill, the Parliamentary Franchise. . . . Everything, in fact, that you would find thoroughly uninteresting.

LORD GORING. And never bonnets?

LADY CHILTERN (*with mock indignation*). Never bonnets, never!

LADY CHILTERN *goes through the door leading to her boudoir.*

SIR ROBERT CHILTERN (*takes* LORD GORING'S *hand*). You have been a good friend to me, Arthur, a thoroughly good friend.

LORD GORING. I don't know that I have been able

to do much for you, Robert, as yet. In fact, I have not been able to do anything for you, as far as I can see. I am thoroughly disappointed with myself.

SIR ROBERT CHILTERN. You have enabled me to tell you the truth. That is something. The truth has always stifled me.

LORD GORING. Ah! the truth is a thing I get rid of as soon as possible! Bad habit, by the way. Makes one very unpopular at the club . . . with the older members. They call it being conceited. Perhaps it is.

SIR ROBERT CHILTERN. I would to God that I had been able to tell the truth . . . to live the truth. Ah! that is the great thing in life, to live the truth. (*Sighs, and goes towards the door.*) I'll see you soon again, Arthur, shan't I?

LORD GORING. Certainly. Whenever you like. I'm going to look in at the Bachelors' Ball tonight, unless I find something better to do. But I'll come round tomorrow morning. If you should want me tonight by any chance, send round a note to Curzon Street.

SIR ROBERT CHILTERN. Thank you.

As he reaches the door, LADY CHILTERN *enters from her boudoir.*

LADY CHILTERN. You are not going, Robert?

SIR ROBERT CHILTERN. I have some letters to write, dear.

LADY CHILTERN (*going to him*). You work too hard,

Robert. You seem never to think of yourself, and you are looking so tired.

SIR ROBERT CHILTERN. It is nothing, dear, nothing.

He kisses her and goes out.

LADY CHILTERN (*to* LORD GORING). Do sit down. I am so glad you have called. I want to talk to you about . . . well, not about bonnets, or the Woman's Liberal Association. You take far too much interest in the first subject, and not nearly enough in the second.

LORD GORING. You want to talk to me about Mrs. Cheveley?

LADY CHILTERN. Yes. You have guessed it. After you left last night I found out that what she had said was really true. Of course I made Robert write her a letter at once, withdrawing his promise.

LORD GORING. So he gave me to understand.

LADY CHILTERN. To have kept it would have been the first stain on a career that has been stainless always. Robert must be above reproach. He is not like other men. He cannot afford to do what other men do. (*She looks at* LORD GORING, *who remains silent.*) Don't you agree with me? You are Robert's greatest friend. You are our greatest friend, Lord Goring. No one, except myself, knows Robert better than you do. He has no secrets from me, and I don't think he has any from you.

LORD GORING. He certainly has no secrets from me. At least I don't think so.

LADY CHILTERN. Then am I not right in my estimate of him? I know I am right. But speak to me frankly.

LORD GORING (*looking straight at her*). Quite frankly?

LADY CHILTERN. Surely. You have nothing to conceal have you?

LORD GORING. Nothing. But, my dear Lady Chiltern, I think, if you will allow me to say so, that in practical life—

LADY CHILTERN (*smiling*). Of which you know so little, Lord Goring—

LORD GORING. Of which I know nothing by experience, though I know something by observation. I think that in practical life there is something about success, actual success, that is a little unscrupulous, something about ambition that is unscrupulous always. Once a man has set his heart and soul on getting to a certain point, if he has to climb the crag, he climbs the crag; if he has to walk in the mire—

LADY CHILTERN. Well?

LORD GORING. He walks in the mire. Of course I am only talking generally about life.

LADY CHILTERN (*gravely*). I hope so. Why do you look at me so strangely, Lord Goring?

LORD GORING. Lady Chiltern, I have sometimes thought that . . . perhaps you are a little hard in some of your views on life. I think that . . . often you don't make sufficient allowances. In every nature there are elements of weakness, or worse than weakness. Supposing, for instance, that—that any public man, my father, or Lord Merton, or Robert, say, had, years ago, written some foolish letters to someone . . .

LADY CHILTERN. What do you mean by a foolish letter?

LORD GORING. A letter gravely compromising one's position. I am only putting an imaginary case.

LADY CHILTERN. Robert is as incapable of doing a foolish thing as he is of doing a wrong thing.

LORD GORING (*after a long pause*). Nobody is incapable of doing a foolish thing. Nobody is incapable of doing a wrong thing.

LADY CHILTERN. Are you a Pessimist? What will the other dandies say? They will all have to go into mourning.

LORD GORING (*rising*). No, Lady Chiltern, I am not a Pessimist. Indeed I am not sure that I quite know what Pessimism really means. All I do know is that life cannot be understood without much charity, cannot be lived without much charity. It is love, and not German philosophy, that is the true explanation of this world, whatever may be the explanation of the next. And if you are ever in trouble, Lady Chiltern, trust me absolutely, and I will help you in every way I can. If you ever want me, come to me for my assistance, and you shall have it. Come at once to me.

LADY CHILTERN (*looking at him in surprise*). Lord Goring, you are talking quite seriously. I don't think I ever heard you talk seriously before.

LORD GORING (*laughing*). You must excuse me, Lady Chiltern. It won't occur again, if I can help it.

LADY CHILTERN. But I like you to be serious.

Enter MABEL CHILTERN, *in the most ravishing frock.*

MABEL CHILTERN. Dear Gertrude, don't say such a dreadful thing to Lord Goring. Seriousness would be very unbecoming to him. Good afternoon, Lord Goring! Pray be as trivial as you can.

LORD GORING. I should like to, Miss Mabel, but I am afraid I am . . . a little out of practice this morning; and besides, I have to be going now.

MABEL CHILTERN. Just when I have come in! What dreadful manners you have! I am sure you were very badly brought up.

LORD GORING. I was.

MABEL CHILTERN. I wish I had brought you up!

LORD GORING. I am sorry you didn't.

MABEL CHILTERN. It is too late now, I suppose?

LORD GORING (*smiling*). I am not so sure.

MABEL CHILTERN. Will you ride tomorrow morning?

LORD GORING. Yes, at ten.

MABEL CHILTERN. Don't forget.

LORD GORING. Of course I shan't. By the way, Lady Chiltern, there is no list of your guests in *The Morning Post* of today. It has apparently been crowded out by the County Council, or the Lambeth Conference, or something equally boring. Could you let me have a list? I have a particular reason for asking you.

LADY CHILTERN. I am sure Mr. Trafford will be able to give you one.

LORD GORING. Thanks, so much.

MABEL CHILTERN. Tommy is the most useful person in London.

LORD GORING (*turning to her*). And who is the most ornamental?

MABEL CHILTERN (*triumphantly*). I am.

LORD GORING. How clever of you to guess it! (*Takes up his hat and cane.*) Good-bye, Lady Chiltern! You will remember what I said to you, won't you?

LADY CHILTERN. Yes; but I don't know why you said it to me.

LORD GORING. I hardly know myself. Good-bye, Miss Mabel!

MABEL CHILTERN (*with a little moue of disappointment*). I wish you were not going. I have had four wonderful adventures this morning; four and a half, in fact. You might stop and listen to some of them.

LORD GORING. How very selfish of you to have four and a half! There won't be any left for me.

MABEL CHILTERN. I don't want you to have any. They would not be good for you.

LORD GORING. That is the first unkind thing you have ever said to me. How charmingly you said it! Ten tomorrow.

MABEL CHILTERN. Sharp.

LORD GORING. Quite sharp. But don't bring Mr. Trafford.

MABEL CHILTERN (*with a little toss of the head*). Of

course I shan't bring Tommy Trafford. Tommy
Trafford is in great disgrace.

LORD GORING. I am delighted to hear it.

Bows and goes out.

MABEL CHILTERN. Gertrude, I wish you would speak
to Tommy Trafford.

LADY CHILTERN. What has poor Mr. Trafford done
this time? Robert says he is the best secretary
he has ever had.

MABEL CHILTERN. Well, Tommy has proposed to me
again. Tommy really does nothing but propose to
me. He proposed to me last night in the music-
room, when I was quite unprotected, as there was
an elaborate trio going on. I didn't dare to make
the smallest repartee, I need hardly tell you. If I
had, it would have stopped the music at once.
Musical people are so absurdly unreasonable.
They always want one to be perfectly dumb at the
very moment when one is longing to be absolutely deaf. Then he proposed to me in broad
daylight this morning, in front of that dreadful
statue of Achilles. Really, the things that go on in
front of that work of art are quite appalling. The
police should interfere. At luncheon I saw by the
glare in his eye that he was going to propose
again, and I just managed to check him in time
by assuring him that I was a bimetallist. Fortunately I don't know what bimetallism means.
And I don't believe anybody else does either. But
the observation crushed Tommy for ten minutes.

He looked quite shocked. And then Tommy is so annoying in the way he proposes. If he proposed at the top of his voice, I should not mind so much. That might produce some effect on the public. But he does it in a horrid confidential way. When Tommy wants to be romantic he talks to one just like a doctor. I am very fond of Tommy, but his methods of proposing are quite out of date. I wish, Gertrude, you would speak to him, and tell him that once a week is quite often enough to propose to anyone, and that it should always be done in a manner that attracts some attention.

LADY CHILTERN. Dear Mabel, don't talk like that. Besides, Robert thinks very highly of Mr. Trafford. He believes he has a brilliant future before him.

MABEL CHILTERN. Oh! I wouldn't marry a man with a future before him for anything under the sun.

LADY CHILTERN. Mabel!

MABEL CHILTERN. I know, dear. You married a man with a future, didn't you? But then Robert was a genius, and you have a noble, self-sacrificing character. You can stand geniuses. I have no character at all, and Robert is the only genius I could ever bear. As a rule, I think they are quite impossible. Geniuses talk so much, don't they? Such a bad habit! And they are always thinking about themselves, when I want them to be thinking about me. I must go round now and rehearse at Lady Basildon's. You remember, we are having tableaux, don't you? The Triumph of something, I don't know what! I hope it will be triumph of me. Only triumph I am really interested in at present. (*Kisses* LADY CHILTERN *and goes out; then comes running back.*) Oh, Gertrude, do you know who is coming to see you? That dreadful Mrs. Cheveley, in a most lovely gown. Did you ask her?

LADY CHILTERN (*rising*). Mrs. Cheveley! Coming to see me? Impossible!

MABEL CHILTERN. I assure you she is coming upstairs, as large as life and not nearly so natural.

LADY CHILTERN. You need not wait, Mabel. Remember, Lady Basildon is expecting you.

MABEL CHILTERN. Oh! I must shake hands with Lady Markby. She is delightful. I love being scolded by her.

Enter MASON.

MASON. Lady Markby. Mrs. Cheveley.

Enter LADY MARKBY *and* MRS. CHEVELEY.

LADY CHILTERN (*advancing to meet them*). Dear Lady Markby, how nice of you to come and see me! (*Shakes hands with her, and bows somewhat distantly to* MRS. CHEVELEY.) Won't you sit down, Mrs. Cheveley?

MRS. CHEVELEY. Thanks. Isn't that Miss Chiltern? I should like so much to know her.

LADY CHILTERN. Mabel, Mrs. Cheveley wishes to know you.

71

MABEL CHILTERN *gives a little nod.*

MRS. CHEVELEY (*sitting down*). I thought your frock so charming last night, Miss Chiltern. So simple and . . . suitable.

MABEL CHILDTERN. Really? I must tell my dressmaker. It will be such a surprise to her. Good-bye, Lady Markby!

LADY MARKBY. Going already?

MABEL CHILTERN. I am so sorry but I am obliged to. I am just off to rehearsal. I have got to stand on my head in some tableaux.

LADY MARKBY. On your head, child? Oh! I hope not. I believe it is most unhealthy.

Takes a seat on the sofa next LADY CHILTERN.

MABEL CHILTERN. But it is for an excellent charity: in aid of the Undeserving, the only people I am really interested in. I am the secretary, and Tommy Trafford is treasurer.

MRS. CHEVELEY. And what is Lord Goring?

MABEL CHILTERN. Oh! Lord Goring is president.

MRS. CHEVELEY. The post should suit him admirably, unless he has deteriorated since I knew him first.

LADY MARKBY (*reflecting*). You are remarkably modern, Mabel. A little too modern perhaps. Nothing is so dangerous as being too modern. One is apt to grow old-fashioned quite suddenly. I have known many instances of it.

MABEL CHILTERN. What a dreadful prospect!

LADY MARKBY. Ah! My dear, you need not be nervous. You will always be as pretty as possible. That is the best fashion there is, and the only fashion that England succeeds in setting.

MABEL CHILTERN (*with a curtsey*). Thank you so much, Lady Markby, for England . . . and myself.

Goes out.

LADY MARKBY (*turning to* LADY CHILTERN). Dear Gertrude, we just called to know if Mrs. Cheveley's diamond brooch has been found.

LADY CHILTERN. Here?

MRS. CHEVELEY. Yes. I missed it when I got back to Claridge's, and I thought I might possibly have dropped it here.

LADY CHILTERN. I have heard nothing about it. But I will send for the butler and ask. (*Touches the bell.*)

MRS. CHEVELEY. Oh, pray don't trouble, Lady Chiltern. I dare say I lost it at the Opera, before we came on here.

LADY MARKBY. Ah yes, I suppose it must have been at the Opera. The fact is, we all scramble and jostle so much nowadays that I wonder we have anything at all left on us at the end of an evening. I know myself that, when I am coming back from the Drawing Room, I always feel as if I hadn't a shred on me, except a small shred of decent reputation, just enough to prevent the lower classes making painful observations through the windows of the carriage. The fact is that our Society is terribly over-populated. Really, someone should arrange a proper scheme of assisted emigration. It would do a great deal of good.

MRS. CHEVELEY. I quite agree with you, Lady Markby. It is nearly six years since I have been in London for the Season, and I must say Society has become dreadfully mixed. One sees the oddest people everywhere.

LADY MARKBY. That is quite true, dear. But one needn't know them. I'm sure I don't know half the people who come to my house. Indeed, from all I hear, I shouldn't like to.

Enter MASON.

LADY CHILTERN. What sort of a brooch was it that you lost, Mrs. Cheveley?

MRS. CHEVELEY. A diamond snake-brooch with a ruby, a rather large ruby.

LADY MARKBY. I thought you said there was a sapphire on the head, dear?

MRS. CHEVELEY (*smiling*). No, Lady Markby—a ruby.

LADY MARKBY (*nodding her head*). And very becoming, I am quite sure.

LADY CHILTERN. Has a ruby and diamond brooch been found in any of the rooms this morning, Mason?

MASON. No, my lady.

MRS. CHEVELEY. It really is of no consequence, Lady Chiltern. I am so sorry to have put you to any inconvenience.

LADY CHILTERN (*coldly*). Oh, it has been no inconvenience. That will do, Mason. You can bring tea.

Exit MASON.

LADY MARKBY. Well, I must say it is most annoying to lose anything. I remember once at Bath, years ago, losing in the Pump Room an exceedingly handsome cameo bracelet that Sir John had given me. I don't think he has ever given me anything since, I am sorry to say. He has sadly degenerated. Really, this horrid House of Commons quite ruins our husbands for us. I think the Lower House by far the greatest blow to a happy married life that there has been since that terrible thing called the Higher Education of Women was invented.

LADY CHILTERN. Ah! it is heresy to say that in this house, Lady Markby. Robert is a great champion of the Higher Education of Women, and so, I am afraid, am I.

MRS. CHEVELEY. The higher education of men is what I should like to see. Men need it so sadly.

LADY MARKBY. They do, dear. But I am afraid such a scheme would be quite unpractical. I don't think man has much capacity for development. He has got as far as he can, and that is not far, is it? With regard to women, well, dear Gertrude, you belong to the younger generation, and I am sure it is all right if you approve of it. In my time, of course, we were taught not to understand anything. That was the old system, and wonderfully interesting it was. I assure you that the amount of things I and my poor dear sister were taught not to understand was quite extraordinary. But modern women understand everything, I am told.

MRS. CHEVELEY. Except their husbands. That is the one thing the modern woman never understands.

LADY MARKBY. And a very good thing too, dear, I dare say. It might break up many a happy home if they did. Not yours, I need hardly say, Gertrude. You have married a pattern husband. I wish I could say as much for myself. But since Sir John has taken to attending the debates regularly, which he never used to do in the good old days, his language has become quite impossible. He always seems to think that he is addressing the House, and consequently whenever he discusses the state of the agricultural labourer, or the Welsh Church, or something quite improper of that kind, I am obliged to send all the servants out of the room. It is not pleasant to see one's own butler, who has been with one for twenty-three years, actually blushing at the side-board, and the footmen making contortions in corners like persons in circuses. I assure you my life will be quite ruined unless they send John at once to the Upper House. He won't take any interest in politics then, will he? The House of Lords is so sensible. An assembly of gentlemen. But in his present state, Sir John is really a great trial. Why, this morning before breakfast was half-over, he stood up on the hearthrug, put his hands in his pockets, and appealed to the country at the top of his voice. I left the table as soon as I had my second cup of tea, I need hardly say. But his violent language could be heard all over the house! I trust, Gertrude, that Sir Robert is not like that?

LADY CHILTERN. But I am very much interested in politics, Lady Markby. I love to hear Robert talk about them.

LADY MARKBY. Well, I hope he is not as devoted to Blue Books as Sir John is. I don't think they can be quite improving reading for anyone.

MRS. CHEVELEY (*languidly*). I have never read a Blue Book. I prefer books . . . in yellow covers.

LADY MARKBY (*genially unconscious*). Yellow is a gayer colour, is it not? I used to wear yellow a good deal in my early days, and would do so now if Sir John was not so painfully personal in his observations, and a man on the question of dress is always ridiculous, is he not?

MRS. CHEVELEY. Oh, no! I think men are the only authorities on dress.

LADY MARKBY. Really? One wouldn't say so from the sort of hats they wear, would one?

The butler enters, followed by the footman. Tea is set on a small table close to LADY CHILTERN.

LADY CHILTERN. May I give you some tea, Mrs. Cheveley?

MRS. CHEVELEY. Thanks.

The butler hands MRS. CHEVELEY *a cup of tea on a salver.*

LADY CHILTERN. Some tea, Lady Markby?

LADY MARKBY. No thanks, dear. (*The servants go out.*) The fact is, I have promised to go round for ten minutes to see poor Lady Brancaster, who is in very great trouble. Her daughter, quite a well-brought-up girl, too, has actually become engaged to be married to a curate in Shropshire. It is very sad, very sad indeed. I can't understand this modern mania for curates. In my time we girls saw them, of course, running about the place like rabbits. But we never took any notice of them, I need hardly say. But I am told that nowadays country society is quite honeycombed with them. I think it most irreligious. And then the eldest son has quarrelled with his father, and it is said that when they meet at the club Lord Brancaster always hides himself behind the money article in *The Times*. However, I believe that is quite a common occurrence nowadays and that they have to take in extra copies of *The Times* at all the clubs in St James's Street; there are so many sons who won't have anything to do with their fathers, and so many fathers who won't speak to their sons. I think myself, it is very much to be regretted.

MRS. CHEVELEY. So do I. Fathers have so much to learn from their sons nowadays.

LADY MARKBY. Really, dear? What?

MRS. CHEVELEY. The art of living. The only really Fine Art we have produced in modern times.

LADY MARKBY (*shaking her head*). Ah! I am afraid Lord Brancaster knew a good deal about that. More than his poor wife ever did. (*Turning to* LADY CHILTERN.) You know Lady Brancaster, don't you, dear?

LADY CHILTERN. Just slightly. She was staying at Langton last autumn, when we were there.

LADY MARKBY. Well, like all stout women, she looks the very picture of happiness, as no doubt you noticed. But there are many tragedies in her family, besides this affair of the curate. Her own sister, Mrs. Jekyll, had a most unhappy life; through no fault of her own, I am sorry to say. She ultimately was so broken-hearted that she went into a convent, or on to the operatic stage, I forget which. No; I think it was decorative art-needlework she took up. I know she had lost all sense of pleasure in life. (*Rising.*) And now, Gertrude, if you will allow me, I shall leave Mrs. Cheveley in your charge and call back for her in a quarter of an hour. Or perhaps, dear Mrs. Cheveley, you wouldn't mind waiting in the carriage while I am with Lady Brancaster. As I intend it to be a visit of condolence, I shan't stay long.

MRS. CHEVELEY (*rising*). I don't mind waiting in the carriage at all, provided there is somebody to look at one.

LADY MARKBY. Well, I hear the curate is always prowling about the house.

MRS. CHEVELEY. I am afraid I am not fond of girl friends.

LADY CHILTERN (*rising*). Oh, I hope Mrs. Cheveley will stay here a little. I should like to have a few minutes' conversation with her.

MRS. CHEVELEY. How very kind of you, Lady Chiltern! Believe me, nothing would give me greater pleasure.

LADY MARKBY. Ah! no doubt you both have many pleasant reminiscences of your schooldays to talk over together. Good-bye, dear Gertrude! Shall I see you at Lady Bonar's tonight? She has discovered a wonderful new genius. He does . . . nothing at all, I believe. That is a great comfort, is it not?

LADY CHILTERN. Robert and I are dining at home by ourselves tonight, and I don't think I shall go anywhere afterwards. Robert, of course, will have to be in the House. But there is nothing interesting on.

LADY MARKBY. Dining at home by yourselves? Is that quite prudent? Ah, I forgot, your husband is an exception. Mine is the general rule, and nothing ages a woman so rapidly as having married the general rule.

Exit LADY MARKBY.

MRS. CHEVELEY. Wonderful woman, Lady Markby, isn't she? Talks more and says less than anybody I ever met. She is made to be a public speaker. Much more so than her husband, though he is a typical Englishman, always dull and usually violent.

LADY CHILTERN (*makes no answer, but remains standing. There is a pause. Then the eyes of the two women meet.* LADY CHILTERN *looks stern and pale.* MRS. CHEVELEY *seems rather amused*). Mrs. Cheveley, I think it is right to tell you quite frankly, had I known who you really were, I should not have invited you to my house last night.

MRS. CHEVELEY (*with an impertinent smile*). Really?

LADY CHILTERN I could not have done so.

MRS. CHEVELEY. I see that after all these years you have not changed a bit, Gertrude.

LADY CHILTERN. I never change.

MRS. CHEVELEY (*elevating her eyebrows*). Then life has taught you nothing?

LADY CHILTERN. It has taught me that a person who has once been guilty of a dishonest and dishonourable action may be guilty of it a second time, and should be shunned.

MRS. CHEVELEY. Would you apply that rule to everyone?

LADY CHILTERN. Yes, to everyone, without exception.

MRS. CHEVELEY. Then I am sorry for you, Gertrude, very sorry for you.

LADY CHILTERN. You see now, I am sure, that for many reasons any further acquaintance between us during your stay in London is quite impossible?

MRS. CHEVELEY (*leaning back in her chair*). Do you know, Gertrude, I don't mind your talking morality a bit. Morality is simply the attitude we adopt towards people whom we personally dislike. You dislike me. I am quite aware of that. And I have always detested you. And yet I have come here to do you a service.

LADY CHILTERN (*contemptuously*). Like the service you wished to render my husband last night, I suppose. Thank heaven, I saved him from that.

MRS. CHEVELEY (*starting to her feet*). It was you who made him write that insolent letter to me? It was you who made him break his promise?

LADY CHILTERN. Yes.

MRS. CHEVELEY. Then you must make him keep it. I give you till tomorrow morning—no more. If by that time your husband does not solemnly bind himself to help me in this great scheme in which I am interested—

LADY CHILTERN. This fraudulent speculation—

MRS. CHEVELEY. Call it what you choose. I hold your husband in the hollow of my hand, and if you are wise you will make him do what I tell him.

LADY CHILTERN (*rising and going towards her*). You are impertinent. What has my husband to do with you? With a woman like you?

MRS. CHEVELEY (*with a bitter laugh*). In this world like meets like. It is because your husband is himself fraudulent and dishonest that we pair so well together. Between you and him there are chasms. He and I are closer than friends. We are enemies linked together. The same sin binds us.

LADY CHILTERN. How dare you class my husband

with yourself? How dare you threaten him or me? Leave my house. You are unfit to enter it.

SIR ROBERT CHILTERN *enters from behind. He hears his wife's last words, and sees to whom they are addressed. He grows deadly pale.*

MRS. CHEVELEY. Your house! A house bought with the price of dishonour. A house, everything in which has been paid for by fraud. (*Turns round and sees* SIR ROBERT CHILTERN.) Ask him what the origin of his fortune is! Get him to tell you how he sold to a stockbroker a Cabinet secret. Learn from him to what you owe your position.

LADY CHILTERN. It is not true! Robert! It is not true!

MRS. CHEVELEY (*pointing at him with outstretched finger*). Look at him! Can he deny it? Does he dare to?

SIR ROBERT CHILTERN. Go! Go at once. You have done your worst now.

MRS. CHEVELEY. My worst? I have not finished with you, with either of you. I give you both till to-morrow at noon. If by then you don't do what I bid you to do, the whole world shall know the origin of Robert Chiltern.

SIR ROBERT CHILTERN *strikes the bell. Enter* MASON.

SIR ROBERT CHILTERN. Show Mrs. Cheveley out.

MRS. CHEVELEY *starts; then bows with somewhat exaggerated politeness to* LADY CHILTERN, *who makes*

no sign of response. As she passes by SIR ROBERT
CHILTERN, *who is standing close to the door, she
pauses for a moment and looks him straight in the
face. She then goes out, followed by the servant, who
closes the door after him. The husband and wife are
left alone.* LADY CHILTERN *stands like someone in a
dreadful dream. Then she turns round and looks at
her husband. She looks at him with strange eyes, as
though she was seeing him for the first time.*

LADY CHILTERN. You sold a Cabinet secret for
money! You began your life with fraud! You
built up your career on dishonour! Oh, tell me
it is not true! Lie to me! Lie to me! Tell me it is
not true!

SIR ROBERT CHILTERN. What this woman said is quite
true. But, Gertrude, listen to me. You don't realize how I was tempted. Let me tell you the
whole thing. (*Goes towards her.*)

LADY CHILTERN. Don't come near me. Don't touch
me. I feel as if you had soiled me for ever. Oh!
what a mask you have been wearing all these
years! A horrible painted mask! You sold yourself for money. Oh! a common thief were better.
You put yourself up to sale to the highest bid-
der! You were bought in the market. You lie to
the whole world. And yet you will not lie to me.

SIR ROBERT CHILTERN (*rushing towards her*). Gertrude! Gertrude!

LADY CHILTERN (*thrusting him back with outstretched
hands*). No, don't speak! Say nothing! Your voice
wakes terrible memories—memories of things

that made me love you—memories of words that made me love you—memories that now are horrible to me. And how I worshipped you! You were to me something apart from common life, a thing pure, noble, honest, without stain. The world seemed to me finer because you were in it, and goodness more real because you lived. And now—oh, when I think that I made of a man like you my ideal! the ideal of my life!

SIR ROBERT CHILTERN. There was your mistake. There was your error. The error all women commit. Why can't you women love us, faults and all? Why do you place us on monstrous pedestals? We have all feet of clay, women as well as men; but when we men love woman, we love them knowing their weaknesses, their follies, their imperfections, love them all the more, it may be, for that reason. It is not the perfect, but the imperfect, who have need of love. It is when we are wounded by our own hands, or by the hands of others, that love should come to cure us—else what use is love at all? All sins, except a sin against itself, Love should forgive. All lives, save loveless lives, true Love should pardon. A man's love is like that. It is wider, larger, more human than a woman's. Women think that they are making ideals of men. What they are making of us are false idols merely. You made your false idol of me, and I had not the courage to come down, show you my wounds, tell you my weaknesses. I was afraid that I might lose your love, as I have lost it now. And so, last night you ruined my life for me—yes, ruined it! What this woman asked of me was nothing compared to what she offered to me. She offered security, peace, stability. The sin of my youth, that I had thought was buried, rose up in front of me, hideous, horrible, with its hands at my throat. I could have killed it for ever, sent it back into its tomb, destroyed its record, burned the one witness against me. You prevented me. No one but you, you know it. And now what is there before me but public disgrace, ruin, terrible shame, the mockery of the world, a lonely dishonoured life, a lonely dishonoured death, it may be, some day? Let women make no more ideals of men! let them not put them on altars and bow before them, or they may ruin other lives as completely as you—you whom I have so wildly loved—have ruined mine!

He passes from the room. LADY CHILTERN *rushes towards him, but the door is closed when she reaches it. Pale with anguish, bewildered, helpless, she sways like a plant in the water. Her hands, outstretched, seem to tremble in the air like blossoms in the wind. Then she flings herself down beside a sofa and buries her face. Her sobs are like the sobs of a child.*

Act Drop

Third Act

SCENE

The Library in Lord Goring's house. An Adam room. On the right is the door leading into the hall. On the left, the door of the smoking-room. A pair of folding doors at the back open into the drawing-room. The fire is lit. Phipps, the Butler, is arranging some newspapers on the writing-table. The distinction of Phipps is his impassivity. He has been termed by enthusiasts the Ideal Butler. The Sphinx is not so incommunicable. He is a mask with a manner. Of his intellectual or emotional life, history knows nothing. He represents the dominance of form.

Enter LORD GORING *in evening dress with a buttonhole. He is wearing a silk hat and Inverness cape. White-gloved, he carries a Louis Seize cane. His are all the delicate fopperies of Fashion. One sees that he stands in immediate relation to modern life, makes it indeed, and so masters it. He is the first well-dressed philosopher in the history of thought.*

LORD GORING. Got my second buttonhole for me, Phipps?

PHIPPS. Yes, my lord.

Takes his hat, cane, and cape, and presents new buttonhole on salver.

LORD GORING. Rather distinguished thing, Phipps. I am the only person of the smallest importance in London at present who wears a buttonhole.

PHIPPS. Yes, my lord. I have observed that.

LORD GORING (*taking out old buttonhole*). You see, Phipps, Fashion is what one wears oneself. What is unfashionable is what other people wear.

PHIPPS. Yes, my lord.

LORD GORING. Just as vulgarity is simply the conduct of other people.

PHIPPS. Yes, my lord.

LORD GORING (*putting in new buttonhole*). And falsehoods the truths of other people.

PHIPPS. Yes, my lord.

LORD GORING. Other people are quite dreadful. The only possible society is oneself.

PHIPPS. Yes, my lord.

LORD GORING. To love oneself is the beginning of a lifelong romance, Phipps.

PHIPPS. Yes, my lord.

LORD GORING (*looking at himself in the glass*). Don't think I quite like this buttonhole, Phipps. Makes me look a little too old. Makes me almost in the prime of life, eh, Phipps?

PHIPPS. I don't observe any alteration in your lordship's appearance.

LORD GORING. You don't, Phipps?

PHIPPS. No, my lord.

LORD GORING. I am not quite sure. For the future a more trivial buttonhole, Phipps, on Thursday evenings.

PHIPPS. I will speak to the florist, my lord. She has had a loss in her family lately, which perhaps accounts for the lack of triviality your lordship complains of in the buttonhole.

LORD GORING. Extraordinary thing about the lower class in England—they are always losing their relations.

PHIPPS. Yes, my lord! They are extremely fortunate in that respect.

LORD GORING (*turns round and looks at him.* PHIPPS *remains impassive*). Hum! Any letters, Phipps?

PHIPPS. Three, my lord. (*Hands letters on a salver.*)

LORD GORING (*takes letters*). Want my cab round in twenty minutes.

PHIPPS. Yes, my lord. (*Goes towards door.*)

LORD GORING (*holds up letter in pink envelope*). Ahem! Phipps, when did this letter arrive?

PHIPPS. It was brought by hand just after your lordship went to the club.

LORD GORING. That will do. (*Exit* PHIPPS.) Lady Chiltern's handwriting on Lady Chiltern's pink notepaper. That is rather curious. I thought Robert was to write. Wonder what Lady Chiltern has got to say to me? (*Sits at bureau, opens letter, and reads it.*) 'I want you. I trust you. I am coming to you. Gertrude.' (*Puts down the letter with a puzzled look. Then takes it up, and reads it again slowly.*) 'I want you. I trust you. I am coming to you.' So she has found out everything! Poor woman! Poor woman! (*Pulls out watch and looks at it.*) But what an hour to call! Ten o'clock! I shall have to give up going to the Berkshires. However, it is always nice to be expected, and not to arrive. I am not expected at the Bachelors', so I shall certainly go there. Well, I will make her stand by her husband. That is the only thing for her to do. That is the only thing for any woman to do. It is the growth of the moral sense in women that makes marriage such a hopeless, one-sided institution. Ten o'clock. She should be here soon. I must tell Phipps I am not in to anyone else.

(*Goes towards bell.*)

Enter PHIPPS.

PHIPPS. Lord Caversham.

LORD GORING. Oh, why will parents always appear at the wrong time? Some extraordinary mistake in nature, I suppose. (*Enter* LORD CAVERSHAM.) Delighted to see you, my dear father. (*Goes to meet him.*)

LORD CAVERSHAM. Take my cloak off.

LORD GORING. Is it worth while, father?

LORD CAVERSHAM. Of course it is worth while, sir. Which is the most comfortable chair?

LORD GORING. This one, father. It is the chair I use myself, when I have visitors.

LORD CAVERSHAM. Thank ye. No draught, I hope, in this room?

LORD GORING. No, father.

LORD CAVERSHAM (*sitting down*). Glad to hear it. Can't stand draughts. No draughts at home.

LORD GORING. Good many breezes, father.

LORD CAVERSHAM. Eh? Eh? Don't understand what you mean. Want to have a serious conversation with you, sir.

LORD GORING. My dear father! At this hour?

LORD CAVERSHAM. Well, sir, it is only ten o'clock. What is your objection to the hour? I think the hour is an admirable hour!

LORD GORING. Well, the fact is, father, this is not my day for talking seriously. I am very sorry, but it is not my day.

LORD CAVERSHAM. What do you mean, sir?

LORD GORING. During the Season, father, I only talk seriously on the first Tuesday in every month, from four to seven.

LORD CAVERSHAM. Well, make it Tuesday, sir, make it Tuesday.

LORD GORING. But it is after seven, father, and my doctor says I must not have any serious conversation after seven. It makes me talk in my sleep.

LORD CAVERSHAM. Talk in your sleep, sir? What does that matter? You are not married.

LORD GORING. No, father, I am not married.

LORD CAVERSHAM. Hum! That is what I have come to talk to you about, sir. You have got to get married, and at once. Why, when I was your age, sir, I had been an inconsolable widower for three months, and was already paying my addresses to your admirable mother. Damme,

91

sir, it is your duty to get married. You can't be always living for pleasure. Every man of position is married nowadays. Bachelors are not fashionable any more. They are a damaged lot. Too much is known about them. You must get a wife, sir. Look where your friend Robert Chiltern has got to by probity, hard work, and a sensible marriage with a good woman. Why don't you imitate him, sir? Why don't you take him for your model?

LORD GORING. I think I shall, father.

LORD CAVERSHAM. I wish you would, sir. Then I should be happy. At present I make your mother's life miserable on your account. You are heartless, sir, quite heartless.

LORD GORING. I hope not, father.

LORD CAVERSHAM. And it is high time for you to get married. You are thirty-four years of age, sir.

LORD GORING. Yes, father, but I only admit to thirty-two—thirty-one and a half when I have a really good buttonhole. This buttonhole is not . . . trivial enough.

LORD CAVERSHAM. I tell you you are thirty-four, sir. And there is a draught in your room, besides, which makes your conduct worse. Why did you tell me there was no draught, sir? I feel a draught, sir, I feel it distinctly.

LORD GORING. So do I, father. It is a dreadful draught. I will come and see you tomorrow, father. We can talk over anything you like. Let me help you on with your cloak, father.

LORD CAVERSHAM. No, sir; I have called this evening for a definite purpose, and I am going to see it through at all costs to my health or yours. Put down my cloak, sir.

LORD GORING. Certainly, father. But let us go into another room. (*Rings bell.*) There is a dreadful draught here. (*Enter* PHIPPS.) Phipps, is there a good fire in the smoking-room?

PHIPPS. Yes, my lord.

LORD GORING. Come in there, father. Your sneezes are quite heartrending.

LORD CAVERSHAM. Well, sir, I suppose I have a right to sneeze when I choose?

LORD GORING (*apologetically*). Quite so, father. I was merely expressing sympathy.

LORD CAVERSHAM. Oh, damn sympathy. There is a great deal too much of that sort of thing going on nowadays.

LORD GORING. I quite agree with you, father. If there was less sympathy in the world there would be less trouble in the world.

LORD CAVERSHAM (*going towards the smoking room*). That is a paradox, sir. I hate paradoxes.

LORD GORING. So do I, father. Everybody one meets is a paradox nowadays. It is a great bore. It makes society so obvious.

LORD CAVERSHAM (*turning round, and looking at his son beneath his bushy eyebrows*). Do you always really understand what you say, sir?

LORD GORING (*after some hesitation*). Yes, father, if I listen attentively.

LORD CAVERSHAM (*indignantly*). If you listen attentively! . . . Conceited young puppy!

Goes off grumbling into the smoking-room. PHIPPS *enters.*

LORD GORING. Phipps, there is a lady coming to see me this evening on particular business. Show her into the drawing-room when she arrives. You understand?

PHIPPS. Yes, my lord.

LORD GORING. It is a matter of the gravest importance, Phipps.

PHIPPS. I understand, my lord.

LORD GORING. No one else is to be admitted, under any circumstances.

PHIPPS. I understand, my lord.

Bell rings.

LORD GORING. Ah! that is probably the lady. I shall see her myself.

Just as he is going towards the door LORD CAVERSHAM *enters from the smoking-room.*

LORD CAVERSHAM. Well, sir? am I to wait attendance on you?

LORD GORING (*considerably perplexed*). In a moment, father. Do excuse me. (LORD CAVERSHAM *goes back.*) Well, remember my instructions, Phipps—into that room.

PHIPPS. Yes, my lord.

LORD GORING *goes into the smoking-room.* HAROLD, *the footman, shows* MRS. CHEVELEY *in. Lamia-like, she is in green and silver. She has a cloak of black satin, lined with dead rose-leaf silk.*

HAROLD. What name, madam?

MRS. CHEVELEY (*to* PHIPPS, *who advances towards her*). Is Lord Goring not here? I was told he was at home?

PHIPPS. His lordship is engaged at present with Lord Caversham, madam.

Turns a cold, glassy eye on HAROLD, *who at once retires.*

MRS. CHEVELEY (*to herself*). How very filial!

PHIPPS. His lordship told me to ask you, madam, to be kind enough to wait in the drawing-room for him. His lordship will come to you there.

MRS. CHEVELEY (*with a look of surprise*). Lord Goring expects me?

PHIPPS. Yes, madam.

MRS. CHEVELEY. Are you quite sure?

PHIPPS. His lordship told me that if a lady called I was to ask her to wait in the drawing-room. (*Goes to the door of the drawing-room and opens it.*) His lordship's directions on the subject were very precise.

MRS. CHEVELEY (*to herself*). How thoughtful of him! To expect the unexpected shows a thoroughly modern intellect. (*Goes towards the drawing-room and looks in*). Ugh! How dreary a bachelor's drawing-room always looks. I shall have to alter all this. (PHIPPS *brings the lamp from the writing-*

table.) No, I don't care for that lamp. It is far too glaring. Light some candles.

PHIPPS (*replaces lamp*). Certainly, madam.

MRS. CHEVELEY. I hope the candles have very becoming shades.

PHIPPS. We have had no complaints about them, madam, as yet.

Passes into the drawing-room and begins to light the candles.

MRS. CHEVELEY (*to herself*). I wonder what woman he is waiting for tonight. It will be delightful to catch him. Men always look so silly when they are caught. And they are always being caught. (*Looks about room and approaches the writing-table.*) What a very interesting room! What a very interesting picture! Wonder what his correspondence is like. (*Takes up letters.*) Oh, what a very uninteresting correspondence! Bills and cards, debts and dowagers! Who on earth writes to him on pink paper! How silly to write on pink paper! It looks like the beginning of a middle-class romance. Romance should never begin with sentiment. It should begin with science and end with a settlement. (*Puts letter down, then takes it up again.*) I know that handwriting. That is Gertrude Chiltern's. I remember it perfectly. The ten commandments in every stroke of the pen, and the moral law all over the page. Wonder what Gertrude is writing to him about? Something horrid about me, I suppose. How I detest that woman! (*Reads it.*) 'I trust

you. I want you. I am coming to you. Gertrude.'
'I trust you. I want you. I am coming to you.'

A look of triumph comes over her face. She is just about to steal the letter, when PHIPPS *comes in.*

PHIPPS. The candles in the drawing-room are lit, madam, as you directed.
MRS. CHEVELEY. Thank you.

Rises hastily and slips the letter under a large silver-cased blotting-book that is lying on the table.

PHIPPS. I trust the shades will be to your liking, madam. They are the most becoming we have. They are the same as his lordship uses himself when he is dressing for dinner.
MRS. CHEVELEY (*with a smile*). Then I am sure they will be perfectly right.
PHIPPS (*gravely*). Thank you, madam.

MRS. CHEVELEY goes into the drawing-room. PHIPPS closes the door and retires. The door is then slowly opened, and MRS. CHEVELEY comes out and creeps stealthily towards the writing-table. Suddenly voices are heard from the smoking-room. MRS. CHEVELEY grows pale, and stops. The voices grow louder, and she goes back into the drawing-room, biting her lip. Enter LORD GORING and LORD CAVERSHAM.

LORD GORING (*expostulating*). My dear father, if I am to get married, surely you will allow me to choose the time, place, and person? Particularly the person.

LORD CAVERSHAM (*testily*). That is a matter for me, sir. You would probably make a very poor choice. It is I who should be consulted, not you. There is property at stake. It is not a matter for affection. Affection comes later on in married life.

LORD GORING. Yes. In married life affection comes when people thoroughly dislike each other, father, doesn't it?

Puts on LORD CAVERSHAM'S *cloak for him.*

LORD CAVERSHAM. Certainly, sir. I mean certainly not, sir. You are talking very foolishly tonight. What I say is that marriage is a matter for common sense.

LORD GORING. But women who have common sense are so curiously plain, father, aren't they? Of course I only speak from hearsay.

LORD CAVERSHAM. No woman, plain or pretty, has any common sense at all, sir. Common sense is the privilege of our sex.

LORD GORING. Quite so. And we men are so self-sacrificing that we never use it, do we, father?

LORD CAVERSHAM. I use it, sir. I use nothing else.

LORD GORING. So my mother tells me.

LORD CAVERSHAM. It is the secret of your mother's happiness. You are very heartless, sir, very heartless.

LORD GORING. I hope not, father.

Goes out for a moment. Then returns, looking rather put out, with SIR ROBERT CHILTERN.

SIR ROBERT CHILTERN. My dear Arthur, what a piece of good luck meeting you on the doorstep! Your servant had just told me you were not at home. How extraordinary!

LORD GORING. The fact is, I am horribly busy tonight, Robert, and I gave orders I was not at home to anyone. Even my father had a comparatively cold reception. He complained of a draught the whole time.

SIR ROBERT CHILTERN. Ah! you must be at home to me, Arthur. You are my best friend. Perhaps by tomorrow you will be my only friend. My wife has discovered everything.

LORD GORING. Ah! I guessed as much!

SIR ROBERT CHILTERN (*looking at him*). Really! How?

LORD GORING (*after some hesitation*). Oh merely by something in the expression of your face as you came in. Who told her?

SIR ROBERT CHILTERN. Mrs. Cheveley herself. And the woman I love knows that I began my career with an act of low dishonesty, that I built up my life upon sands of shame—that I sold, like a common huckster, the secret that had been intrusted to me as a man of honour. I thank heaven poor Lord Radley died without knowing that I betrayed him. I would to God I had died before I had been so horribly tempted, or had fallen so low. (*Burying his face in his hands*).

LORD GORING (*after a pause*). You have heard nothing from Vienna yet, in answer to your wire?

SIR ROBERT CHILTERN (*looking up*). Yes; I got a telegram from the first secretary at eight o'clock tonight.

LORD GORING. Well?

SIR ROBERT CHILTERN. Nothing is absolutely known against her. On the contrary, she occupies a rather high position in society. It is a sort of open secret that Baron Arnheim left her the greater portion of his immense fortune. Beyond that I can learn nothing.

LORD GORING. She doesn't turn out to be a spy, then?

SIR ROBERT CHILTERN. Oh! spies are of no use nowadays. Their profession is over. The newspapers do their work instead.

LORD GORING. And thunderingly well they do it.

SIR ROBERT CHILTERN. Arthur, I am parched with thirst. May I ring for something? Some hock and seltzer?

LORD GORING. Certainly. Let me. (*Rings the bell.*)

SIR ROBERT CHILTERN. Thanks! I don't know what to do, Arthur, I don't know what to do, and you are my only friend. But what a friend you are— the one friend I can trust. I can trust you absolutely, can't I?

Enter PHIPPS.

LORD GORING. My dear Robert, of course. Oh! (*To* PHIPPS.) Bring some hock and seltzer.

PHIPPS. Yes, my lord.

LORD GORING. And Phipps!

PHIPPS. Yes, my lord.

LORD GORING. Will you excuse me for a moment, Robert! I want to give some directions to my servant.

SIR ROBERT CHILTERN. Certainly.

LORD GORING. When that lady calls, tell her that I am not expected home this evening. Tell her that I have been suddenly called out of town. You understand?

PHIPPS. The lady is in that room, my lord. You told me to show her into that room, my lord.

LORD GORING. You did perfectly right. (*Exit* PHIPPS.) What a mess I am in. No; I think I shall get through it. I'll give her a lecture through the door. Awkward thing to manage, though.

SIR ROBERT CHILTERN. Arthur, tell me what I should do. My life seems to have crumbled about me, I am a ship without a rudder in a night without a star.

LORD GORING. Robert, you love your wife, don't you?

SIR ROBERT CHILTERN. I love her more than anything in the world. I used to think ambition the great thing. It is not. Love is the great thing in the world. There is nothing but love, and I love her. But I am defamed in her eyes. I am ignoble in her eyes. There is a wide gulf between us now. She has found me out, Arthur, she has found me out.

LORD GORING. Has she never in her life done some

folly—some indiscretion—that she should not forgive your sin?

SIR ROBERT CHILTERN. My wife! Never! She does not know what weakness or temptation is. I am of clay like other men. She stands apart as good women do—pitiless in her perfection—cold and stern and without mercy. But I love her, Arthur. We are childless, and I have no one else to love, no one else to love me. Perhaps if God had sent us children she might have been kinder to me. But God has given us a lonely house. And she has cut my heart in two. Don't let us talk of it. I was brutal to her this evening. But I suppose when sinners talk to saints they are brutal always. I said to her things that were hideously true, on my side, from my standpoint, from the standpoint of men. But don't let us talk of that.

LORD GORING. Your wife will forgive you. Perhaps at this moment she is forgiving you. She loves you, Robert. Why should she not forgive?

SIR ROBERT CHILTERN. God grant it! God grant it! (*Buries his face in his hands.*) But there is something more I have to tell you, Arthur.

Enter PHIPPS *with drinks.*

PHIPPS (*hands hock and seltzer to* SIR ROBERT CHILTERN). Hock and seltzer, sir.

SIR ROBERT CHILTERN. Thank you.

LORD GORING. Is your carriage here, Robert?

SIR ROBERT CHILTERN. No; I walked from the club.

LORD GORING. Sir Robert will take my cab, Phipps.

PHIPPS. Yes, my lord.

Exit.

LORD GORING. Robert, you don't mind my sending you away?

SIR ROBERT CHILTERN. Arthur, you must let me stay for five minutes. I have made up my mind what I am going to do tonight in the House. The debate on the Argentine Canal is to begin at eleven. (*A chair falls in the drawing-room.*) What is that?

LORD GORING. Nothing.

SIR ROBERT CHILTERN. I heard a chair fall in the next room. Someone has been listening.

LORD GORING. No, no; there is no one there.

SIR ROBERT CHILTERN. There is someone. There are lights in the room and the door is ajar. Someone has been listening to every secret of my life. Arthur, what does this mean?

LORD GORING. Robert, you are excited, unnerved. I tell you there is no one in that room. Sit down, Robert.

SIR ROBERT CHILTERN. Do you give me your word that there is no one there?

LORD GORING. Yes.

SIR ROBERT CHILTERN. Your word of honour? (*Sits down.*)

LORD GORING. Yes.

SIR ROBERT CHILTERN (*rises*). Arthur, let me see for myself.

LORD GORING. No, no.

SIR ROBERT CHILTERN. If there is no one there why should I not look in that room? Arthur, you must let me go into that room and satisfy myself. Let me know that no eavesdropper has heard my life's secret. Arthur, you don't realize what I am going through.

LORD GORING. Robert, this must stop. I have told you that there is no one in that room—that is enough.

SIR ROBERT CHILTERN (*rushes to the door of the room*). It is not enough. I insist on going into this room. You have told me there is no one there, so what reason can you have for refusing me?

LORD GORING. For God's sake, don't! There is someone there. Someone whom you must not see.

SIR ROBERT CHILTERN. Ah, I thought so!

LORD GORING. I forbid you to enter that room.

SIR ROBERT CHILTERN. Stand back. My life is at stake. And I don't care who is there. I will know who it is to whom I have told my secret and my shame. (*Enters room.*)

LORD GORING. Great heavens! his own wife!

SIR ROBERT CHILTERN *comes back, with a look of scorn and anger on his face.*

SIR ROBERT CHILTERN. What explanation have you to give me for the presence of that woman here?

LORD GORING. Robert, I swear to you on my honour that that lady is stainless and guiltless of all offences towards you.

SIR ROBERT CHILTERN. She is a vile, an infamous thing!

LORD GORING. Don't say that, Robert! It was for your sake she came here. It was to try and save you she came here. She loves you and no one else.

SIR ROBERT CHILTERN. You are mad. What have I to do with her intrigues with you? Let her remain your mistress! You are well suited to each other. She, corrupt and shameful—you, false as a friend, treacherous as an enemy even—

LORD GORING. It is not true, Robert. Before heaven, it is not true. In her presence and in yours I will explain all.

SIR ROBERT CHILTERN. Let me pass, sir. You have lied enough upon your word of honour.

SIR ROBERT CHILTERN *goes out.* LORD GORING *rushes to the door of the drawing-room, when* MRS. CHEVE-LEY *comes out, looking radiant and much amused.*

MRS. CHEVELEY (*with a mock curtsey*). Good evening, Lord Goring!

LORD GORING. Mrs. Cheveley! Great heavens! . . . May I ask what you were doing in my drawing-room?

MRS. CHEVELEY. Merely listening. I have a perfect passion for listening through keyholes. One always hears such wonderful things through them.

LORD GORING. Doesn't that sound rather like tempting Providence?

MRS. CHEVELEY. Oh! surely Providence can resist temptation by this time.

Makes a sign to him to take her cloak off, which he does.

LORD GORING. I am glad you have called. I am going to give you some good advice.

MRS. CHEVELEY. Oh! pray don't. One should never give a woman anything that she can't wear in the evening.

LORD GORING. I see you are quite as wilful as you used to be.

MRS. CHEVELEY. Far more! I have greatly improved. I have had more experience.

LORD GORING. Too much experience is a dangerous thing. Pray have a cigarette. Half the pretty women in London smoke cigarettes. Personally I prefer the other half.

MRS. CHEVELEY. Thanks. I never smoke. My dressmaker wouldn't like it, and a woman's first duty in life is to her dressmaker, isn't it? What the second duty is, no one has as yet discovered.

LORD GORING. You have come here to sell me Robert Chiltern's letter, haven't you?

MRS. CHEVELEY. To offer it to you on conditions. How did you guess that?

LORD GORING. Because you haven't mentioned the subject. Have you got it with you?

MRS. CHEVELEY (*sitting down*). Oh, no! A well-made dress has no pockets.

LORD GORING. What is your price for it?

MRS. CHEVELEY. How absurdly English you are! The English think that a cheque-book can solve every problem in life. Why, my dear Arthur, I have very much more money than you have, and quite as much as Robert Chiltern has got hold of. Money is not what I want.

LORD GORING. What do you want then, Mrs. Cheveley?

MRS. CHEVELEY. Why don't you call me Laura?

LORD GORING. I don't like the name.

MRS. CHEVELEY. You used to adore it.

LORD GORING. Yes: that's why.

MRS. CHEVELEY *motions to him to sit down beside her. He smiles, and does so.*

MRS. CHEVELEY. Arthur, you loved me once.

LORD GORING. Yes.

MRS. CHEVELEY. And you asked me to be your wife.

LORD GORING. That was the natural result of my loving you.

MRS. CHEVELEY. And you threw me over because you saw, or said you saw, poor old Lord Mortlake trying to have a violent flirtation with me in the conservatory at Tenby.

LORD GORING. I am under the impression that my lawyer settled the matter with you on certain terms . . . dictated by yourself.

MRS. CHEVELEY. At the time I was poor; you were rich.

LORD GORING. Quite so. That is why you pretended to love me.

MRS. CHEVELEY (*shrugging her shoulders*). Poor old Lord Mortlake, who had only two topics of conversation, his gout and his wife! I never could quite make out which of the two he was talking about. He used the most horrible language about them both. Well, you were silly, Arthur. Why, Lord Mortlake was never anything more to me than amusement. One of those utterly tedious amusements one only finds at an English country house on an English country Sunday. I don't think anyone at all morally responsible for what he or she does at an English country house.

LORD GORING. Yes. I know lots of people think that.

MRS. CHEVELEY. I loved you, Arthur.

LORD GORING. My dear Mrs. Cheveley, you have always been far too clever to know anything about love.

MRS. CHEVELEY. I did love you. And you loved me. You know you loved me; and love is a very wonderful thing. I suppose that when a man has once loved a woman, he will do anything for her, except continue to love her? (*Puts her hand on his.*)

LORD GORING (*taking his hand away quietly*). Yes; except that.

MRS. CHEVELEY (*after a pause*). I am tired of living abroad. I want to come back to London. I want to have a charming house here. I want to have a salon. If one could only teach the English how to talk, and the Irish how to listen, society here would be quite civilized. Besides, I have arrived at the romantic stage. When I saw you last night at the Chilterns', I knew you were the only person I had ever cared for, if I ever have cared for anybody, Arthur. And so, on the morning of the day you marry me, I will give you Robert Chiltern's letter. That is my offer. I will give it to you now, if you promise to marry me.

LORD GORING. Now?

MRS. CHEVELEY (smiling). Tomorrow.

LORD GORING. Are you really serious?

MRS. CHEVELEY. Yes, quite serious.

LORD GORING. I should make you a very bad husband.

MRS. CHEVELEY. I don't mind bad husbands. I have had two. They amused me immensely.

LORD GORING. You mean that you amused yourself immensely, don't you?

MRS. CHEVELEY. What do you know about my married life?

LORD GORING. Nothing: but I can read it like a book.

MRS. CHEVELEY. What book?

LORD GORING (rising). The Book of Numbers.

MRS. CHEVELEY. Do you think it is quite charming of you to be so rude to a woman in your own house?

LORD GORING. In the case of very fascinating women, sex is a challenge, not a defence.

MRS. CHEVELEY. I suppose that is meant for a compliment. My dear Arthur, women are never disarmed by compliments. Men always are. That is the difference between the two sexes.

LORD GORING. Women are never disarmed by anything, as far as I know them.

MRS. CHEVELEY (*after a pause*). Then you are going to allow your greatest friend, Robert Chiltern, to be ruined, rather than marry someone who really has considerable attractions left. I thought you would have risen to some great height of self-sacrifice, Arthur. I think you should. And the rest of your life you could spend in contemplating your own perfections.

LORD GORING. Oh! I do that as it is. And self-sacrifice is a thing that should be put down by law. It is so demoralizing to the people for whom one sacrifices oneself. They always go to the bad.

MRS. CHEVELEY. As if anything could demoralize Robert Chiltern! You seem to forget that I know his real character.

LORD GORING. What you know about him is not his real character. It was an act of folly done in his youth, dishonourable, I admit, shameful, I admit, unworthy of him, I admit, and therefore . . . not his true character.

MRS. CHEVELEY. How you men stand up for each other!

LORD GORING. How you women war against each other!

MRS. CHEVELEY (*bitterly*). I only war against one woman, against Gertrude Chiltern. I hate her. I hate her now more than ever.

LORD GORING. Because you have brought a real tragedy into her life, I suppose?

MRS. CHEVELEY (*with a sneer*). Oh, there is only one real tragedy in a woman's life. The fact that her past is always her lover, and her future invariably her husband.

LORD GORING. Lady Chiltern knows nothing of the kind of life to which you are alluding.

MRS. CHEVELEY. A woman whose size in gloves is seven and three-quarters never knows much about anything. You know Gertrude has always worn seven and three-quarters? That is one of the reasons why there was never any moral sympathy between us. . . . Well, Arthur, I suppose this romantic interview may be regarded as at an end. You admit it was romantic, don't you? For the privilege of being your wife I was ready to surrender a great prize, the climax of my diplomatic career. You decline. Very well. If Sir Robert doesn't uphold my Argentine scheme, I expose him. *Voilà tout.*

LORD GORING. You mustn't do that. It would be vile, horrible, infamous.

MRS. CHEVELEY (*shrugging her shoulders*). Oh! don't use big words. They mean so little. It is a commercial transaction. That is all. There is no good mixing sentimentality in it. I offered to sell Robert Chiltern a certain thing. If he won't pay me my price, he will have to pay the world a greater price. There is no more to be said. I must go. Good-bye. Won't you shake hands?

LORD GORING. With you? No. Your transaction with Robert Chiltern may pass as a loathsome commercial transaction of a loathsome commercial age; but you seem to have forgotten that you came here tonight to talk of love, you whose lips desecrated the word love, you to whom the thing is a book closely sealed, went this afternoon to the house of one of the most noble and gentle women in the world to degrade her husband in her eyes, to try and kill her love for him, to put poison in her heart, and bitterness in her life, to break her idol, and, it may be, spoil her soul. That I cannot forgive you. That was horrible. For that there can be no forgiveness.

MRS. CHEVELEY. Arthur, you are unjust to me. Believe me, you are quite unjust to me. I didn't go to taunt Gertrude at all. I had no idea of doing anything of the kind when I entered. I called with Lady Markby simply to ask whether an ornament, a jewel, that I lost somewhere last night, had been found at the Chilterns'. If you don't believe me, you can ask Lady Markby. She will tell you it is true. The scene that occurred happened after Lady Markby had left, and was really forced on me by Gertrude's rudeness and sneers. I called, oh!—a little out of malice if you like—but really to ask if a diamond brooch of mine had been found. That was the origin of the whole thing.

LORD GORING. A diamond snake-brooch with a ruby?

MRS. CHEVELEY. Yes. How do you know?

LORD GORING. Because it is found. In point of fact, I found it myself, and stupidly forgot to tell the butler anything about it as I was leaving. (*Goes over to the writing-table and pulls out the drawers.*) It is in this drawer. No, that one. This is the brooch, isn't it? (*Holds up the brooch.*)

MRS. CHEVELEY. Yes. I am so glad to get it back. It was . . . a present.

LORD GORING. Won't you wear it?

MRS. CHEVELEY. Certainly, if you pin it in. (LORD GORING *suddenly clasps it on her arm.*) Why do you put it on as a bracelet? I never knew it could be worn as a bracelet.

LORD GORING. Really?

MRS. CHEVELEY (*holding out her handsome arm*). No; but it looks very well on me as a bracelet, doesn't it?

LORD GORING. Yes; much better than when I saw it last.

MRS. CHEVELEY. When did you see it last?

LORD GORING (*calmly*). Oh, ten years ago, on Lady Berkshire, from whom you stole it.

MRS. CHEVELEY (*starting*). What do you mean?

LORD GORING. I mean that you stole that ornament from my cousin, Mary Berkshire, to whom I gave it when she was married. Suspicion fell on a wretched servant, who was sent away in disgrace. I recognized it last night. I determined to say nothing about it till I had found the thief. I have found the thief now, and I have heard her own confession.

MRS. CHEVELEY (*tossing her head*). It is not true.

LORD GORING. You know it is true. Why, thief is written across your face at this moment.

113

MRS. CHEVELEY. I will deny the whole affair from beginning to end. I will say that I have never seen this wretched thing, that it was never in my possession.

MRS. CHEVELEY *tries to get the bracelet off her arm, but fails.* LORD GORING *looks on amused. Her thin fingers tear at the jewel to no purpose. A curse breaks from her.*

LORD GORING. The drawback of stealing a thing, Mrs. Cheveley, is that one never knows how wonderful the thing that one steals is. You can't get that bracelet off, unless you know where the spring is. And I see you don't know where the spring is. It is rather difficult to find.

MRS. CHEVELEY. You brute! You coward! (*She tries again to unclasp the bracelet, but fails.*)

LORD GORING. Oh! don't use big words. They mean so little.

MRS. CHEVELEY (*again tears at the bracelet in a paroxysm of rage, with inarticulate sounds. Then stops, and looks at* LORD GORING). What are you going to do?

LORD GORING. I am going to ring for my servant. He is an admirable servant. Always comes in the moment one rings for him. When he comes I will tell him to fetch the police.

MRS. CHEVELEY (*trembling*). The police? What for?

LORD GORING. Tomorrow the Berkshires will prosecute you. That is what the police are for.

MRS. CHEVELEY (*is now in an agony of physical terror.*

Her face is distorted. Her mouth awry. A mask has fallen from her. She is, for the moment, dreadful to look at). Don't do that. I will do anything you want. Anything in the world you want.

LORD GORING. Give me Robert Chiltern's letter.

MRS. CHEVELEY. Stop! Stop! Let me have time to think.

LORD GORING. Give me Robert Chiltern's letter.

MRS CHEVELEY. I have not got it with me. I will give it to you tomorrow.

LORD GORING. You know you are lying. Give it to me at once.

MRS. CHEVELEY *pulls the letter out, and hands it to him. She is horribly pale.*

This is it?

MRS. CHEVELEY *(in a hoarse voice).* Yes.

LORD GORING *(takes the letter, examines it, sighs, and burns it over the lamp).* For so well-dressed a woman, Mrs. Cheveley, you have moments of admirable common sense. I congratulate you.

MRS. CHEVELEY *(catches sight of* LADY CHILTERN'S *letter, the cover of which is just showing from under the blotting-book).* Please get me a glass of water.

LORD GORING. Certainly.

Goes to the corner of the room and pours out a glass of water. While his back is turned MRS. CHEVELEY *steals* LADY CHILTERN'S *letter. When* LORD GORING *returns with the glass she refuses it with a gesture.*

MRS. CHEVELEY. Thank you. Will you help me on with my cloak?

LORD GORING. With pleasure. (*Puts her cloak on.*)

MRS. CHEVELEY. Thanks. I am never going to try to harm Robert Chiltern again.

LORD GORING. Fortunately you have not the chance, Mrs. Cheveley.

MRS. CHEVELEY. Well, even if I had the chance, I wouldn't. On the contrary, I am going to render him a great service.

LORD GORING. I am charmed to hear it. It is a reformation.

MRS. CHEVELEY. Yes. I can't bear so upright a gentleman, so honourable an English gentleman, being so shamefully deceived, and so—

LORD GORING. Well?

MRS. CHEVELEY. I find that somehow Gertrude Chiltern's dying speech and confession has strayed into my pocket.

LORD GORING. What do you mean?

MRS. CHEVELEY (*with a bitter note of triumph in her voice*). I mean that I am going to send Robert Chiltern the love-letter his wife wrote to you tonight.

LORD GORING. Love-letter?

MRS. CHEVELEY (*laughing*). 'I want you. I trust you, I am coming to you. Gertrude.'

LORD GORING *rushes to the bureau and takes up the envelope, finds it empty, and turns round.*

LORD GORING. You wretched woman, must you always be thieving? Give me back that letter. I'll take it from you by force. You shall not leave my room till I have got it.

He rushes towards her, but MRS. CHEVELEY *at once puts her hand on the electric bell that is on the table. The bell sounds with shrill reverberations, and* PHIPPS *enters.*

MRS. CHEVELEY (*after a pause*). Lord Goring merely rang that you should show me out. Good night, Lord Goring!

Goes out followed by PHIPPS. *Her face is illuminated with evil triumph. There is joy in her eyes. Youth seems to have come back to her. Her last glance is like a swift arrow.* LORD GORING *bites his lip, and lights a cigarette.*

Act Drop

Fourth Act

Same as Act II. LORD GORING is standing by the fireplace with his hands in his pockets. He is looking rather bored.

LORD GORING (*pulls out his watch, inspects it, and rings the bell*). It is a great nuisance. I can't find anyone in this house to talk to. And I am full of interesting information. I feel like the latest edition of something or other.

Enter servant.

JAMES. Sir Robert is still at the Foreign Office, my lord.
LORD GORING. Lady Chiltern not down yet?
JAMES. Her ladyship has not yet left her room. Miss Chiltern has just come in from riding.
LORD GORING (*to himself*). Ah! that is something.
JAMES. Lord Caversham has been waiting some time in the library for Sir Robert. I told him your lordship was here.

LORD GORING. Thank you. Would you kindly tell him I've gone?

JAMES (*bowing*). I shall do so, my lord.

Exit servant.

LORD GORING. Really, I don't want to meet my father three days running. It is a great deal too much excitement for any son. I hope to goodness he won't come up. Fathers should be neither seen nor heard. That is the only proper basis for family life. Mothers are different. Mothers are darlings.

Throws himself down into a chair, picks up a paper and begins to read it. Enter LORD CAVERSHAM.

LORD CAVERSHAM. Well, sir, what are you doing here? Wasting your time as usual, I suppose?

LORD GORING (*throws down paper and rises*). My dear father, when one pays a visit it is for the purpose of wasting other people's time, not one's own.

LORD CAVERSHAM. Have you been thinking over what I spoke to you about last night?

LORD GORING. I have been thinking about nothing else.

LORD CAVERSHAM. Engaged to be married yet?

LORD GORING (*genially*). Not yet; but I hope to be before lunch-time.

LORD CAVERSHAM (*caustically*). You can have till

119

dinner-time if it would be of any convenience to you.

LORD GORING. Thanks awfully, but I think I'd sooner be engaged before lunch.

LORD CAVERSHAM. Humph! Never know when you are serious or not.

LORD GORING. Neither do I, father.

A pause.

LORD CAVERSHAM. I suppose you have read *The Times* this morning?

LORD GORING (*airily*). *The Times*? Certainly not. I only read *The Morning Post*. All that one should know about modern life is where the Duchesses are; anything else is quite demoralizing.

LORD CAVERSHAM. Do you mean to say you have not read *The Times* leading article on Robert Chiltern's career?

LORD GORING. Good heavens! No. What does it say?

LORD CAVERSHAM. What should it say, sir? Everything complimentary, of course. Chiltern's speech last night on this Argentine Canal scheme was one of the finest pieces of oratory ever delivered in the House since Canning.

LORD GORING. Ah! Never heard of Canning. Never wanted to. And did . . . did Chiltern uphold the scheme?

LORD CAVERSHAM. Uphold it, sir? How little you know him! Why, he denounced it roundly, and the whole system of modern political finance. This speech is the turning-point in his career, as

The Times points out. You should read this article, sir. (*Opens* The Times.) 'Sir Robert Chiltern . . . most rising of our young statesmen . . . Brilliant orator . . . Unblemished career . . . Well-known integrity of character . . . Represents what is best in English public life . . . Noble contrast to the lax morality so common among foreign politicians.' They will never say that of you, sir.

LORD GORING. I sincerely hope not, father. However, I am delighted at what you tell me about Robert, thoroughly delighted. It shows he has got pluck.

LORD CAVERSHAM. He has got more than pluck, sir, he has got genius.

LORD GORING. Ah! I prefer pluck. It is not so common, nowadays, as genius is.

LORD CAVERSHAM. I wish you would go into Parliament.

LORD GORING. My dear father, only people who look dull ever get into the House of Commons, and only people who are dull ever succeed there.

LORD CAVERSHAM. Why don't you try to do something useful in life?

LORD GORING. I am far too young.

LORD CAVERSHAM (*testily*). I hate this affectation of youth, sir. It is a great deal too prevalent nowadays.

LORD GORING. Youth isn't an affectation. Youth is an art.

LORD CAVERSHAM. Why don't you propose to that pretty Miss Chiltern?

LORD GORING. I am a very nervous disposition, especially in the morning.

LORD CAVERSHAM. I don't suppose there is the smallest chance of her accepting you.

LORD GORING. I don't know how the betting stands today.

LORD CAVERSHAM. If she did accept you she would be the prettiest fool in England.

LORD GORING. That is just what I should like to marry. A thoroughly sensible wife would reduce me to a condition of absolute idiocy in less than six months.

LORD CAVERSHAM. You don't deserve her, sir.

LORD GORING. My dear father, if we men married the women we deserved, we should have a very bad time of it.

Enter MABEL CHILTERN.

MABEL CHILTERN. Oh! . . . How do you do, Lord Caversham? I hope Lady Caversham is quite well?

LORD CAVERSHAM. Lady Caversham is as usual, as usual.

LORD GORING. Good morning, Miss Mabel!

MABEL CHILTERN (*taking no notice at all of* LORD GORING, *and addressing herself exclusively to* LORD CAVERSHAM). And Lady Caversham's bonnets . . . are they at all better?

LORD CAVERSHAM. They have had a serious relapse, I am sorry to say.

LORD GORING. Good morning, Miss Mabel!

MABEL CHILTERN (*to* LORD CAVERSHAM). I hope an operation will not be necessary.

LORD CAVERSHAM (*smiling at her pertness*). If it is, we shall have to give Lady Caversham a narcotic. Otherwise she would never consent to have a feather touched.

LORD GORING (*with increased emphasis*). Good morning, Miss Mabel!

MABEL CHILTERN (*turning round with feigned surprise*). Oh, are you here? Of course you understand that after your breaking your appointment I am never going to speak to you again.

LORD GORING. Oh, please don't say such a thing. You are the one person in London I really like to have to listen to me.

MABEL CHILTERN. Lord Goring. I never believe a single word that either you or I say to each other.

LORD CAVERSHAM. You are quite right, my dear, quite right . . . as far as he is concerned, I mean.

MABEL CHILTERN. Do you think you could possibly make your son behave a little better occasionally? Just as a change.

LORD CAVERSHAM. I regret to say, Miss Chiltern, that I have no influence at all over my son. I wish I had. If I had, I know what I would make him do.

MABEL CHILTERN. I am afraid that he has one of those terribly weak natures that are not susceptible to influence.

LORD CAVERSHAM. He is very heartless, very heartless.

LORD GORING. It seems to me that I am a little in the way here.

MABEL CHILTERN. It is very good for you to be in the way, and to know what people say of you behind your back.

LORD GORING. I don't at all like knowing what people say of me behind my back. It makes me far too conceited.

LORD CAVERSHAM. After that, my dear, I really must bid you good morning.

MABEL CHILTERN. Oh! I hope you are not going to leave me all alone with Lord Goring? Especially at such an early hour in the day.

LORD CAVERSHAM. I am afraid I can't take him with me to Downing Street. It is not the Prime Minister's day for seeing the unemployed.

Shakes hands with MABEL CHILTERN, *takes up his hat and stick, and goes out, with a parting glare of indignation at* LORD GORING.

MABEL CHILTERN (*takes up roses and begins to arrange them in a bowl on the table*). People who don't keep their appointments in the Park are horrid.

LORD GORING. Detestable.

MABEL CHILTERN. I am glad you admit it. But I wish you wouldn't look so pleased about it.

LORD GORING. I can't help it. I always look pleased when I am with you.

MABEL CHILTERN (*sadly*). Then I suppose it is my duty to remain with you?

LORD GORING. Of course it is.

MABEL CHILTERN. Well, my duty is a thing I never do, on principle. It always depresses me. So I am afraid I must leave you.

LORD GORING. Please don't, Miss Mabel. I have something very particular to say to you.

MABEL CHILTERN (*rapturously*). Oh, is it a proposal?

LORD GORING (*somewhat taken aback*). Well, yes, it is—I am bound to say it is.

MABEL CHILTERN (*with a sigh of pleasure*). I am so glad. That makes the second today.

LORD GORING (*indignantly*). The second today? What conceited ass has been impertinent enough to dare to propose to you before I had proposed to you?

MABEL CHILTERN. Tommy Trafford, of course. It is one of Tommy's days for proposing. He always proposes on Tuesdays and Thursdays, during the Season.

LORD GORING. You didn't accept him, I hope?

MABEL CHILTERN. I make it a rule never to accept Tommy. That is why he goes on proposing. Of course, as you didn't turn up this morning, I very nearly said yes. It would have been an excellent lesson both for him and for you if I had. It would have taught you both better manners.

LORD GORING. Oh! bother Tommy Trafford. Tommy is a silly little ass. I love you.

MABEL CHILTERN. I know. And I think you might

have mentioned it before. I am sure I have given you heaps of opportunities.

LORD GORING. Mabel, do be serious. Please be serious.

MABEL CHILTERN. Ah! that is the sort of thing a man always says to a girl before he has been married to her. He never says it afterwards.

LORD GORING (*taking hold of her hand*). Mabel, I have told you that I love you. Can't you love me a little in return?

MABEL CHILTERN. You silly Arthur! If you knew anything about . . . anything, which you don't, you would know that I adore you. Everyone in London knows it except you. It is a public scandal the way I adore you. I have been going about for the last six months telling the whole of society that I adore you. I wonder you consent to have anything to say to me. I have no character left at all. At least, I feel so happy that I am quite sure I have no character left at all.

LORD GORING (*catches her in his arms and kisses her. Then there is a pause of bliss*). Dear! Do you know I was awfully afraid of being refused!

MABEL CHILTERN (*looking up at him*). But you never have been refused yet by anybody, have you, Arthur? I can't imagine anyone refusing you.

LORD GORING (*after kissing her again*). Of course I'm not nearly good enough for you, Mabel.

MABEL CHILTERN (*nestling close to him*). I am so glad, darling. I was afraid you were.

LORD GORING (*after some hesitation*). And I'm . . . I'm a little over thirty.

MABEL CHILTERN. Dear, you look weeks younger than that.

LORD GORING (*enthusiastically*). How sweet of you to say so! . . . And it is only fair to tell you frankly that I am fearfully extravagant.

MABEL CHILTERN. But so am I, Arthur. So we're sure to agree. And now I must go and see Gertrude.

LORD GORING. Must you really? (*Kisses her.*)

MABEL CHILTERN. Yes.

LORD GORING. Then do tell her I want to talk to her particularly. I have been waiting here all the morning to see either her or Robert.

MABEL CHILTERN. Do you mean to say you didn't come here expressly to propose to me?

LORD GORING (*triumphantly*). No; that was a flash of genius.

MABEL CHILTERN. Your first.

LORD GORING (*with determination*). My last.

MABEL CHILTERN. I am delighted to hear it. Now don't stir. I'll be back in five minutes. And don't fall into any temptations while I am away.

LORD GORING. Dear Mabel, while you are away, there are none. It makes me horribly dependent on you.

Enter LADY CHILTERN.

LADY CHILTERN. Good morning, dear! How pretty you are looking!

MABEL CHILTERN. How pale you are looking, Gertrude! It is most becoming!

LADY CHILTERN. Good morning, Lord Goring!

127

LORD GORING (*bowing*). Good morning, Lady Chiltern.

MABEL CHILTERN (*aside to* LORD GORING). I shall be in the conservatory, under the second palm tree on the left.

LORD GORING. Second on the left?

MABEL CHILTERN (*with a look of mock surprise*). Yes; the usual palm tree.

Blows a kiss to him, unobserved by LADY CHILTERN, *and goes out.*

LORD GORING. Lady Chiltern, I have a certain amount of very good news to tell you. Mrs. Cheveley gave me up Robert's letter last night, and I burned it. Robert is safe.

LADY CHILTERN (*sinking on the sofa*). Safe! Oh! I am so glad of that. What a good friend you are to him—to us!

LORD GORING. There is only one person now that could be said to be in any danger.

LADY CHILTERN. Who is that?

LORD GORING (*sitting down beside her*). Yourself.

LADY CHILTERN. I! In danger? What do you mean?

LORD GORING. Danger is too great a word. It is a word I should not have used. But I admit I have something to tell you that may distress you, that terribly distresses me. Yesterday evening you wrote me a very beautiful, womanly letter, asking me for my help. You wrote to me as one of your oldest friends, one of your husband's oldest friends. Mrs. Cheveley stole that letter from my rooms.

LADY CHILTERN. Well, what use is it to her? Why should she not have it?

LORD GORING (*rising*). Lady Chiltern, I will be quite frank with you. Mrs. Cheveley puts a certain construction on that letter and proposes to send it to your husband.

LADY CHILTERN. But what construction could she put on it? . . . Oh! not that! not that! If I in—in trouble, and wanting your help, trusting you, propose to come to you . . . that you may advise me . . . assist me . . . Oh! are there women so horrible as that . . . ? And she proposes to send it to my husband? Tell me what happened. Tell me all that happened.

LORD GORING. Mrs. Cheveley was concealed in a room adjoining my library, without my knowledge. I thought that the person who was waiting in that room to see me was yourself. Robert came in unexpectedly. A chair or something fell in the room. He forced his way in, and he discovered her. We had a terrible scene. I still thought it was you. He left me in anger. At the end of everything Mrs. Cheveley got possession of your letter—she stole it, when or how, I don't know.

LADY CHILTERN. At what hour did this happen?

LORD GORING. At half past ten. And now I propose that we tell Robert the whole thing at once.

LADY CHILTERN (*looking at him with amazement that is almost terror*). You want me to tell Robert that the woman you expected was not Mrs. Cheveley, but myself? That it was I whom you

129

thought was concealed in a room in your house, at half-past ten o'clock at night? You want me to tell him that?

LORD GORING. I think it is better that he should know the exact truth.

LADY CHILTERN (rising). Oh, I couldn't, I couldn't!

LORD GORING. May I do it?

LADY CHILTERN. No.

LORD GORING (gravely). You are wrong, Lady Chiltern.

LADY CHILTERN. No. The letter must be intercepted. That is all. But how can I do it? Letters arrive for him every moment of the day. His secretaries open them and hand them to him. I dare not ask the servants to bring me his letters. It would be impossible. Oh! why don't you tell me what do to?

LORD GORING. Pray be calm, Lady Chiltern, and answer the questions I am going to put to you. You said his secretaries open his letters.

LADY CHILTERN. Yes.

LORD GORING. Who is with him today? Mr. Trafford, isn't it?

LADY CHILTERN. No. Mr. Montford, I think.

LORD GORING. You can trust him?

LADY CHILTERN (with a gesture of despair). Oh! how do I know?

LORD GORING. He would do what you asked him, wouldn't he?

LADY CHILTERN. I think so.

LORD GORING. Your letter was on pink paper. He

could recognize it without reading it, couldn't he? By the colour?

LADY CHILTERN. I suppose so.

LORD GORING. Is he in the house now?

LADY CHILTERN. Yes.

LORD GORING. Then I will go and see him myself, and tell him that a certain letter, written on pink paper, is to be forwarded to Robert today, and that at all costs it must not reach him. (*Goes to the door, and opens it.*) Oh! Robert is coming upstairs with the letter in his hand. It has reached him already.

LADY CHILTERN (*with a cry of pain*). Oh! you have saved his life; what have you done with mine?

Enter SIR ROBERT CHILTERN. *He has the letter in his hand, and is reading it. He comes towards his wife, not noticing* LORD GORING'S *presence.*

SIR ROBERT CHILTERN. 'I want you. I trust you. I am coming to you, Gertrude.' Oh, my love! is this true? Do you indeed trust me, and want me? If so, it was for me to come to you, not for you to write of coming to me. This letter of yours, Gertrude, makes me feel that nothing that the world may do can hurt me now. You want me, Gertrude?

LORD GORING, *unseen by* SIR ROBERT CHILTERN, *makes an imploring sign to* LADY CHILTERN *to accept the situation and* SIR ROBERT'S *error.*

LADY CHILTERN. Yes.

SIR ROBERT CHILTERN. You trust me, Gertrude?

LADY CHILTERN. Yes.

SIR ROBERT CHILTERN. Ah! why did you not add you loved me?

LADY CHILTERN (*taking his hand*). Because I loved you.

LORD GORING *passes into the conservatory.*

SIR ROBERT CHILTERN (*kisses her*). Gertrude, you don't know what I feel. When Montford passed me your letter across the table—he had opened it by mistake, I suppose, without looking at the handwriting on the envelope—and I read it—oh! I did not care what disgrace or punishment was in store for me, I only thought you loved me still.

LADY CHILTERN. There is no disgrace in store for you, nor any public shame. Mrs. Cheveley has handed over to Lord Goring the document that was in her possession, and he has destroyed it.

SIR ROBERT CHILTERN. Are you sure of this, Gertrude?

LADY CHILTERN. Yes; Lord Goring has just told me.

SIR ROBERT CHILTERN. Then I am safe! Oh! What a wonderful thing to be safe! For two days I have been in terror. I am safe now. How did Arthur destroy my letter? Tell me.

LADY CHILTERN. He burned it.

SIR ROBERT CHILTERN. I wish I had seen that one sin of my youth burning to ashes. How many men there are in modern life who would like to see

their past burning to white ashes before them!
Is Arthur still here?

LADY CHILTERN. Yes; he is in the conservatory.

SIR ROBERT CHILTERN. I am so glad now I made that
speech last night in the House, so glad. I made
it thinking that public disgrace might be the result. But it has not been so.

LADY CHILTERN. Public honour has been the result.

SIR ROBERT CHILTERN. I think so. I fear so, almost.
For although I am safe from detection, although
every proof against me is destroyed, I suppose,
Gertrude . . . I suppose I should retire from
public life? (*He looks anxiously at his wife.*)

LADY CHILTERN (*eagerly*). Oh yes, Robert, you
should do that. It is your duty to do that.

SIR ROBERT CHILTERN. It is much to surrender.

LADY CHILTERN. No; it will be much to gain.

SIR ROBERT CHILTERN *walks up and down the room
with a troubled expression. Then comes over to his
wife, and puts his hand on her shoulder.*

SIR ROBERT CHILTERN. And you would be happy living somewhere alone with me, abroad perhaps,
or in the country away from London, away
from public life? You would have no regrets?

LADY CHILTERN. Oh! none, Robert.

SIR ROBERT CHILTERN (*sadly*). And your ambition for
me? You used to be ambitious for me.

LADY CHILTERN. Oh, my ambition! I have none now,
but that we two may love each other. It was

your ambition that led you astray. Let us not talk about ambition.

LORD GORING *returns from the conservatory, looking very pleased with himself, and with an entirely new buttonhole that someone has made for him.*

SIR ROBERT CHILTERN (*going towards him*). Arthur, I have to thank you for what you have done for me. I don't know how I can repay you.

Shakes hands with him.

LORD GORING. My dear fellow, I'll tell you at once. At the present moment, under the usual palm tree . . . I mean in the conservatory . . .

Enter MASON.

MASON. Lord Caversham.

LORD GORING. That admirable father of mine really makes a habit of turning up at the wrong moment. It is very heartless of him, very heartless indeed.

Enter LORD CAVERSHAM. MASON *goes out.*

LORD CAVERSHAM. Good morning, Lady Chiltern! Warmest congratulations to you, Chiltern, on your brilliant speech last night. I have just left the Prime Minister, and you are to have the vacant seat in the Cabinet.

SIR ROBERT CHILTERN (*with a look of joy and triumph*). A seat in the Cabinet?

LORD CAVERSHAM. Yes; here is the Prime Minister's letter. (*Hands letter.*)

SIR ROBERT CHILTERN (*takes letter and reads it*). A seat in the cabinet!

LORD CAVERSHAM. Certainly, and you well deserve it too. You have got what we want so much in political life nowadays—high character, high moral tone, high principles. (*To* LORD GORING.) Everything that you have not got, sir, and never will have.

LORD GORING. I don't like principles, father. I prefer prejudices.

SIR ROBERT CHILTERN *is on the brink of accepting the Prime Minister's offer, when he sees his wife looking at him with clear, candid eyes. He then realizes that it is impossible.*

SIR ROBERT CHILTERN. I cannot accept this offer, Lord Caversham. I have made up my mind to decline it.

LORD CAVERSHAM. Decline it, sir!

SIR ROBERT CHILTERN. My intention is to retire at once from public life.

LORD CAVERSHAM (*angrily*). Decline a seat in the Cabinet, and retire from public life? Never heard such damned nonsense in the whole course of my existence. I beg your pardon, Lady

Chiltern. Chiltern, I beg your pardon. (*To* LORD GORING.) Don't grin like that, sir.

LORD GORING. No, father.

LORD CAVERSHAM. Lady Chiltern, you are a sensible woman, the most sensible woman in London, the most sensible woman I know. Will you kindly prevent your husband from making such a . . . from talking such . . . Will you kindly do that, Lady Chiltern?

LADY CHILTERN. I think my husband is right in his determination, Lord Caversham. I approve of it.

LORD CAVERSHAM. You approve of it? Good heavens!

LADY CHILTERN (*taking her husband's hand*). I admire him for it. I admire him immensely for it. I have never admired him so much before. He is finer than even I thought him. (*To* SIR ROBERT CHILTERN.) You will go and write your letter to the Prime Minister now, won't you? Don't hesitate about it, Robert.

SIR ROBERT CHILTERN (*with a touch of bitterness*). I suppose I had better write it at once. Such offers are not repeated. I will ask you to excuse me for a moment, Lord Caversham.

LADY CHILTERN. I may come with you, Robert, may I not?

SIR ROBERT CHILTERN. Yes, Gertrude.

LADY CHILTERN *goes out with him.*

LORD CAVERSHAM. What is the matter with the family? Something wrong here, eh? (*Tapping his fore-*

head.) Idiocy? Hereditary, I suppose. Both of them, too, Wife as well as husband. Very sad. Very sad indeed! And they are not an old family. Can't understand it.

LORD GORING. It is not idiocy, father, I assure you.

LORD CAVERSHAM. What is it then, sir.

LORD GORING (*after some hesitation*). Well, it is what is called nowadays a high moral tone, father. That is all.

LORD CAVERSHAM. Hate these new-fangled names. Same thing as we used to call idiocy fifty years ago. Shan't stay in this house any longer.

LORD GORING (*taking his arm*). Oh! just go in here for a moment, father. Second palm tree to the left, the usual palm tree.

LORD CAVERSHAM. What, sir?

LORD GORING. I beg your pardon, father, I forgot. The conservatory, father, the conservatory— there is someone there that I want you to talk to.

LORD CAVERSHAM. What about, sir?

LORD GORING. About me, father.

LORD CAVERSHAM (*grimly*). Not a subject on which much eloquence is possible.

LORD GORING. No, father; but the lady is like me. She doesn't care much for eloquence in others. She thinks it a little loud.

LORD CAVERSHAM *goes into the conservatory.* LADY CHILTERN *enters.*

LORD GORING. Lady Chiltern, why are you playing Mrs. Cheveley's cards?

137

LADY CHILTERN (*startled*). I don't understand you.

LORD GORING. Mrs. Cheveley made an attempt to ruin your husband. Either to drive him from public life, or to make him adopt a dishonourable position. From the latter tragedy you saved him. The former you are now thrusting on him. Why should you do him the wrong Mrs. Cheveley tried to do and failed?

LADY CHILTERN. Lord Goring?

LORD GORING (*pulling himself together for a great effort, and showing the philosopher that underlies the dandy*). Lady Chiltern, allow me. You wrote me a letter last night in which you said you trusted me and wanted my help. Now is the moment when you really want my help, now is the time when you have got to trust me, to trust in my counsel and judgement. You love Robert. Do you want to kill his love for you? What sort of existence will he have if you rob him of the fruits of his ambition, if you take him from the splendour of a great political career, if you close the doors of public life against him, if you condemn him to sterile failure, he who was made for triumph and success? Women are not meant to judge us, but to forgive us when we need forgiveness. Pardon, not punishment, is their mission. Why should you scourge him with rods for a sin done in his youth, before he knew you, before he knew himself? A man's life is of more value than a woman's. It has larger issues, wider scope, greater ambitions. A woman's life revolves in curves of emotions. It is upon lines of intellect that a man's life progresses. Don't make any terrible mistake, Lady Chiltern. A woman who can keep a man's love, and love him in return, has done all the world wants of women, or should want of them.

LADY CHILTERN (*troubled and hesitating*). But it is my husband himself who wishes to retire from public life. He feels it is his duty. It was he who first said so.

LORD GORING. Rather than lose your love, Robert would do anything, wreck his whole career, as he is on the brink of doing now. He is making for you a terrible sacrifice. Take my advice, Lady Chiltern, and do not accept a sacrifice so great. If you do you will live to repent it bitterly. We men and women are not made to accept such sacrifices from each other. We are not worthy of them. Besides, Robert has been punished enough.

LADY CHILTERN. We have both been punished. I set him up too high.

LORD GORING (*with deep feelings in his voice*). Do not for that reason set him down now too low. If he has fallen from his altar, do not thrust him into the mire. Failure to Robert would be the very mire of shame. Power is his passion. He would lose everything, even his power to feel love. Your husband's life is at this moment in your hands, your husband's love is in your hands. Don't mar both for him.

Enter SIR ROBERT CHILTERN.

SIR ROBERT CHILTERN. Gertrude, here is the draft of my letter. Shall I read it to you?

LADY CHILTERN. Let me see it.

SIR ROBERT *hands her the letter. She reads it, and then with a gesture of passion, tears it up.*

SIR ROBERT CHILTERN. What are you doing?

LADY CHILTERN. A man's life is of more value than a woman's. It has larger issues, wider scope, greater ambitions. Our lives revolve in curves of emotions. It is upon lines of intellect that a man's life progresses. I have just learnt this, and much else with it, from Lord Goring. And I will not spoil your life for you, nor see you spoil it as a sacrifice to me, a useless sacrifice!

SIR ROBERT CHILTERN. Gertrude! Gertrude!

LADY CHILTERN. You can forget. Men easily forget. And I forgive. That is how women help the world. I see that now.

SIR ROBERT CHILTERN (*deeply overcome by emotion, embraces her*). My wife! my wife! (*To* LORD GORING.) Arthur, it seems that I am always to be in your debt.

LORD GORING. Oh dear no, Robert. Your debt is to Lady Chiltern, not to me!

SIR ROBERT CHILTERN. I owe you much. And now tell me what you were going to ask me just now as Lord Caversham came in.

LORD GORING. Robert, you are your sister's guardian, and I want your consent to my marriage with her. That is all.

LADY CHILTERN. Oh, I am so glad! I am so glad!

Shakes hands with LORD GORING.

LORD GORING. Thank you, Lady Chiltern.

SIR ROBERT CHILTERN (*with a troubled look*). My sister to be your wife?

LORD GORING. Yes.

SIR ROBERT CHILTERN (*speaking with great firmness*). Arthur, I am very sorry, but the thing is quite out of the question. I have to think of Mabel's future happiness. And I don't think her happiness would be safe in your hands. And I cannot have her sacrificed!

LORD GORING: Sacrificed!

SIR ROBERT CHILTERN. Yes, utterly sacrificed. Loveless marriages are horrible. But there is one thing worse than an absolutely loveless marriage. A marriage in which there is love, but on one side only; faith, but on one side only; devotion, but on one side only, and in which of the two hearts one is sure to be broken.

LORD GORING. But I love Mabel. No other woman has any place in my life.

LADY CHILTERN. Robert, if they love each other, why should they not be married?

SIR ROBERT CHILTERN. Arthur cannot bring Mabel the love that she deserves.

LORD GORING. What reason have you for saying that?

141

SIR ROBERT CHILTERN (*after a pause*). Do you really require me to tell you?

LORD GORING. Certainly I do.

SIR ROBERT CHILTERN. As you choose. When I called on you yesterday evening I found Mrs. Cheveley concealed in your rooms. It was between ten and eleven o'clock at night. I do not wish to say anything more. Your relations with Mrs. Cheveley have, as I said to you last night, nothing whatsoever to do with me. I know you were engaged to be married to her once. The fascination she exercised over you then seems to have returned. You spoke to me last night of her as of a woman pure and stainless, a woman whom you respected and honoured. That may be so. But I cannot give my sister's life into your hands. It would be wrong of me. It would be unjust, infamously unjust to her.

LORD GORING. I have nothing more to say.

LADY CHILTERN. Robert, it was not Mrs. Cheveley whom Lord Goring expected last night.

SIR ROBERT CHILTERN. Not Mrs. Cheveley! Who was it then?

LORD GORING. Lady Chiltern!

LADY CHILTERN. It was your own wife. Robert, yesterday afternoon Lord Goring told me that if ever I was in trouble I could come to him for help, as he was our oldest and best friend. Later on, after that terrible scene in this room, I wrote to him telling him that I trusted him, that I had need of him, that I was coming to him for help and advice. (SIR ROBERT CHILTERN *takes the letter*

out of his pocket.) Yes, that letter. I didn't go to
Lord Goring's, after all. I felt that it is from ourselves alone that help can come. Pride made me
think that. Mrs. Cheveley went. She stole my
letter and sent it anonymously to you this morning, that you should think . . . Oh! Robert, I
cannot tell you what she wished you to
think . . .

SIR ROBERT CHILTERN. What! Had I fallen so low in
your eyes that you thought that even for a moment I could have doubted your goodness? Gertrude, Gertrude, you are to me the white image
of all good things, and sin can never touch you.
Arthur, you can go to Mabel, and you have my
best wishes! Oh! stop a moment. There is no
name at the beginning of this letter. The brilliant
Mrs. Cheveley does not seem to have noticed
that. There should be a name.

LADY CHILTERN. Let me write yours. It is you I trust
and need. You and none else.

LORD GORING. Well, really, Lady Chiltern, I think I
should have back my own letter.

LADY CHILTERN (*smiling*). No; you shall have Mabel.
(*Takes the letter and writes her husband's name on
it.*)

LORD GORING. Well, I hope she hasn't changed
her mind. It's nearly twenty minutes since I
saw her last. (*Enter* MABEL CHILTERN *and* LORD
CAVERSHAM.)

MABEL CHILTERN. Lord Goring, I think your father's
conversation much more improving than yours.
I am only going to talk to Lord Caversham in

143

the future, and always under the usual palm tree.

LORD GORING. Darling!

Kisses her.

LORD CAVERSHAM (*considerably taken aback*). What does this mean, sir? You don't mean to say that this charming, clever young lady has been so foolish as to accept you?

LORD GORING. Certainly, father! And Chiltern's been wise enough to accept the seat in the Cabinet.

LORD CAVERSHAM. I am very glad to hear that, Chiltern . . . I congratulate you, sir. If the country doesn't go to the dogs or the radicals, we shall have you Prime Minister, some day.

Enter MASON.

MASON. Luncheon is on the table, my Lady!

MASON *goes out.*

MABEL CHILTERN. You'll stop to luncheon, Lord Caversham, won't you?

LORD CAVERSHAM. With pleasure, and I'll drive you down to Downing Street afterwards, Chiltern. You have a great future before you, a great future. (*To* LORD GORING.) Wish I could say the same for you, sir. But your career will have to be entirely domestic.

144

LORD GORING. Yes, father, I prefer it domestic.

LORD CAVERSHAM. And if you don't make this young lady an ideal husband, I'll cut you off with a shilling.

MABEL CHILTERN. An ideal husband! Oh, I don't think I should like that. It sounds like something in the next world.

LORD CAVERSHAM. What do you want him to be then, dear?

MABEL CHILTERN. He can be what he chooses. All I want is to be . . . to be . . . oh! a real wife to him.

LORD CAVERSHAM. Upon my word, there is a good deal of common sense in that, Lady Chiltern.

They all go out except SIR ROBERT CHILTERN. *He sinks into a chair, wrapt in thoughts. After a little time* LADY CHILTERN *returns to look for him.*

LADY CHILTERN (*leaning over the back of the chair*). Aren't you coming in, Robert?

SIR ROBERT CHILTERN (*taking her hand*). Gertrude, is it love you feel for me, or is it pity merely?

LADY CHILTERN (*kisses him*). It is love, Robert. Love, and only love. For both of us a new life is beginning.

Curtain

A Woman of No
Importance

To
Gladys
Countess De Grey

A Woman of No Importance was first performed at the Theatre Royal, Haymarket, London on 19 April 1893, produced by Beerbohm Tree.

Characters

LORD ILLINGWORTH	Mr Beerbohm Tree
SIR JOHN PONTEFRACT	Mr Holman Clarke
LORD ALFRED RUFFORD	Mr Lawford
MR. KELVIL, M.P.	Mr Allan
THE VEN. ARCHDEACON DAUBENY, D.D.	Mr Kemble
GERALD ARBUTHNOT	Mr Fred Tree
FARQUHAR, *Butler*	Mr Hay
FRANCIS, *Footman*	Mr Montagu
SERVANTS	
LADY HUNSTANTON	Miss Rose Leclerq
LADY CAROLINE PONTEFRACT	Miss LeThiere
LADY STUTFIELD	Miss Horlock
MRS. ALLONBY	Mrs Tree
MISS HESTER WORSLEY	Miss Julia Neilson
ALICE, *Maid*	Miss Kelly
MRS. ARBUTHNOT	Mrs Bernard Beere

Lessee and Manager: Mr Herbert Beerbohm Tree

THE SCENES OF THE PLAY

ACT I Lawn in front of the terrace at Hunstanton Chase.
ACT II Drawing-room at Hunstanton Chase.
ACT III The picture gallery at Hunstanton Chase.
ACT IV Sitting-room at Mrs. Arbuthnot's house at Wrockley.

The action of the play takes place within twenty-four hours.

Time: The last decade of the nineteenth century.

FIRST ACT

SCENE

Lawn in front of the terrace at Hunstanton Chase. SIR JOHN *and* LADY CAROLINE PONTEFRACT, MISS WORSLEY, *on chairs under large yew tree.*

LADY CAROLINE. I believe this is the first English country house you have stayed at, Miss Worsley?

HESTER. Yes, Lady Caroline.

LADY CAROLINE. You have no country houses, I am told, in America?

HESTER. We have not many.

LADY CAROLINE. Have you any country? What we should call country?

HESTER (*smiling*). We have the largest country in the world, Lady Caroline. They used to tell us at school that some of our states are as big as France and England put together.

LADY CAROLINE. Ah! you must find it very draughty, I should fancy. (*To* SIR JOHN.) John, you should have your muffler. What is the use of my always knitting mufflers for you if you won't wear them?

SIR JOHN. I am quite warm, Caroline, I assure you.

LADY CAROLINE. I think not, John. Well, you couldn't come to a more charming place than this, Miss Worsley, though the house is excessively damp, quite unpardonably damp, and dear Lady Hunstanton is sometimes a little lax about the people she asks down here. (*To* SIR JOHN.) Jane mixes too much. Lord Illingworth, of course, is a man of high distinction. It is a privilege to meet him. And that member of Parliament, Mr. Kettle—

SIR JOHN. Kelvil, my love, Kelvil.

LADY CAROLINE. He must be quite respectable. One has never heard his name before in the whole course of one's life, which speaks volumes for a man, nowadays. But Mrs. Allonby is hardly a very suitable person.

HESTER. I dislike Mrs. Allonby. I dislike her more than I can say.

LADY CAROLINE. I am not sure, Miss Worsley, that foreigners like yourself should cultivate likes or dislikes about the people they are invited to meet. Mrs. Allonby is very well born. She is a niece of Lord Brancaster's. It is said, of course, that she ran away twice before she was married. But you know how unfair people often are. I myself don't believe she ran away more than once.

HESTER. Mr. Arbuthnot is very charming.

LADY CAROLINE. Ah, yes! the young man who has

a post in a bank. Lady Hunstanton is most kind in asking him here, and Lord Illingworth seems to have quite a fancy to him. I am not sure, however, that Jane is right in taking him out of his position. In my young days, Miss Worsley, one never met any one in society who worked for their living. It was not considered the thing.

HESTER. In America those are the people we respect most.

LADY CAROLINE. I have no doubt of it.

HESTER. Mr. Arbuthnot has a beautiful nature! He is so simple, so sincere. He has one of the most beautiful natures I have ever come across. It is a privilege to meet *him*.

LADY CAROLINE. It is not customary in England, Miss Worsley, for a young lady to speak with such enthusiasm of any person of the opposite sex. English women conceal their feelings till after they are married. They show them then.

HESTER. Do you, in England, allow no friendship to exist between a young man and a young girl?

Enter LADY HUNSTANTON, *followed by* FOOTMAN *with shawls and a cushion.*

LADY CAROLINE. We think it very inadvisable. Jane, I was just saying what a pleasant party you have asked us to meet. You have a wonderful power of selection. It is quite a gift.

LADY HUNSTANTON. Dear Caroline, how kind of you! I think we all do fit in very nicely together. And I hope our charming American visitor will carry back pleasant recollections of our English country life (*To* FOOTMAN.) The cushion, there, Francis. And my shawl. The Shetland. Get the Shetland.

Exit FOOTMAN *for shawl. Enter* GERALD ARBUTHNOT.

GERALD. Lady Hunstanton, I have such good news to tell you. Lord Illingworth has just offered to make me his secretary.

LADY HUNSTANTON. His secretary? That is good news indeed, Gerald. It means a very brilliant future in store for you. Your dear mother will be delighted. I really must try and induce her to come up here to-night. Do you think she would, Gerald? I know how difficult it is to get her to go anywhere.

GERALD. Oh! I am sure she would, Lady Hunstanton, if she knew Lord Illingworth had made me such an offer.

Enter FOOTMAN *with shawl.*

LADY HUNSTANTON. I will write and tell her about it, and ask her to come up and meet him. (*To* FOOTMAN.) Just wait, Francis. (*Writes letter.*)

LADY CAROLINE. That is a very wonderful opening for so young a man as you are, Mr. Arbuthnot.

GERALD. It is indeed, Lady Caroline. I trust I shall be able to show myself worthy of it.

LADY CAROLINE. I trust so.

GERALD (*to* HESTER). You have not congratulated me yet, Miss Worsley.

HESTER. Are you very pleased about it?

GERALD. Of course I am. It means everything to me—things that were out of the reach of hope before may be within hope's reach now.

HESTER. Nothing should be out of the reach of hope. Life is a hope.

LADY HUNSTANTON. I fancy, Caroline, that Diplomacy is what Lord Illingworth is aiming at. I heard that he was offered Vienna. But that may not be true.

LADY CAROLINE. I don't think that England should be represented abroad by an unmarried man, Jane. It might lead to complications.

LADY HUNSTANTON. You are too nervous, Caroline. Believe me, you are too nervous. Besides, Lord Illingworth may marry any day. I was in hopes he would have married Lady Kelso. But I believe he said her family was too large. Or was it her feet? I forget which. I regret it very much. She was made to be an ambassador's wife.

LADY CAROLINE. She certainly has a wonderful faculty of remembering people's names, and forgetting their faces.

LADY HUNSTANTON. Well, that is very natural, Caroline, is it not? (*To* FOOTMAN.) Tell Henry to wait for an answer. I have written a line to your dear mother, Gerald, to tell her your good news, and to say she really must come to dinner.

Exit FOOTMAN.

157

GERALD. That is awfully kind of you, Lady Hunstanton. (*To* HESTER.) Will you come for a stroll, Miss Worsley?

HESTER. With pleasure. (*Exit with* GERALD.)

LADY HUNSTANTON. I am very much gratified at Gerald Arbuthnot's good fortune. He is quite a *protegé* of mine. And I am particularly pleased that Lord Illingworth should have made the offer of his own accord without my suggesting anything. Nobody likes to be asked favours. I remember poor Charlotte Pagden making herself quite unpopular one season, because she had a French governess she wanted to recommend to every one.

LADY CAROLINE. I saw the governess, Jane. Lady Pagden sent her to me. It was before Eleanor came out. She was far too good-looking to be in any respectable household. I don't wonder Lady Pagden was so anxious to get rid of her.

LADY HUNSTANTON. Ah, that explains it.

LADY CAROLINE. John, the grass is too damp for you. You had better go and put on your overshoes at once.

SIR JOHN. I am quite comfortable, Caroline, I assure you.

LADY CAROLINE. You must allow me to be the best judge of that, John. Pray do as I tell you.

SIR JOHN *gets up and goes off.*

LADY HUNSTANTON. You spoil him, Caroline, you do indeed!

Enter MRS. ALLONBY *and* LADY STUTFIELD.

(*To* MRS. ALLONBY.) Well, dear, I hope you like the park. It is said to be well timbered.

MRS. ALLONBY. The trees are wonderful, Lady Hunstanton.

LADY STUTFIELD. Quite, quite wonderful.

MRS. ALLONBY. But somehow, I feel sure that if I lived in the country for six months, I should become so unsophisticated that no one would take the slightest notice of me.

LADY HUNSTANTON. I assure you, dear, that the country has not that effect at all. Why, it was from Melthorpe, which is only two miles from here, that Lady Belton eloped with Lord Fethersdale. I remember the occurrence perfectly. Poor Lord Belton died three days after wards of joy, or gout. I forget which. We had a large party staying here at the time, so we were all very much interested in the whole affair.

MRS. ALLONBY. I think to elope is cowardly. It's running away from danger. And danger has become so rare in modern life.

LADY CAROLINE. As far as I can make out, the young women of the present day seem to make it the sole object of their lives to be always playing with fire.

MRS. ALLONBY. The one advantage of playing with fire, Lady Caroline, is that one never gets even singed. It is the people who don't know how to play with it who get burned up.

LADY STUTFIELD. Yes; I see that. It is very, very helpful.

LADY HUNSTANTON. I don't know how the world would get on with such a theory as that, dear Mrs. Allonby.

LADY STUTFIELD. Ah! The world was made for men and not for women.

MRS. ALLONBY. Oh, don't say that, Lady Stutfield. We have a much better time than they have. There are far more things forbidden to us than are forbidden to them.

LADY STUTFIELD. Yes; that is quite, quite true. I had not thought of that.

Enter SIR JOHN *and* MR. KELVIL.

LADY HUNSTANTON. Well, Mr. Kelvil, have you got through your work?

KELVIL. I have finished my writing for the day, Lady Hunstanton. It has been an arduous task. The demands on the time of a public man are very heavy nowadays, very heavy indeed. And I don't think they meet with adequate recognition.

LADY CAROLINE. John, have you got your overshoes on?

SIR JOHN. Yes, my love.

LADY CAROLINE. I think you had better come over here, John. It is more sheltered.

SIR JOHN. I am quite comfortable, Caroline.

LADY CAROLINE. I think not, John. You had better sit beside me.

SIR JOHN *rises and goes across.*

LADY STUTFIELD. And what have you been writing about this morning, Mr. Kelvil?

KELVIL. On the usual subject, Lady Stutfield. On Purity.

LADY STUTFIELD. That must be such a very, very interesting thing to write about.

KELVIL. It is the one subject of really national importance, nowadays, Lady Stutfield. I purpose addressing my constituents on the question before Parliament meets. I find that the poorer classes of this country display a marked desire for a higher ethical standard.

LADY STUTFIELD. How quite, quite nice of them.

LADY CAROLINE. Are you in favour of women taking part in politics, Mr. Kettle?

SIR JOHN. Kelvil, my love, Kelvil.

KELVIL. The growing influence of women is the one reassuring thing in our political life, Lady Caroline. Women are always on the side of morality, public and private.

LADY STUTFIELD. It is so very, very gratifying to hear you say that.

LADY HUNSTANTON. Ah, yes!—the moral qualities in women—that is the important thing. I am afraid, Caroline, that dear Lord Illingworth doesn't value the moral qualities in women as much as he should.

Enter LORD ILLINGWORTH.

LADY STUTFIELD. The world says that Lord Illingworth is very, very wicked.

LORD ILLINGWORTH. But what world says that, Lady Stutfield? It must be the next world. This world and I are on excellent terms. (*Sits down beside* MRS. ALLONBY.)

LADY STUTFIELD. Every one *I* know says you are very, very wicked.

LORD ILLINGWORTH. It is perfectly monstrous the way people go about, nowadays, saying things against one behind one's back that are absolutely and entirely true.

LADY HUNSTANTON. Dear Lord Illingworth is quite hopeless, Lady Stutfield. I have given up trying to reform him. It would take a Public Company with a Board of Directors and a paid Secretary to do that. But you have the secretary already, Lord Illingworth, haven't you? Gerald Arbuthnot has told us of his good fortune; it is really most kind of you.

LORD ILLINGWORTH. Oh, don't say that, Lady Hunstanton. Kind is a dreadful word. I took a great fancy to young Arbuthnot the moment I met him, and he'll be of considerable use to me in something I am foolish enough to think of doing.

LADY HUNSTANTON. He is an admirable young man. And his mother is one of my dearest friends. He has just gone for a walk with our pretty American. She is very pretty, is she not?

LADY CAROLINE. Far too pretty. These American girls carry off all the good matches. Why can't they stay in their own country? They are always telling us it is the Paradise of women.

LORD ILLINGWORTH. It is, Lady Caroline. That is why, like Eve, they are so extremely anxious to get out of it.

LADY CAROLINE. Who are Miss Worsley's parents?

LORD ILLINGWORTH. American women are wonderfully clever in concealing their parents.

LADY HUNSTANTON. My dear Lord Illingworth, what do you mean? Miss Worsley, Caroline, is an orphan. Her father was a very wealthy millionaire or philanthropist, or both, I believe, who entertained my son quite hospitably, when he visited Boston. I don't know how he made his money, originally.

KELVIL. I fancy in American dry goods.

LADY HUNSTANTON. What are American dry goods?

LORD ILLINGWORTH. American novels.

LADY HUNSTANTON. How very singular! . . . Well, from whatever source her large fortune came, I have a great esteem for Miss Worsley. She dresses exceedingly well. All Americans do dress well. They get their clothes in Paris.

MRS. ALLONBY. They say, Lady Hunstanton, that when good Americans die they go to Paris.

LADY HUNSTANTON. Indeed? And when bad Americans die, where do they go to?

LORD ILLINGWORTH. Oh, they go to America.

KELVIL. I am afraid you don't appreciate America, Lord Illingworth. It is a very remarkable country, especially considering its youth.

LORD ILLINGWORTH. The youth of America is their

oldest tradition. It has been going on now for three hundred years. To hear them talk one would imagine they were in their first childhood. As far as civilisation goes they are in their second.

KELVIL. There is undoubtedly a great deal of corruption in American politics. I suppose you allude to that?

LORD ILLINGWORTH. I wonder.

LADY HUNSTANTON. Politics are in a sad way, everywhere, I am told. They certainly are in England. Dear Mr. Cardew is ruining the country. I wonder Mrs. Cardew allows him. I am sure, Lord Illingworth, you don't think that uneducated people should be allowed to have votes?

LORD ILLINGWORTH. I think they are the only people who should.

KELVIL. Do you take no side then in modern politics, Lord Illingworth?

LORD ILLINGWORTH. One should never take sides in anything, Mr. Kelvil. Taking sides is the beginning of sincerity, and earnestness follows shortly afterwards, and the human being becomes a bore. However, the House of Commons really does very little harm. You can't make people good by Act of Parliament—that is something.

KELVIL. You cannot deny that the House of Commons has always shown great sympathy with the sufferings of the poor.

LORD ILLINGWORTH. That is its special vice. That is the special vice of the age. One should sympathise with the joy, the beauty, the colour of life. The less said about life's sores the better, Mr. Kelvil.

KELVIL. Still our East End is a very important problem.

LORD ILLINGWORTH. Quite so. It is the problem of slavery. And we are trying to solve it by amusing the slaves.

LADY HUNSTANTON. Certainly, a great deal may be done by means of cheap entertainments, as you say, Lord Illingworth. Dear Dr. Daubeny, our rector here, provides, with the assistance of his curates, really admirable recreations for the poor during the winter. And much good may be done by means of a magic lantern, or a missionary, or some popular amusement of that kind.

LADY CAROLINE. I am not at all in favour of amusements for the poor, Jane. Blankets and coals are sufficient. There is too much love of pleasure amongst the upper classes as it is. Health is what we want in modern life. The tone is not healthy, not healthy at all.

KELVIL. You are quite right, Lady Caroline.

LADY CAROLINE. I believe I am usually right.

MRS. ALLONBY. Horrid word 'health'.

LORD ILLINGWORTH. Silliest word in our language, and one knows so well the popular idea of health. The English country gentleman galloping after a fox—the unspeakable in full pursuit of the uneatable.

KELVIL. May I ask, Lord Illingworth, if you regard

the House of Lords as a better institution than the House of Commons?

LORD ILLINGWORTH. A much better institution, of course. We in the House of Lords are never in touch with public opinion. That makes us a civilised body.

KELVIL. Are you serious in putting forward such a view?

LORD ILLINGWORTH. Quite serious, Mr. Kelvil. (*To* MRS. ALLONBY.) Vulgar habit that is people have nowadays of asking one, after one has given them an idea, whether one is serious or not. Nothing is serious except passion. The intellect is not a serious thing, and never has been. It is an instrument on which one plays, that is all. The only serious form of intellect I know is the British intellect. And on the British intellect the illiterates play the drum.

LADY HUNSTANTON. What are you saying, Lord Illingworth, about the drum?

LORD ILLINGWORTH. I was merely talking to Mrs. Allonby about the leading articles in the London newspapers.

LADY HUNSTANTON. But do you believe all that is written in the newspapers?

LORD ILLINGWORTH. I do. Nowadays it is only the unreadable that occurs. (*Rises with* MRS. ALLONBY.)

LADY HUNSTANTON. Are you going, Mrs. Allonby?

MRS. ALLONBY. Just as far as the conservatory. Lord Illingworth told me this morning that there was an orchid there as beautiful as the seven deadly sins.

LADY HUNSTANTON. My dear, I hope there is nothing of the kind. I will certainly speak to the gardener.

Exit MRS. ALLONBY *and* LORD ILLINGWORTH.

LADY CAROLINE. Remarkable type, Mrs. Allonby.

LADY HUNSTANTON. She lets her clever tongue run away with her sometimes.

LADY CAROLINE. Is that the only thing, Jane, Mrs. Allonby allows to run away with her?

LADY HUNSTANTON. I hope so, Caroline, I am sure.

Enter LORD ALFRED.
Dear Lord Alfred, do join us.

LORD ALFRED *sits down beside* LADY STUTFIELD.

LADY CAROLINE. You believe good of every one, Jane. It is a great fault.

LADY STUTFIELD. Do you really, really think, Lady Caroline, that one should believe evil of every one?

LADY CAROLINE. I think it is much safer to do so, Lady Stutfield. Until, of course, people are found out to be good. But that requires a great deal of investigation nowadays.

LADY STUTFIELD. But there is so much unkind scandal in modern life.

LADY CAROLINE. Lord Illingworth remarked to me

last night at dinner that the basis of every scandal is an absolutely immoral certainty.

KELVIL. Lord Illingworth is, of course, a very brilliant man, but he seems to me to be lacking in that fine faith in the nobility and purity of life which is so important in this century.

LADY STUTFIELD. Yes, quite, quite important, is it not?

KELVIL. He gives me the impression of a man who does not appreciate the beauty of our English home-life. I would say that he was tainted with foreign ideas on the subject.

LADY STUTFIELD. There is nothing, nothing like the beauty of home-life, is there?

KELVIL. It is the mainstay of our moral system in England, Lady Stutfield. Without it we would become like our neighbours.

LADY STUTFIELD. That would be so, so sad, would it not?

KELVIL. I am afraid, too, that Lord Illingworth regards woman simply as a toy. Now, I have never regarded woman as a toy. Woman is the intellectual helpmeet of man in public as in private life. Without her we should forget the true ideals. (*Sits down beside* LADY STUTFIELD.)

LADY STUTFIELD. I am so very, very glad to hear you say that.

LADY CAROLINE. You are a married man, Mr. Kettle?

SIR JOHN. Kelvil, dear, Kelvil.

KELVIL. I am married, Lady Caroline.

LADY CAROLINE. Family?

KELVIL. Yes.

LADY CAROLINE. How many?

KELVIL. Eight.

LADY STUTFIELD *turns her attention to* LORD ALFRED.

LADY CAROLINE. Mrs. Kettle and the children are, I suppose, at the seaside?

SIR JOHN *shrugs his shoulders.*

KELVIL. My wife is at the seaside with the children, Lady Caroline.

LADY CAROLINE. You will join them later on, no doubt?

KELVIL. If my public engagements permit me.

LADY CAROLINE. Your public life must be a great source of gratification to Mrs. Kettle.

SIR JOHN. Kelvil, my love, Kelvil.

LADY STUTFIELD (*to* LORD ALFRED). How very, very charming those gold-tipped cigarettes of yours are, Lord Alfred.

LORD ALFRED. They are awfully expensive. I can only afford them when I'm in debt.

LADY STUTFIELD. It must be terribly, terribly distressing to be in debt.

LORD ALFRED. One must have some occupation nowadays. If I hadn't my debts I shouldn't have anything to think about. All the chaps I know are in debt.

LADY STUTFIELD. But don't the people to whom you

owe the money give you a great, great deal of annoyance?

Enter FOOTMAN.

LORD ALFRED. Oh, no, they write; I don't.

LADY STUTFIELD. How very, very strange.

LADY HUNSTANTON. Ah, here is a letter, Caroline, from dear Mrs. Arbuthnot. She won't dine. I am so sorry. But she will come in the evening. I am very pleased, indeed. She is one of the sweetest of women. Writes a beautiful hand, too, so large, so firm. (*Hands letter to* LADY CAROLINE.)

LADY CAROLINE (*looking at it*). A little lacking in femininity, Jane. Femininity is the quality I admire most in women.

LADY HUNSTANTON (*taking back letter and leaving it on table*). Oh! she is very feminine, Caroline, and so good, too. You should hear what the Archdeacon says of her. He regards her as his right hand in the parish. (FOOTMAN *speaks to her.*) In the Yellow Drawing-room. Shall we all go in? Lady Stutfield, shall we go in to tea?

LADY STUTFIELD. With pleasure, Lady Hunstanton.

They rise and proceed to go off. SIR JOHN *offers to carry* LADY STUTFIELD's *cloak.*

LADY CAROLINE. John! If you would allow your nephew to look after Lady Stutfield's cloak, you might help me with my work-basket.

Enter LORD ILLINGWORTH *and* MRS. ALLONBY.

SIR JOHN. Certainly, my love.

Exeunt.

MRS. ALLONBY. Curious thing, plain women are always jealous of their husbands, beautiful women never are!

LORD ILLINGWORTH. Beautiful women never have time. They are always so occupied in being jealous of other people's husbands.

MRS. ALLONBY. I should have thought Lady Caroline would have grown tired of conjugal anxiety by this time! Sir John is her fourth!

LORD ILLINGWORTH. So much marriage is certainly not becoming. Twenty years of romance make a woman look like a ruin; but twenty years of marriage make her something like a public building.

MRS. ALLONBY. Twenty years of romance! Is there such a thing?

LORD ILLINGWORTH. Not in our day. Women have become too brilliant. Nothing spoils a romance so much as a sense of humour in the woman.

MRS. ALLONBY. Or the want of it in the man.

LORD ILLINGWORTH. You are quite right. In a Temple every one should be serious, except the thing that is worshipped.

MRS. ALLONBY. And that should be man?

LORD ILLINGWORTH. Women kneel so gracefully; men don't.

MRS. ALLONBY. You are thinking of Lady Stutfield!

LORD ILLINGWORTH. I assure you I have not thought of Lady Stutfield for the last quarter of an hour.

MRS. ALLONBY. Is she such a mystery?

LORD ILLINGWORTH. She is more than a mystery— she is a mood.

MRS. ALLONBY. Moods don't last.

LORD ILLINGWORTH. It is their chief charm.

Enter HESTER *and* GERALD.

GERALD. Lord Illingworth, every one has been congratulating me, Lady Hunstanton and Lady Caroline, and . . . every one. I hope I shall make a good secretary.

LORD ILLINGWORTH. You will be the pattern secretary, Gerald. (*Talks to him.*)

MRS. ALLONBY. You enjoy country life, Miss Worsley?

HESTER. Very much, indeed.

MRS. ALLONBY. Don't you find yourself longing for a London dinner-party?

HESTER. I dislike London dinner-parties.

MRS. ALLONBY. I adore them. The clever people never listen, and the stupid people never talk.

HESTER. I think the stupid people talk a great deal.

MRS. ALLONBY. Ah, I never listen!

LORD ILLINGWORTH. My dear boy, if I didn't like you I wouldn't have made you the offer. It is because I like you so much that I want to have you with me.

Exit HESTER *with* GERALD.

Charming fellow, Gerald Arbuthnot!

MRS. ALLONBY. He is very nice; very nice indeed. But I can't stand the American young lady.

LORD ILLINGWORTH. Why?

MRS. ALLONBY. She told me yesterday, and in quite a loud voice too, that she was only eighteen. It was most annoying.

LORD ILLINGWORTH. One should never trust a woman who tells one her real age. A woman who would tell one that would tell one anything.

MRS. ALLONBY. She is a Puritan besides—

LORD ILLINGWORTH. Ah, that is inexcusable. I don't mind plain women being Puritans. It is the only excuse they have for being plain. But she is decidedly pretty. I admire her immensely. (*Looks steadfastly at* MRS. ALLONBY.)

MRS. ALLONBY. What a thoroughly bad man you must be!

LORD ILLINGWORTH. What do you call a bad man?

MRS. ALLONBY. The sort of man who admires innocence.

LORD ILLINGWORTH. And a bad woman?

MRS. ALLONBY. Oh! the sort of woman a man never gets tired of.

LORD ILLINGWORTH. You are severe—on yourself.

MRS. ALLONBY. Define us as a sex.

LORD ILLINGWORTH. Sphinxes without secrets.

MRS. ALLONBY. Does that include the Puritan women?

LORD ILLINGWORTH. Do you know, I don't believe in the existence of Puritan women? I don't think there is a woman in the world who would not be a little flattered if one made love to her. It is that which makes women so irresistibly adorable.

MRS. ALLONBY. You think there is no woman in the world who would object to being kissed?

LORD ILLINGWORTH. Very few.

MRS. ALLONBY. Miss Worsley would not let you kiss her.

LORD ILLINGWORTH. Are you sure?

MRS. ALLONBY. Quite.

LORD ILLINGWORTH. What do you think she'd do if I kissed her?

MRS. ALLONBY. Either marry you, or strike you across the face with her glove. What would you do if she struck you across the face with her glove?

LORD ILLINGWORTH. Fall in love with her, probably.

MRS. ALLONBY. Then it is lucky you are not going to kiss her!

LORD ILLINGWORTH. Is that a challenge?

MRS. ALLONBY. It is an arrow shot into the air.

LORD ILLINGWORTH. Don't you know that I always succeed in whatever I try?

MRS. ALLONBY. I am sorry to hear it. We women adore failures. They lean on us.

LORD ILLINGWORTH. You worship successes. You cling to them.

MRS. ALLONBY. We are the laurels to hide their baldness.

LORD ILLINGWORTH. And they need you always, except at the moment of triumph.

MRS. ALLONBY. They are uninteresting then.

LORD ILLINGWORTH. How tantalising you are! (*A pause.*)

MRS. ALLONBY. Lord Illingworth, there is one thing I shall always like you for.

LORD ILLINGWORTH. Only one thing? And I have so many bad qualities.

MRS. ALLONBY. Ah, don't be too conceited about them. You may lose them as you grow old.

LORD ILLINGWORTH. I never intend to grow old. The soul is born old but grows young. That is the comedy of life.

MRS. ALLONBY. And the body is born young and grows old. That is life's tragedy.

LORD ILLINGWORTH. Its comedy also, sometimes. But what is the mysterious reason why you will always like me?

MRS. ALLONBY. It is that you have never made love to me.

LORD ILLINGWORTH. I have never done anything else.

MRS. ALLONBY. Really? I have not noticed it.

LORD ILLINGWORTH. How unfortunate! It might have been a tragedy for both of us.

MRS. ALLONBY. We should each have survived.

LORD ILLINGWORTH. One can survive everything nowadays, except death, and live down anything except a good reputation.

MRS. ALLONBY. Have you tried a good reputation?

LORD ILLINGWORTH. It is one of the many annoyances to which I have never been subjected.

MRS. ALLONBY. It may come.

LORD ILLINGWORTH. Why do you threaten me?

MRS. ALLONBY. I will tell you when you have kissed the Puritan.

Enter FOOTMAN.

FRANCIS. Tea is served in the Yellow Drawing-room, my lord.

LORD ILLINGWORTH. Tell her ladyship we are coming in.

FRANCIS. Yes, my lord. (*Exit.*)

LORD ILLINGWORTH. Shall we go in to tea?

MRS. ALLONBY. Do you like such simple pleasures?

LORD ILLINGWORTH. I adore simple pleasures. They are the last refuge of the complex. But, if you wish, let us stay here. Yes, let us stay here. The Book of Life begins with a man and a woman in a garden.

MRS. ALLONBY. It ends with Revelations.

LORD ILLINGWORTH. You fence divinely. But the button has come off your foil.

MRS. ALLONBY. Thank you. Come.

LORD ILLINGWORTH (*sees* MRS. ARBUTHNOT'S *letter on table, and takes it up and looks at envelope*). What a curious handwriting! It reminds me of the handwriting of a woman I used to know years ago.

MRS. ALLONBY. Who?

LORD ILLINGWORTH. Oh! no one. No one in particular. A woman of no importance. (*Throws letter down, and passes up the steps of the terrace with* MRS. ALLONBY. *They smile at each other.*)

Curtain.

SECOND ACT

1a. A woman of no importance/2 hours after
noon, and passes in the style of that vertue with
Mrs. Allonby. They seldom of mid-day.

Curtain.

Second Act

SCENE

Drawing-room at Hunstanton Chase, after dinner,
lamps lit. Door L.C. Door R.C.
  Ladies seated on sofa.

MRS. ALLONBY. What a comfort it is to have got rid
  of the men for a little!

LADY STUTFIELD. Yes; men persecute us dreadfully,
  don't they?

MRS. ALLONBY. Persecute us? I wish they did.

LADY HUNSTANTON. My dear?

MRS. ALLONBY. The annoying thing is that the
  wretches can be perfectly happy without us.
  That is why I think it is every woman's duty
  never to leave them alone for a single moment,
  except during this short breathing space after
  dinner; without which, I believe, we poor
  women would be absolutely worn to shadows.

Enter SERVANTS *with coffee.*

LADY HUNSTANTON. Worn to shadows, dear?

MRS. ALLONBY. Yes, Lady Hunstanton. It is such a strain keeping men up to the mark. They are always trying to escape from us.

LADY STUTFIELD. It seems to me that it is we who are always trying to escape from them. Men are so very, very heartless. They know their power and use it.

LADY CAROLINE (*takes coffee from* SERVANT). What stuff and nonsense all this about men is! The thing to do is to keep men in their proper place.

MRS. ALLONBY. But what is their proper place, Lady Caroline?

LADY CAROLINE. Looking after their wives, Mrs. Allonby.

MRS. ALLONBY (*takes coffee from* SERVANT). Really? And if they're not married?

LADY CAROLINE. If they are not married, they would be looking after a wife. It's perfectly scandalous the amount of bachelors who are going about society. There should be a law passed to compel them all to marry within twelve months.

LADY STUTFIELD (*refuses coffee*). But if they're in love with some one who, perhaps, is tied to another?

LADY CAROLINE. In that case, Lady Stutfield, they would be married off in a week to some plain respectable girl, in order to teach them not to meddle with other people's property.

MRS. ALLONBY. I don't think that we should ever be spoken of as other people's property. All men are married women's property. That is the only true definition of what married women's property really is. But we don't belong to any one.

LADY STUTFIELD. Oh, I am so very, very glad to hear you say so.

LADY HUNSTANTON. But do you really think, dear Caroline, that legislation would improve matters in any way? I am told that, nowadays, all the married men live like bachelors, and all the bachelors like married men.

MRS. ALLONBY. I certainly never know one from the other.

LADY STUTFIELD. Oh, I think one can always know at once whether a man has home claims upon his life or not. I have noticed a very, very sad expression in the eyes of so many married men.

MRS. ALLONBY. Ah, all that I have noticed is that they are horribly tedious when they are good husbands, and abominably conceited when they are not.

LADY HUNSTANTON. Well, I suppose the type of husband has completely changed since my young days, but I'm bound to state that poor dear Hunstanton was the most delightful of creatures, and as good as gold.

MRS. ALLONBY. Ah, my husband is a sort of promissory note; I'm tired of meeting him.

LADY CAROLINE. But you renew him from time to time, don't you?

MRS. ALLONBY. Oh no, Lady Caroline. I have only had one husband as yet. I suppose you look upon me as quite an amateur.

LADY CAROLINE. With your views on life I wonder you married at all.

MRS. ALLONBY. So do I.

LADY HUNSTANTON. My dear child, I believe you are really very happy in your married life, but that you like to hide your happiness from others.

MRS. ALLONBY. I assure you I was horribly deceived in Ernest.

LADY HUNSTANTON. Oh, I hope not, dear. I knew his mother quite well. She was a Stratton, Caroline, one of Lord Crowland's daughters.

LADY CAROLINE. Victoria Stratton? I remember her perfectly. A silly, fair-haired woman with no chin.

MRS. ALLONBY. Ah, Ernest has a chin. He has a very strong chin, a square chin. Ernest's chin is far too square.

LADY STUTFIELD. But do you really think a man's chin can be too square? I think a man should look very, very strong, and that his chin should be quite, quite square.

MRS. ALLONBY. Then you should certainly know Ernest, Lady Stutfield. It is only fair to tell you beforehand he has got no conversation at all.

LADY STUTFIELD. I adore silent men.

MRS. ALLONBY. Oh, Ernest isn't silent. He talks the whole time. But he has got no conversation. What he talks about I don't know. I haven't listened to him for years.

LADY STUTFIELD. Have you never forgiven him

then? How sad that seems! But all life is very, very sad, is it not?

MRS. ALLONBY. Life, Lady Stutfield, is simply a *mauvais quart d'heure* made up of exquisite moments.

LADY STUTFIELD. Yes, there are moments, certainly. But was it something very, very wrong that Mr. Allonby did? Did he become angry with you, and say anything that was unkind or true?

MRS. ALLONBY. Oh, dear, no. Ernest is invariably calm. That is one of the reasons he always gets on my nerves. Nothing is so aggravating as calmness. There is something positively brutal about the good temper of most modern men. I wonder we women stand it as well as we do.

LADY STUTFIELD. Yes; men's good temper shows they are not so sensitive as we are, not so finely strung. It makes a great barrier often between husband and wife, does it not? But I would so much like to know what was the wrong thing Mr. Allonby did.

MRS. ALLONBY. Well, I will tell you, if you solemnly promise to tell everybody else.

LADY STUTFIELD. Thank you, thank you. I will make a point of repeating it.

MRS. ALLONBY. When Ernest and I were engaged, he swore to me positively on his knees that he had never loved any one before in the whole course of his life. I was very young at the time, so I didn't believe him, I needn't tell you. Unfortunately, however, I made no inquiries of any kind till after I had been actually married four or five months. I found out then that what he had told me was perfectly true. And that sort of thing makes a man so absolutely uninteresting.

LADY HUNSTANTON. My dear!

MRS. ALLONBY. Men always want to be a woman's first love. That is their clumsy vanity. We women have a more subtle instinct about things. What we like is to be a man's last romance.

LADY STUTFIELD. I see what you mean. It's very, very beautiful.

LADY HUNSTANTON. My dear child, you don't mean to tell me that you won't forgive your husband because he never loved any one else? Did you ever hear such a thing, Caroline? I am quite surprised.

LADY CAROLINE. Oh, women have become so highly educated, Jane, that nothing should surprise us nowadays, except happy marriages. They apparently are getting remarkably rare.

MRS. ALLONBY. Oh, they're quite out of date.

LADY STUTFIELD. Except amongst the middle classes, I have been told.

MRS. ALLONBY. How like the middle classes!

LADY STUTFIELD. Yes—is it not?—very, very like them.

LADY CAROLINE. If what you tell us about the middle classes is true, Lady Stutfield, it redounds greatly to their credit. It is much to be regretted that in our rank of life the wife should be so persistently frivolous, under the impression apparently that it is the proper thing to be. It is to that I attribute the unhappiness of so many marriages we all know of in society.

MRS. ALLONBY. Do you know, Lady Caroline, I don't think the frivolity of the wife has ever anything to do with it. More marriages are ruined nowadays by the common sense of the husband than by anything else. How can a woman be expected to be happy with a man who insists on treating her as if she was a perfectly rational being?

LADY HUNSTANTON. My dear!

MRS. ALLONBY. Man, poor, awkward, reliable, necessary man belongs to a sex that has been rational for millions and millions of years. He can't help himself. It is in his race. The History of Woman is very different. We have always been picturesque protests against the mere existence of common sense. We saw its dangers from the first.

LADY STUTFIELD. Yes, the common sense of husbands is certainly most, most trying. Do tell me your conception of the Ideal Husband. I think it would be so very, very helpful.

MRS. ALLONBY. The Ideal Husband? There couldn't be such a thing. The institution is wrong.

LADY STUTFIELD. The Ideal Man, then, in his relations to us.

LADY CAROLINE. He would probably be extremely realistic.

MRS. ALLONBY. The Ideal Man! Oh, the Ideal Man should talk to us as if we were goddesses, and treat us as if we were children. He should refuse all our serious requests, and gratify every one of our whims. He should encourage us to have caprices, and forbid us to have missions. He

should always say much more than he means,
and always mean much more than he says.

LADY HUNSTANTON. But how could he do both,
dear?

MRS. ALLONBY. He should never run down other
pretty women. That would show he had no
taste, or make one suspect that he had too
much. No; he should be nice about them all, but
say that somehow they don't attract him.

LADY STUTFIELD. Yes, that is always very, very
pleasant to hear about other women.

MRS. ALLONBY. If we ask him a question about anything, he should give us an answer all about
ourselves. He should invariably praise us for
whatever qualities he knows we haven't got.
But he should be pitiless, quite pitiless, in re-
proaching us for the virtues that we have never
dreamed of possessing. He should never believe
that we know the use of useful things. That
would be unforgivable. But he should shower
on us everything we don't want.

LADY CAROLINE. As far as I can see, he is to do
nothing but pay bills and compliments.

MRS. ALLONBY. He should persistently compromise
us in public, and treat us with absolute respect
when we are alone. And yet he should always
be ready to have a perfectly terrible scene,
whenever we want one, and to become miserable, absolutely miserable, at a moment's notice,
and to overwhelm us with reproaches in less
than twenty minutes, and to be positively violent at the end of half an hour, and to leave us

for ever at a quarter to eight, when we have to go and dress for dinner. And when, after that, one has seen him for really the last time, and he has refused to take back the little things he has given one, and promised never to communicate with one again, or to write one any foolish letters, he should be perfectly broken-hearted, and telegraph to one all day long, and send one little notes every half-hour by a private hansom, and dine quite alone at the club, so that every one should know how unhappy he was. And after a whole dreadful week, during which one has gone about everywhere with one's husband, just to show how absolutely lonely one was, he may be given a third last parting, in the evening, and then, if his conduct has been quite irreproachable, and one has behaved really badly to him, he should be allowed to admit that he has been entirely in the wrong, and when he has admitted that, it becomes a woman's duty to forgive, and one can do it all over again from the beginning, with variations.

LADY HUNSTANTON. How clever you are, my dear! You never mean a single word you say.

LADY STUTFIELD. Thank you, thank you. It has been quite, quite entrancing. I must try and remember it all. There are such a number of details that are so very, very important.

LADY CAROLINE. But you have not told us yet what the reward of the Ideal Man is to be.

MRS. ALLONBY. His reward? Oh, infinite expectation. That is quite enough for him.

LADY STUTFIELD. But men are so terribly, terribly exacting, are they not?

MRS. ALLONBY. That makes no matter. One should never surrender.

LADY STUTFIELD. Not even to the Ideal Man?

MRS. ALLONBY. Certainly not to him. Unless, of course, one wants to grow tired of him.

LADY STUTFIELD. Oh! . . . Yes. I see that. It is very, very helpful. Do you think, Mrs. Allonby, I shall ever meet the Ideal Man? Or are there more than one?

MRS. ALLONBY. There are just four in London, Lady Stutfield.

LADY HUNSTANTON. Oh, my dear!

MRS. ALLONBY (*going over to her*). What has happened? Do tell me.

LADY HUNSTANTON (*in a low voice*). I had completely forgotten that the American young lady has been in the room all the time. I am afraid some of this clever talk may have shocked her a little.

MRS. ALLONBY. Ah, that will do her so much good!

LADY HUNSTANTON. Let us hope she didn't understand much. I think I had better go over and talk to her. (*Rises and goes across to* HESTER WORS-LEY.) Well, dear Miss Worsley. (*Sitting down beside her.*) How quiet you have been in your nice little corner all this time! I suppose you have been reading a book? There are so many books here in the library.

HESTER. No, I have been listening to the conversation.

LADY HUNSTANTON. You mustn't believe everything that was said, you know, dear.

HESTER. I didn't believe any of it.

LADY HUNSTANTON. That is quite right, dear.

HESTER (*continuing*). I couldn't believe that any women could really hold such views of life as I have heard to-night from some of your guests. (*An awkward pause.*)

LADY HUNSTANTON. I hear you have such pleasant society in America. Quite like our own in places, my son wrote to me.

HESTER. There are cliques in America as elsewhere, Lady Hunstanton. But true American society consists simply of all the good women and good men we have in our country.

LADY HUNSTANTON. What a sensible system, and I dare say quite pleasant, too. I am afraid in England we have too many artificial social barriers. We don't see as much as we should of the middle and lower classes.

HESTER. In America we have no lower classes.

LADY HUNSTANTON. Really? What a very strange arrangement!

MRS. ALLONBY. What is that dreadful girl talking about?

LADY STUTFIELD. She is painfully natural, is she not?

LADY CAROLINE. There are a great many things you haven't got in America, I am told, Miss Worsley. They say you have no ruins, and no curiosities.

MRS. ALLONBY (*to* LADY STUTFIELD). What nonsense! They have their mothers and their manners.

HESTER. The English aristocracy supply us with our

curiosities, Lady Caroline. They are sent over to us every summer, regularly, in the steamers, and propose to us the day after they land. As for ruins, we are trying to build up something that will last longer than brick or stone. (*Gets up to take her fan from table.*)

LADY HUNSTANTON. What is that, dear? Ah, yes, an iron Exhibition, is it not, at that place that has the curious name?

HESTER (*standing by table*). We are trying to build up life, Lady Hunstanton, on a better, truer, purer basis than life rests on here. This sounds strange to you all, no doubt. How could it sound other than strange? You rich people in England, you don't know how you are living. How could you know? You shut out from your society the gentle and the good. You laugh at the simple and the pure. Living, as you all do, on others and by them, you sneer at self-sacrifice, and if you throw bread to the poor, it is merely to keep them quiet for a season. With all your pomp and wealth and art you don't know how to live—you don't even know that. You love the beauty that you can see and touch and handle, the beauty that you can destroy, and do destroy, but of the unseen beauty of life, of the unseen beauty of a higher life you know nothing. You have lost life's secret. Oh, your English society seems to me shallow, selfish, foolish. It has blinded its eyes, and stopped its ears. It lies like a leper in purple. It sits like a dead thing smeared with gold. It is all wrong, all wrong.

LADY STUTFIELD. I don't think one should know of these things. It is not very, very nice, is it?

LADY HUNSTANTON. My dear Miss Worsley, I thought you liked English society so much. You were such a success in it. And you were so much admired by the best people. I quite forget what Lord Henry Weston said of you—but it was most complimentary, and you know what an authority he is on beauty.

HESTER. Lord Henry Weston! I remember him, Lady Hunstanton. A man with a hideous smile and a hideous past. He is asked everywhere. No dinner-party is complete without him. What of those whose ruin is due to him? They are outcasts. They are nameless. If you met them in the street you would turn your head away. I don't complain of their punishment. Let all women who have sinned be punished.

MRS. ARBUTHNOT *enters from terrace behind in a cloak with a lace veil over her head. She hears the last words and starts.*

LADY HUNSTANTON. My dear young lady!

HESTER. It is right that they should be punished, but don't let them be the only ones to suffer. If a man and woman have sinned, let them both go forth into the desert to love or loathe each other there. Let them both be branded. Set a mark, if you wish, on each, but don't punish the one and let the other go free. Don't have one law for men and another for women. You are unjust to women in England. And till you count what is a shame in a woman to be infamy in a man, you will always be unjust, and Right, that pillar of fire, and Wrong, that pillar of cloud, will be made dim to your eyes, or be not seen at all, or if seen, not regarded.

LADY CAROLINE. Might I, dear Miss Worsley, as you are standing up, ask you for my cotton that is just behind you? Thank you.

LADY HUNSTANTON. My dear Mrs. Arbuthnot! I am so pleased you have come up. But I didn't hear you announced.

MRS. ARBUTHNOT. Oh I came straight in from the terrace, Lady Hunstanton, just as I was. You didn't tell me you had a party.

LADY HUNSTANTON. Not a party. Only a few guests who are staying in the house, and whom you must know. Allow me. (*Tries to help her. Rings bell.*) Caroline, this is Mrs. Arbuthnot, one of my sweetest friends. Lady Caroline Pontefract, Lady Stutfield, Mrs. Allonby, and my young American friend, Miss Worsley, who has just been telling us all how wicked we are.

HESTER. I am afraid you think I spoke too strongly, Lady Hunstanton. But there are some things in England—

LADY HUNSTANTON. My dear young lady, there was a great deal of truth, I dare say, in what you said, and you looked very pretty while you said it, which is much more important, Lord Illingworth would tell us. The only point where I thought you were a little hard was about Lady

Caroline's brother, about poor Lord Henry. He is really such good company.

Enter FOOTMAN.

Take Mrs. Arbuthnot's things.

Exit FOOTMAN *with wraps.*

HESTER. Lady Caroline, I had no idea it was your brother. I am sorry for the pain I must have caused you—I—

LADY CAROLINE. My dear Miss Worsley, the only part of your little speech, if I may so term it, with which I thoroughly agreed, was the part about my brother. Nothing that you could possibly say could be too bad for him. I regard Henry as infamous, absolutely infamous. But I am bound to state, as you were remarking, Jane, that he is excellent company, and he has one of the best cooks in London, and after a good dinner one can forgive anybody, even one's own relations.

LADY HUNSTANTON (*to* MISS WORSLEY). Now, do come, dear, and make friends with Mrs. Arbuthnot. She is one of the good, sweet, simple people you told us we never admitted into society. I am sorry to say Mrs. Arbuthnot comes very rarely to me. But that is not my fault.

MRS. ALLONBY. What a bore it is the men staying so long after dinner! I expect they are saying the most dreadful things about us.

LADY STUTFIELD. Do you really think so?

MRS. ALLONBY. I am sure of it.

LADY STUTFIELD. How very, very horrid of them! Shall we go on to the terrace?

MRS. ALLONBY. Oh, anything to get away from the dowagers and the dowdies. (*Rises and goes with* LADY STUTFIELD *to door* L.C.) We are only going to look at the stars, Lady Hunstanton.

LADY HUNSTANTON. You will find a great many, dear, a great many. But don't catch cold. (*To* MRS. ARBUTHNOT). We shall all miss Gerald so much, dear Mrs. Arbuthnot.

MRS. ARBUTHNOT. But has Lord Illingworth really offered to make Gerald his secretary?

LADY HUNSTANTON. Oh, yes! He has been most charming about it. He has the highest possible opinion of your boy. You don't know Lord Illingworth, I believe, dear.

MRS. ARBUTHNOT. I have never met him.

LADY HUNSTANTON. You know him by name, no doubt?

MRS. ARBUTHNOT. I am afraid I don't. I live so much out of the world, and see so few people. I remember hearing years ago of an old Lord Illingworth who lived in Yorkshire, I think.

LADY HUNSTANTON. Ah, yes. That would be the last Earl but one. He was a very curious man. He wanted to marry beneath him. Or wouldn't, I believe. There was some scandal about it. The present Lord Illingworth is quite different. He is very distinguished. He does—well, he does nothing, which I am afraid our pretty American visitor here thinks very wrong of anybody, and I don't know that he cares much for the subjects in which you are so interested, dear Mrs. Arbuthnot. Do you think, Caroline, that Lord Illingworth is interested in the Housing of the Poor?

LADY CAROLINE. I should fancy not at all, Jane.

LADY HUNSTANTON. We all have our different tastes, have we not? But Lord Illingworth has a very high position, and there is nothing he couldn't get if he chose to ask for it. Of course, he is comparatively a young man still, and he has only come to his title within—how long exactly is it, Caroline, since Lord Illingworth succeeded?

LADY CAROLINE. About four years, I think, Jane. I know it was the same year in which my brother had his last exposure in the evening newspapers.

LADY HUNSTANTON. Ah, I remember. That would be about four years ago. Of course, there were a great many people between the present Lord Illingworth and the title, Mrs. Arbuthnot. There was—who was there, Caroline?

LADY CAROLINE. There was poor Margaret's baby. You remember how anxious she was to have a boy, and it was a boy, but it died, and her husband died shortly afterwards, and she married almost immediately, one of Lord Ascot's sons, who, I am told, beats her.

LADY HUNSTANTON. Ah, that is in the family, dear, that is in the family. And there was also, I remember, a clergyman who wanted to be a lunatic, or a lunatic who wanted to be a clergyman, I

194

forget which, but I know the Court of Chancery investigated the matter, and decided that he was quite sane. And I saw him afterwards at poor Lord Plumstead's with straws in his hair, or something very odd about him. I can't recall what. I often regret, Lady Caroline, that dear Lady Cecilia never lived to see her son get the title.

MRS. ARBUTHNOT. Lady Cecilia?

LADY HUNSTANTON. Lord Illingworth's mother, dear Mrs. Arbuthnot, was one of the Duchess of Jerningham's pretty daughters, and she married Sir Thomas Harford, who wasn't considered a very good match for her at the time, though he was said to be the handsomest man in London. I knew them all quite intimately, and both the sons, Arthur and George.

MRS. ARBUTHNOT. It was the eldest son who succeeded, of course, Lady Hunstanton?

LADY HUNSTANTON. No, dear, he was killed in the hunting field. Or was it fishing, Caroline? I forget. But George came in for everything. I always tell him that no younger son has ever had good luck as he has had.

MRS. ARBUTHNOT. Lady Hunstanton, I want to speak to Gerald at once. Might I see him? Can he be sent for?

LADY HUNSTANTON. Certainly, dear. I will send one of the servants into the dining-room to fetch him. I don't know what keeps the gentlemen so long. (*Rings bell.*) When I knew Lord Illingworth first as plain George Harford, he was simply a very brilliant young man about town, with not a penny of money except what poor dear Lady Cecilia gave him. She was quite devoted to him. Chiefly, I fancy, because he was on bad terms with his father. Oh, here is the dear Archdeacon. (*To* SERVANT). It doesn't matter.

Enter SIR JOHN *and* DOCTOR DAUBENY. SIR JOHN *goes over to* LADY STUTFIELD, DOCTOR DAUBENY *to* LADY HUNSTANTON.

THE ARCHDEACON. Lord Illingworth has been most entertaining. I have never enjoyed myself more. (*Sees* MRS. ARBUTHNOT.) Ah, Mrs. Arbuthnot.

LADY HUNSTANTON (*to* DOCTOR DAUBENY). You see I have got Mrs. Arbuthnot to come to me at last.

THE ARCHDEACON. That is a great honour, Lady Hunstanton. Mrs. Daubeny will be quite jealous of you.

LADY HUNSTANTON. Ah, I am so sorry Mrs. Daubeny could not come with you to-night. Headache as usual, I suppose.

THE ARCHDEACON. Yes, Lady Hunstanton; a perfect martyr. But she is happiest alone. She is happiest alone.

LADY CAROLINE (*to her husband*). John!

SIR JOHN *goes over to his wife.* DOCTOR DAUBENY *talks to* LADY HUNSTANTON *and* MRS. ARBUTHNOT.

MRS. ARBUTHNOT *watches* LORD ILLINGWORTH *the whole time. He has passed across the room without noticing her, and approaches* MRS. ALLONBY, *who with* LADY STUTFIELD *is standing by the door looking on to the terrace.*

LORD ILLINGWORTH. How is the most charming woman in the world?

MRS. ALLONBY (*taking* LADY STUTFIELD *by the hand*). We are both quite well, thank you, Lord Illingworth. But what a short time you have been in the dining-room! It seems as if we had only just left.

LORD ILLINGWORTH. I was bored to death. Never opened my lips the whole time. Absolutely longing to come in to you.

MRS. ALLONBY. You should have. The American girl has been giving us a lecture.

LORD ILLINGWORTH. Really? All Americans lecture, I believe. I suppose it is something in their climate. What did she lecture about?

MRS. ALLONBY. Oh Puritanism, of course.

LORD ILLINGWORTH. I am going to convert her, am I not? How long do you give me?

MRS. ALLONBY. A week.

LORD ILLINGWORTH. A week is more than enough.

Enter GERALD *and* LORD ALFRED.

GERALD (*going to* MRS. ARBUTHNOT). Dear mother!

MRS. ARBUTHNOT. Gerald, I don't feel at all well. See me home, Gerald. I shouldn't have come.

GERALD. I am so sorry, mother. Certainly. But you

must know Lord Illingworth first. (*Goes across room.*)

MRS. ARBUTHNOT. Not to-night, Gerald.

GERALD. Lord Illingworth, I want you so much to know my mother.

LORD ILLINGWORTH. With the greatest pleasure. (*To* MRS. ALLONBY.) I'll be back in a moment. People's mothers always bore me to death. All women become like their mothers. That is their tragedy.

MRS. ALLONBY. No man does. That is his.

LORD ILLINGWORTH. What a delightful mood you are in to-night! (*Turns round and goes across with* GERALD *to* MRS. ARBUTHNOT. *When he sees her, he starts back in wonder. Then slowly his eyes turn towards* GERALD.)

GERALD. Mother, this is Lord Illingworth, who has offered to take me as his private secretary.

MRS. ARBUTHNOT *bows coldly.*

It is a wonderful opening for me, isn't it? I hope he won't be disappointed in me, that is all. You'll thank Lord Illingworth, mother, won't you?

MRS. ARBUTHNOT. Lord Illingworth is very good, I am sure, to interest himself in you for the moment.

LORD ILLINGWORTH (*putting his hand on* GERALD's *shoulder*). Oh, Gerald and I are great friends already, Mrs. . . . . Arbuthnot.

MRS. ARBUTHNOT. There can be nothing in common between you and my son, Lord Illingworth.

GERALD. Dear mother, how can you say so? Of course, Lord Illingworth is awfully clever and that sort of thing. There is nothing Lord Illingworth doesn't know.

LORD ILLINGWORTH. My dear boy!

GERALD. He knows more about life than any one I have ever met. I feel an awful duffer when I am with you, Lord Illingworth. Of course, I have had so few advantages. I have not been to Eton or Oxford like other chaps. But Lord Illingworth doesn't seem to mind that. He has been awfully good to me, mother.

MRS. ARBUTHNOT. Lord Illingworth may change his mind. He may not really want you as his secretary.

GERALD. Mother!

MRS. ARBUTHNOT. You must remember, as you said yourself, you have had so few advantages.

MRS. ALLONBY. Lord Illingworth, I want to speak to you for a moment. Do come over.

LORD ILLINGWORTH. Will you excuse me, Mrs. Arbuthnot? Now, don't let your charming mother make any more difficulties, Gerald. The thing is quite settled, isn't it?

GERALD. I hope so.

LORD ILLINGWORTH *goes across to* MRS. ALLONBY.

MRS. ALLONBY. I thought you were never going to leave the lady in black velvet.

LORD ILLINGWORTH. She is excessively handsome. (*Looks at* MRS. ARBUTHNOT.)

LADY HUNSTANTON. Caroline, shall we all make a move to the music-room? Miss Worsley is going to play. You'll come too, dear Mrs. Arbuthnot, won't you? You don't know what a treat is in store for you. (*To* DOCTOR DAUBENY.) I must really take Miss Worsley down some afternoon to the rectory. I should so much like dear Mrs. Daubeny to hear her on the violin. Ah, I forgot. Dear Mrs. Daubeny's hearing is a little defective, is it not?

THE ARCHDEACON. Her deafness is a great privation to her. She can't even hear my sermons now. She reads them at home. But she has many resources in herself, many resources.

LADY HUNSTANTON. She reads a good deal, I suppose?

THE ARCHDEACON. Just the very largest print. The eyesight is rapidly going. But she's never morbid, never morbid.

GERALD (*to* LORD ILLINGWORTH). Do speak to my mother, Lord Illingworth, before you go into the music-room. She seems to think, somehow, you don't mean what you said to me.

MRS. ALLONBY. Aren't you coming?

LORD ILLINGWORTH. In a few moments. Lady Hunstanton, if Mrs. Arbuthnot would allow me, I would like to say a few words to her, and we will join you later on.

LADY HUNSTANTON. Ah, of course. You will have a great deal to say to her, and she will have a great deal to thank you for. It is not every son

who gets such an offer, Mrs. Arbuthnot. But I
know you appreciate that, dear.

LADY CAROLINE. John!

LADY HUNSTANTON. Now, don't keep Mrs. Arbuthnot too long, Lord Illingworth. We can't spare
her.

*Exit following the other guests. Sound of violin
heard from music-room.*

LORD ILLINGWORTH. So that is our son, Rachel! Well,
I am very proud of him. He is a Harford, every
inch of him. By the way, why Arbuthnot,
Rachel?

MRS. ARBUTHNOT. One name is as good as another,
when one has no right to any name.

LORD ILLINGWORTH. I suppose so—but why Gerald?

MRS. ARBUTHNOT. After a man whose heart I
broke—after my father.

LORD ILLINGWORTH. Well, Rachel, what is over is
over. All I have got to say now is that I am very,
very much pleased with our boy. The world will
know him merely as my private secretary, but
to me he will be something very near, and very
dear. It is a curious thing, Rachel; my life
seemed to be quite complete. It was not so. It
lacked something, it lacked a son. I have found
my son now. I am glad I have found him.

MRS. ARBUTHNOT. You have no right to claim him,
or the smallest part of him. The boy is entirely
mine, and shall remain mine.

LORD ILLINGWORTH. My dear Rachel, you have had

him to yourself for over twenty years. Why not let me have him for a little now? He is quite as much mine as yours.

MRS. ARBUTHNOT. Are you talking of the child you abandoned? Of the child who, as far as you are concerned, might have died of hunger and of want?

LORD ILLINGWORTH. You forget, Rachel, it was you who left me. It was not I who left you.

MRS. ARBUTHNOT. I left you because you refused to give the child a name. Before my son was born, I implored you to marry me.

LORD ILLINGWORTH. I had no expectations then. And besides, Rachel, I wasn't much older than you were. I was only twenty-two. I was twenty-one, I believe, when the whole thing began in your father's garden.

MRS. ARBUTHNOT. When a man is old enough to do wrong he should be old enough to do right also.

LORD ILLINGWORTH. My dear Rachel, intellectual generalities are always interesting, but generalities in morals mean absolutely nothing. As for saying I left our child to starve, that, of course, is untrue and silly. My mother offered you six hundred a year. But you wouldn't take anything. You simply disappeared, and carried the child away with you.

MRS. ARBUTHNOT. I wouldn't have accepted a penny from her. Your father was different. He told you, in my presence, when we were in Paris, that it was your duty to marry me.

LORD ILLINGWORTH. Oh, duty is what one expects

from others, it is not what one does oneself. Of course, I was influenced by my mother. Every man is when he is young.

MRS. ARBUTHNOT. I am glad to hear you say so. Gerald shall certainly not go away with you.

LORD ILLINGWORTH. What nonsense, Rachel!

MRS. ARBUTHNOT. Do you think I would allow my son—

LORD ILLINGWORTH. Our son.

MRS. ARBUTHNOT. My son—(LORD ILLINGWORTH *shrugs his shoulders.*)—to go away with the man who spoiled my youth, who ruined my life, who has tainted every moment of my days? You don't realise what my past has been in suffering and in shame.

LORD ILLINGWORTH. My dear Rachel, I must candidly say that I think Gerald's future considerably more important than your past.

MRS. ARBUTHNOT. Gerald cannot separate his future from my past.

LORD ILLINGWORTH. That is exactly what he should do. That is exactly what you should help him to do. What a typical woman you are! You talk sentimentally and you are thoroughly selfish the whole time. But don't let us have a scene. Rachel, I want you to look at this matter from the common-sense point of view, from the point of view of what is best for our son, leaving you and me out of the question. What is our son at present? An underpaid clerk in a small Provincial Bank in a third-rate English town. If you imagine he is quite happy in such a position, you are mistaken. He is thoroughly discontented.

MRS. ARBUTHNOT. He was not discontented till he met you. You have made him so.

LORD ILLINGWORTH. Of course I made him so. Discontent is the first step in the progress of a man or a nation. But I did not leave him with a mere longing for things he could not get. No, I made him a charming offer. He jumped at it, I need hardly say. Any young man would. And now, simply because it turns out that I am the boy's own father and he my own son, you propose practically to ruin his career. That is to say, if I were a perfect stranger, you would allow Gerald to go away with me, but as he is my own flesh and blood you won't. How utterly illogical you are!

MRS. ARBUTHNOT. I will not allow him to go.

LORD ILLINGWORTH. How can you prevent it? What excuse can you give to him for making him decline such an offer as mine? I won't tell him in what relations I stand to him, I need hardly say. But you daren't tell him. You know that. Look how you have brought him up.

MRS. ARBUTHNOT. I have brought him up to be a good man.

LORD ILLINGWORTH. Quite so. And what is the result? You have educated him to be your judge if he ever finds you out. And a bitter, an unjust judge he will be to you. Don't be deceived, Rachel. Children begin by loving their parents.

After a time they judge them. Rarely, if ever, do they forgive them.

MRS. ARBUTHNOT. George, don't take my son away from me. I have had twenty years of sorrow, and I have only had one thing to love me, only one thing to love. You have had a life of joy, and pleasure, and success. You have been quite happy, you have never thought of us. There was no reason, according to your views of life, why you should have remembered us at all. Your meeting us was a mere accident, a horrible accident. Forget it. Don't come now, and rob me of—of all I have in the whole world. You are so rich in other things. Leave me the little vineyard of my life; leave me the walled-in garden and the well of water; the ewe-lamb God sent me, in pity or in wrath, oh! leave me that. George, don't take Gerald from me.

LORD ILLINGWORTH. Rachel, at the present moment you are not necessary to Gerald's career; I am. There is nothing more to be said on the subject.

MRS. ARBUTHNOT. I will not let him go.

LORD ILLINGWORTH. Here is Gerald. He has a right to decide for himself.

Enter GERALD.

GERALD. Well, dear mother, I hope you have settled it all with Lord Illingworth?

MRS. ARBUTHNOT. I have not, Gerald.

LORD ILLINGWORTH. Your mother seems not to like your coming with me, for some reason.

GERALD. Why, mother?

MRS. ARBUTHNOT. I thought you were quite happy here with me, Gerald. I didn't know you were so anxious to leave me

GERALD. Mother, how can you talk like that? Of course I have been quite happy with you. But a man can't stay always with his mother. No chap does. I want to make myself a position, to do something. I thought you would have been proud to see me Lord Illingworth's secretary.

MRS. ARBUTHNOT. I do not think you would be suitable as a private secretary to Lord Illingworth. You have no qualifications.

LORD ILLINGWORTH. I don't wish to seem to interfere for a moment, Mrs. Arbuthnot, but as far as your last objection is concerned, I surely am the best judge. And I can only tell you that your son has all the qualifications I had hoped for. He has more, in fact, than I had even thought of. Far more. (MRS. ARBUTHNOT *remains silent*.) Have you any other reason, Mrs. Arbuthnot, why you don't wish your son to accept this post?

GERALD. Have you, mother? Do answer.

LORD ILLINGWORTH. If you have, Mrs. Arbuthnot, pray, pray say it. We are quite by ourselves here. Whatever it is, I need not say I will not repeat it.

GERALD. Mother?

LORD ILLINGWORTH. If you would like to be alone with your son, I will leave you. You may have some other reason you don't wish me to hear.

MRS. ARBUTHNOT. I have no other reason.

LORD ILLINGWORTH. Then, my dear boy, we may look on the thing as settled. Come, you and I will smoke a cigarette on the terrace together. And Mrs. Arbuthnot, pray let me tell you, that I think you have acted very, very wisely.

Exit with GERALD. MRS. ARBUTHNOT *is left alone. She stands immobile with a look of unutterable sorrow on her face.*

Curtain.

Third Act

SCENE

The Picture Gallery at Hunstanton Chase. Door at back leading on to terrace.

LORD ILLINGWORTH *and* GERALD, *R.C.* LORD ILLINGWORTH *lolling on a sofa.* GERALD *in a chair.*

LORD ILLINGWORTH. Thoroughly sensible woman, your mother, Gerald. I knew she would come round in the end.

GERALD. My mother is awfully conscientious, Lord Illingworth, and I know she doesn't think I am educated enough to be your secretary. She is perfectly right, too. I was fearfully idle when I was at school, and I couldn't pass an examination now to save my life.

LORD ILLINGWORTH. My dear Gerald, examinations are of no value whatsoever. If a man is a gentleman, he knows quite enough, and if he is not a gentleman, whatever he knows is bad for him.

GERALD. But I am so ignorant of the world, Lord Illingworth.

LORD ILLINGWORTH. Don't be afraid, Gerald. Remember that you've got on your side the most wonderful thing in the world—youth! There is nothing like youth. The middle-aged are mortgaged to Life. The old are in life's lumber-room. But youth is the Lord of Life. Youth has a kingdom waiting for it. Every one is born a king, and most people die in exile, like most kings. To win back my youth, Gerald, there is nothing I wouldn't do—except take exercise, get up early, or be a useful member of the community.

GERALD. But you don't call yourself old, Lord Illingworth?

LORD ILLINGWORTH. I am old enough to be your father, Gerald.

GERALD. I don't remember my father; he died years ago.

LORD ILLINGWORTH. So Lady Hunstanton told me.

GERALD. It is very curious, my mother never talks to me about my father. I sometimes think she must have married beneath her.

LORD ILLINGWORTH (*winces slightly*). Really? (*Goes over and puts his hand on* GERALD's *shoulder*.) You have missed not having a father, I suppose, Gerald?

GERALD. Oh, no; my mother has been so good to me. No one ever had such a mother as I have had.

LORD ILLINGWORTH. I am quite sure of that. Still I should imagine that most mothers don't quite understand their sons. Don't realise, I mean, that a son has ambitions, a desire to see life, to make himself a name. After all, Gerald, you couldn't be expected to pass all your life in such a hole as Wrockley, could you?

GERALD. Oh, no! It would be dreadful!

LORD ILLINGWORTH. A mother's love is very touching, of course, but it is often curiously selfish. I mean, there is a good deal of selfishness in it.

GERALD (*slowly*). I suppose there is.

LORD ILLINGWORTH. Your mother is a thoroughly good woman. But good women have such limited views of life, their horizon is so small, their interests are so petty, aren't they?

GERALD. They are awfully interested, certainly, in things we don't care much about.

LORD ILLINGWORTH. I suppose your mother is very religious, and that sort of thing.

GERALD. Oh, yes, she's always going to church.

LORD ILLINGWORTH. Ah! she is not modern, and to be modern is the only thing worth being nowadays. You want to be modern, don't you, Gerald? You want to know life as it really is. Not to be put off with any old-fashioned theories about life. Well, what you have to do at present is simply to fit yourself for the best society. A man who can dominate a London dinner-table can dominate the world. The future belongs to the dandy. It is the exquisites who are going to rule.

GERALD. I should like to wear nice things awfully, but I have always been told that a man should not think so much about his clothes.

LORD ILLINGWORTH. People nowadays are so absolutely superficial that they don't understand the

210

philosophy of the superficial. By the way, Gerald, you should learn how to tie your tie better. Sentiment is all very well for the buttonhole. But the essential thing for a necktie is style. A well-tied tie is the first serious step in life.

GERALD (*laughing*). I might be able to learn how to tie a tie, Lord Illingworth, but I should never be able to talk as you do. I don't know how to talk.

LORD ILLINGWORTH. Oh! talk to every woman as if you loved her, and to every man as if he bored you, and at the end of your first season you will have the reputation of possessing the most perfect social tact.

GERALD. But it is very difficult to get into society, isn't it?

LORD ILLINGWORTH. To get into the best society, nowadays, one has either to feed people, amuse people, or shock people—that is all!

GERALD. I suppose society is wonderfully delightful!

LORD ILLINGWORTH. To be in it is merely a bore. But to be out of it simply a tragedy. Society is a necessary thing. No man has any real success in this world unless he has got women to back him, and women rule society. If you have not got women on your side you are quite over. You might just as well be a barrister or a stockbroker, or a journalist at once.

GERALD. It is very difficult to understand women, is it not?

LORD ILLINGWORTH. You should never try to understand them. Women are pictures. Men are problems. If you want to know what a woman really means—which, by the way, is always a dangerous thing to do—look at her, don't listen to her.

GERALD. But women are awfully clever, aren't they?

LORD ILLINGWORTH. One should always tell them so. But, to the philosopher, my dear Gerald, women represent the triumph of matter over mind—just as men represent the triumph of mind over morals.

GERALD. How then can women have so much power as you say they have?

LORD ILLINGWORTH. The history of women is the history of the worst form of tyranny the world has ever known. The tyranny of the weak over the strong. It is the only tyranny that lasts.

GERALD. But haven't women got a refining influence?

LORD ILLINGWORTH. Nothing refines but the intellect.

GERALD. Still, there are many different kinds of women, aren't there?

LORD ILLINGWORTH. Only two kinds in society: the plain and the coloured.

GERALD. But there are good women in society, aren't there?

LORD ILLINGWORTH. Far too many.

GERALD. But do you think women shouldn't be good?

LORD ILLINGWORTH. One should never tell them so, they'd all become good at once. Women are a fascinatingly wilful sex. Every woman is a rebel, and usually in wild revolt against herself.

GERALD. You have never been married, Lord Illingworth, have you?

LORD ILLINGWORTH. Men marry because they are tired; women because they are curious. Both are disappointed.

GERALD. But don't you think one can be happy when one is married?

LORD ILLINGWORTH. Perfectly happy. But the happiness of a married man, my dear Gerald, depends on the people he has not married.

GERALD. But if one is in love?

LORD ILLINGWORTH. One should always be in love. That is the reason one should never marry.

GERALD. Love is a very wonderful thing, isn't it?

LORD ILLINGWORTH. When one is in love one begins by deceiving oneself. And one ends by deceiving others. That is what the world calls a romance. But a really *grand passion* is comparatively rare nowadays. It is the privilege of people who have nothing to do. That is the one use of the idle classes in a country, and the only possible explanation of us Harfords.

GERALD. Harfords, Lord Illingworth?

LORD ILLINGWORTH. That is my family name. You should study the Peerage, Gerald. It is the one book a young man about town should know thoroughly, and it is the best thing in fiction the English have ever done. And now, Gerald, you are going into a perfectly new life with me, and I want you to know how to live.

MRS. ARBUTHNOT *appears on terrace behind.*

For the world has been made by fools that wise men should live in it!

Enter L.C. LADY HUNSTANTON *and* DOCTOR DAUBENY.

LADY HUNSTANTON. Ah! here you are, dear Lord Illingworth. Well, I suppose you have been telling our young friend, Gerald, what his new duties are to be, and giving him a great deal of good advice over a pleasant cigarette.

LORD ILLINGWORTH. I have been giving him the best of advice, Lady Hunstanton, and the best of cigarettes.

LADY HUNSTANTON. I am so sorry I was not here to listen to you, but I suppose I am too old now to learn. Except from you, dear Archdeacon, when you are in your nice pulpit. But then I always know what you are going to say, so I don't feel alarmed. (*Sees* MRS. ARBUTHNOT.) Ah! dear Mrs. Arbuthnot, do come and join us. Come, dear.

Enter MRS. ARBUTHNOT.

Gerald has been having such a long talk with Lord Illingworth; I am sure you must feel very much flattered at the pleasant way in which everything has turned out for him. Let us sit down. (*They sit down.*) And how is your beautiful embroidery going on?

MRS. ARBUTHNOT. I am always at work, Lady Hunstanton.

LADY HUNSTANTON. Mrs. Daubeny embroiders a little, too, doesn't she?

THE ARCHDEACON. She was very deft with her needle once, quite a Dorcas. But the gout has crippled her fingers a good deal. She has not touched the tambour frame for nine or ten years. But she has many other amusements. She is very much interested in her own health.

LADY HUNSTANTON. Ah! that is always a nice distraction, is it not? Now, what are you talking about, Lord Illingworth? Do tell us.

LORD ILLINGWORTH. I was on the point of explaining to Gerald that the world has always laughed at its own tragedies, that being the only way in which it has been able to bear them. And that, consequently, whatever the world has treated seriously belongs to the comedy side of things.

LADY HUNSTANTON. Now I am quite out of my depth. I usually am when Lord Illingworth says anything. And the Humane Society is most careless. They never rescue me. I am left to sink. I have a dim idea, dear Lord Illingworth, that you are always on the side of the sinners, and I know I always try to be on the side of the saints, but that is as far as I get. And after all, it may be merely the fancy of a drowning person.

LORD ILLINGWORTH. The only difference between

the saint and the sinner is that every saint has a past, and every sinner has a future.

LADY HUNSTANTON. Ah! that quite does for me. I haven't a word to say. You and I, dear Mrs. Arbuthnot, are behind the age. We can't follow Lord Illingworth. Too much care was taken with our education, I am afraid. To have been well brought up is a great drawback nowadays. It shuts one out from so much.

MRS. ARBUTHNOT. I should be sorry to follow Lord Illingworth in any of his opinions.

LADY HUNSTANTON. You are quite right, dear.

GERALD *shrugs his shoulders and looks irritably over at his mother. Enter* LADY CAROLINE.

LADY CAROLINE. Jane, have you seen John any-where?

LADY HUNSTANTON. You needn't be anxious about him, dear. He is with Lady Stutfield; I saw them some time ago, in the Yellow Drawing-room. They seem quite happy together. You are not going, Caroline? Pray sit down.

LADY CAROLINE. I think I had better look after John.

Exit LADY CAROLINE.

LADY HUNSTANTON. It doesn't do to pay men so much attention. And Caroline has really nothing to be anxious about. Lady Stutfield is very sympathetic. She is just as sympathetic about one thing as she is about another. A beautiful nature.

Enter SIR JOHN *and* MRS. ALLONBY.

Ah! here is Sir John! And with Mrs. Allonby too! I suppose it was Mrs. Allonby I saw him with. Sir John, Caroline has been looking everywhere for you.

MRS. ALLONBY. We have been waiting for her in the Music-room, dear Lady Hunstanton.

LADY HUNSTANTON. Ah! the Music-room, of course. I thought it was the Yellow Drawing-room, my memory is getting so defective. (*To the* ARCHDEACON.) Mrs. Daubeny has a wonderful memory, hasn't she?

THE ARCHDEACON. She used to be quite remarkable for her memory, but since her last attack she recalls chiefly the events of her early childhood. But she finds great pleasure in such retrospections, great pleasure.

Enter LADY STUTFIELD *and* MR. KELVIL.

LADY HUNSTANTON. Ah! dear Lady Stutfield! and what has Mr. Kelvil been talking to you about?

LADY STUTFIELD. About Bimetallism, as well as I remember.

LADY HUNSTANTON. Bimetallism! Is that quite a nice subject? However, I know people discuss everything very freely nowadays. What did Sir John talk to you about, dear Mrs. Allonby?

MRS. ALLONBY. About Patagonia.

LADY HUNSTANTON. Really? What a remote topic! But very improving, I have no doubt.

MRS. ALLONBY. He has been most interesting on the subject of Patagonia. Savages seem to have quite the same views as cultured people on almost all subjects. They are excessively advanced.

LADY HUNSTANTON. What do they do?

MRS. ALLONBY. Apparently everything.

LADY HUNSTANTON. Well, it is very gratifying, dear Archdeacon, is it not, to find that Human Nature is permanently one. —On the whole, the world is the same world, is it not?

LORD ILLINGWORTH. The world is simply divided into two classes—those who believe the incredible, like the public—and those who do the improbable—

MRS. ALLONBY. Like yourself?

LORD ILLINGWORTH. Yes; I am always astonishing myself. It is the only thing that makes life worth living.

LADY STUTFIELD. And what have you been doing lately that astonishes you?

LORD ILLINGWORTH. I have been discovering all kinds of beautiful qualities in my own nature.

MRS. ALLONBY. Ah! don't become quite perfect all at once. Do it gradually!

LORD ILLINGWORTH. I don't intend to grow perfect at all. At least, I hope I shan't. It would be most inconvenient. Women love us for our defects. If we have enough of them, they will forgive us for our defects. If we have enough of them, they will forgive us everything, even our gigantic intellects.

MRS. ALLONBY. It is premature to ask us to forgive analysis. We forgive adoration; that is quite as much as should be expected from us.

Enter LORD ALFRED. *He joins* LADY STUTFIELD.

LADY HUNSTANTON. Ah! we women should forgive everything, shouldn't we, dear Mrs. Arbuthnot? I am sure you agree with me in that.

MRS. ARBUTHNOT. I do not, Lady Hunstanton. I think there are many things women should never forgive.

LADY HUNSTANTON. What sort of things?

MRS. ARBUTHNOT. The ruin of another woman's life. (*Moves slowly away to back of stage.*)

LADY HUNSTANTON. Ah! those things are very sad, no doubt, but I believe there are admirable homes where people of that kind are looked after and reformed, and I think on the whole that the secret of life is to take things very, very easily.

MRS. ALLONBY. The secret of life is never to have an emotion that is unbecoming.

LADY STUTFIELD. The secret of life is to appreciate the pleasure of being terribly, terribly deceived.

KELVIL. The secret of life is to resist temptation, Lady Stutfield.

LORD ILLINGWORTH. There is no secret of life. Life's aim, if it has one, is simply to be always looking for temptations. There are not nearly enough. I sometimes pass a whole day without coming across a single one. It is quite dreadful. It makes one so nervous about the future.

LADY HUNSTANTON (*shakes her fan at him*). I don't know how it is, Lord Illingworth, but everything you have said today seems to me excessively immoral. It has been most interesting, listening to you.

LORD ILLINGWORTH. All thought is immoral. Its very essence is destruction. If you think of anything, you kill it. Nothing survives being thought of.

LADY HUNSTANTON. I don't understand a word, Lord Illingworth. But I have no doubt it is all quite true. Personally, I have very little to reproach myself with, on the score of thinking. I don't believe in women thinking too much. Women should think in moderation, as they should do all things in moderation.

LORD ILLINGWORTH. Moderation is a fatal thing, Lady Hunstanton. Nothing succeeds like excess.

LADY HUNSTANTON. I hope I shall remember that. It sounds an admirable maxim. But I'm beginning to forget everything. It's a great misfortune.

LORD ILLINGWORTH. It is one of your most fascinating qualities, Lady Hunstanton. No woman should have a memory. Memory in a woman is the beginning of dowdiness. One can always tell from a woman's bonnet whether she has got a memory or not.

LADY HUNSTANTON. How charming you are, dear Lord Illingworth. You always find out that one's

most glaring fault is one's important virtue. You
have the most comforting view of life.

Enter FARQUHAR.

FARQUHAR. Doctor Daubeny's carriage!

LADY HUNSTANTON. My dear Archdeacon! It is only
half-past ten.

THE ARCHDEACON (*rising*). I am afraid I must go,
Lady Hunstanton. Tuesday is always one of
Mrs. Daubeny's bad nights.

LADY HUNSTANTON (*rising*). Well, I won't keep you
from her. (*Goes with him towards door.*) I have
told Farquhar to put a brace of partridge into
the carriage. Mrs. Daubeny may fancy them.

THE ARCHDEACON. It is very kind of you, but Mrs.
Daubeny never touches solids now. Lives entirely on jellies. But she is wonderfully cheerful,
wonderfully cheerful. She has nothing to complain of.

Exit with LADY HUNSTANTON.

MRS. ALLONBY (*goes over to* LORD ILLINGWORTH).
There is a beautiful moon to-night.

LORD ILLINGWORTH. Let us go and look at it. To
look at anything that is inconstant is charming
nowadays.

MRS. ALLONBY. You have your looking-glass.

LORD ILLINGWORTH. It is unkind. It merely shows
me my wrinkles.

MRS. ALLONBY. Mine is better behaved. It never tells me the truth.

LORD ILLINGWORTH. Then it is in love with you.

Exeunt SIR JOHN, LADY STUTFIELD, MR. KELVIL *and* LORD ALFRED.

GERALD (*to* LORD ILLINGWORTH). May I come too?

LORD ILLINGWORTH. Do, my dear boy. (*Moves towards door with* MRS. ALLONBY *and* GERALD.)

LADY CAROLINE *enters, looks rapidly round and goes out in opposite direction to that taken by* SIR JOHN *and* LADY STUTFIELD.

MRS. ARBUTHNOT. Gerald!

GERALD. What, mother?

Exit LORD ILLINGWORTH *with* MRS. ALLONBY.

MRS. ARBUTHNOT. It is getting late. Let us go home.

GERALD. My dear mother. Do let us wait a little longer. Lord Illingworth is so delightful, and, by the way, mother, I have a great surprise for you. We are starting for India at the end of this month.

MRS. ARBUTHNOT. Let us go home.

GERALD. If you really want to, of course, mother, but I must bid good-bye to Lord Illingworth first. I'll be back in five minutes. (*Exit.*)

MRS. ARBUTHNOT. Let him leave me if he chooses,

but not with him—not with him! I couldn't bear it. (*Walks up and down.*)

Enter HESTER.

HESTER. What a lovely night it is, Mrs. Arbuthnot.

MRS. ARBUTHNOT. Is it?

HESTER. Mrs. Arbuthnot, I wish you would let us be friends. You are so different from the other women here. When you came into the Drawing-room this evening, somehow you brought with you a sense of what is good and pure in life. I had been foolish. There are things that are right to say, but that may be said at the wrong time and to the wrong people.

MRS. ARBUTHNOT. I heard what you said. I agree with it, Miss Worsley.

HESTER. I didn't know you had heard it. But I knew you would agree with me. A woman who has sinned should be punished, shouldn't she?

MRS. ARBUTHNOT. Yes.

HESTER. She shouldn't be allowed to come into the society of good men and women?

MRS. ARBUTHNOT. She should not.

HESTER. And the man should be punished in the same way?

MRS. ARBUTHNOT. In the same way. And the children, if there are children, in the same way also?

HESTER. Yes, it is right that the sins of the parents should be visited on the children. It is a just law. It is God's law.

MRS. ARBUTHNOT. It is one of God's terrible laws. (*Moves away to fireplace.*)

HESTER. You are distressed about your son leaving you, Mrs. Arbuthnot?

MRS. ARBUTHNOT. Yes.

HESTER. Do you like him going away with Lord Illingworth? Of course there is position, no doubt, and money, but position and money are not everything, are they?

MRS. ARBUTHNOT. They are nothing; they bring misery.

HESTER. Then why do you let your son go with him?

MRS. ARBUTHNOT. He wishes it himself.

HESTER. But if you asked him he would stay, would he not?

MRS. ARBUTHNOT. He has set his heart on going.

HESTER. He couldn't refuse you anything. He loves you too much. Ask him to stay. Let me send him to you. He is on the terrace at this moment with Lord Illingworth. I heard them laughing together as I passed through the Music-room.

MRS. ARBUTHNOT. Don't trouble, Miss Worsley, I can wait. It is of no consequence.

HESTER. No, I'll tell him you want him. Do—do ask him to stay.

Exit HESTER.

MRS. ARBUTHNOT. He won't come—I know he won't come.

Enter LADY CAROLINE. *She looks round anxiously.*
Enter GERALD.

LADY CAROLINE. Mr. Arbuthnot, may I ask you is Sir John anywhere on the terrace?

GERALD. No, Lady Caroline, he is not on the terrace.

LADY CAROLINE. It is very curious. It is time for him to retire.

Exit LADY CAROLINE.

GERALD. Dear mother, I am afraid I kept you waiting. I forgot all about it. I am so happy to-night, mother; I have never been so happy.

MRS. ARBUTHNOT. At the prospect of going away?

GERALD. Don't put it like that, mother. Of course I am sorry to leave you. Why, you are the best mother in the whole world. But after all, as Lord Illingworth says, it is impossible to live in such a place as Wrockley. You don't mind it. But I'm ambitious; I want something more than that. I want to have a career. I want to do something that will make you proud of me, and Lord Illingworth is going to help me. He is going to do everything for me.

MRS. ARBUTHNOT. Gerald, don't go away with Lord Illingworth. I implore you not to. Gerald I beg you!

GERALD. Mother, how changeable you are! You don't seem to know your own mind for a single moment. An hour and a half ago in the Drawing-room you agreed to the whole thing; now you turn round and make objections, and try to force me to give up my one chance in life. Yes, my one chance. You don't suppose that men like Lord Illingworth are to be found every day, do you, mother? It is very strange that when I have had such a wonderful piece of good luck, the one person to put difficulties in my way should be my own mother. Besides, you know, mother, I love Hester Worsley. Who could help loving her? I love her more than I ever have told you, far more. And if I had a position, if I had prospects, I could—I could ask her to. . . . Don't you understand now, mother, what it means to me to be Lord Illingworth's secretary? To start like that is to find a career ready for one—before one—waiting for one. If I were Lord Illingworth's secretary I could ask Hester to be my wife. As a wretched bank clerk with a hundred a year it would be an impertinence.

MRS. ARBUTHNOT. I fear you need have no hopes of Miss Worsley. I know her views on life. She has just told them to me. (*A pause.*)

GERALD. Then I have my ambition left, at any rate. That is something—I am glad I have that! You have always tried to crush my ambition, mother—haven't you? You have told me that the world is a wicked place, that success is not worth having, that society is shallow, and all that sort of thing—well, I don't believe it, mother. I think the world must be delightful. I think society must be exquisite. I think success is a thing worth having. You have been wrong in all that you taught me, mother, quite wrong. Lord Illingworth is a successful man. He is a fashionable man. He is a man who lives in the world and for it. Well, I would give anything to be just like Lord Illingworth.

MRS. ARBUTHNOT. I would sooner see you dead.

GERALD. Mother, what is your objection to Lord Illingworth? Tell me—tell me right out. What is it?

MRS. ARBUTHNOT. He is a bad man.

GERALD. In what way bad? I don't understand what you mean.

MRS. ARBUTHNOT. I will tell you.

GERALD. I suppose you think him bad, because he doesn't believe the same things as you do. Well, men are different from women, mother. It is natural that they should have different views.

MRS. ARBUTHNOT. It is not what Lord Illingworth believes, or what he does not believe, that makes him bad. It is what he is.

GERALD. Mother, is it something you know of him? Something you actually know?

MRS. ARBUTHNOT. It is something I know.

GERALD. Something you are quite sure of?

MRS. ARBUTHNOT. Quite sure of.

GERALD. How long have you known it?

MRS. ARBUTHNOT. For twenty years.

GERALD. Is it fair to go back twenty years in any man's career? And what have you or I to do with Lord Illingworth's early life? What business is it of ours?

MRS. ARBUTHNOT. What this man has been, he is now, and will be always.

GERALD. Mother, tell me what Lord Illingworth

did? If he did anything shameful, I will not go away with him. Surely you know me well enough for that?

MRS. ARBUTHNOT. Gerald, come near to me. Quite close to me, as you used to do when you were a little boy, when you were mother's own boy.

GERALD *sits down beside his mother. She runs her fingers through his hair, and strokes his hands.*

Gerald, there was a girl once, she was very young, she was little over eighteen at the time. George Harford—that was Lord Illingworth's name then—George Harford met her. She knew nothing about life. He—knew everything. He made this girl love him. He made her love so much that she left her father's house with him one morning. She loved him so much, and he had promised to marry her! He had solemnly promised to marry her, and she had believed him. She was very young—and ignorant of what life really is. But he put the marriage off from week to week, and month to month. —She trusted in him all the while. She loved him. —Before her child was born—for she had a child—she implored him for the child's sake to marry her, that the child might have a name, that her sin might not be visited on the child, who was innocent. He refused. After the child was born she left him, taking the child away, and her life was ruined, and her soul ruined, and all that was sweet and good and pure in her ruined also. She suffered terribly—she suffers now. She will always suffer. For her there is no joy, no peace, no atonement. She is a woman who drags a chain like a guilty thing. She is a woman who wears a mask, like a thing that is a leper. The fire cannot purify her. The waters cannot quench her anguish. Nothing can heal her! no anodyne can give her sleep! no poppies forgetfulness! She is lost! She is a lost soul! That is why I call Lord Illingworth a bad man. That is why I don't want my boy to be with him.

GERALD. My dear mother, it all sounds very tragic, of course. But I dare say the girl was just as much to blame as Lord Illingworth was. —After all, would a really nice girl, a girl with any nice feelings at all, go away from her home with a man to whom she was not married, and live with him as his wife? No nice girl would.

MRS. ARBUTHNOT (*after a pause*). Gerald, I withdraw all my objections. You are at liberty to go away with Lord Illingworth, when and where you choose.

GERALD. Dear mother, I knew you wouldn't stand in my way. You are the best woman God ever made. And, as for Lord Illingworth, I don't believe he is capable of anything infamous or base. I can't believe it of him—I can't.

HESTER (*outside*). Let me go! Let me go!

Enter HESTER *in terror, and rushes over to* GERALD *and flings herself in his arms.*

HESTER. Oh! save me—save me from him!

GERALD. From whom?

HESTER. He has insulted me! Horribly insulted me! Save me!

GERALD. Who? Who has dared—?

LORD ILLINGWORTH *enters at back of stage.* HESTER *breaks from* GERALD's *arms and points to him.*

GERALD (*quite beside himself with rage and indignation*). Lord Illingworth, you have insulted the purest thing on God's earth, a thing as pure as my own mother. You have insulted the woman I love most in the world with my own mother. As there is a God in Heaven, I will kill you!

MRS. ARBUTHNOT (*rushing across and catching hold of him*). No! no!

GERALD (*thrusting her back*). Don't hold me, mother. Don't hold me—I'll kill him!

MRS. ARBUTHNOT. Gerald!

GERALD. Let me go, I say!

MRS. ARBUTHNOT. Stop, Gerald, stop! He is your own father!

GERALD *clutches his mother's hands and looks into her face. She sinks slowly on the ground in shame.* HESTER *steals towards the door.* LORD ILLINGWORTH *frowns and bites his lip. After a time* GERALD *raises his mother up, puts his arm round her, and leads her from the room.*

Curtain.

Fourth Act

SCENE

Sitting-room at Mrs. Arbuthnot's house at Wrockley. Large open French window at back, looking on to garden. Doors R.C. and L.C.

GERALD ARBUTHNOT *writing at table.*

Enter ALICE R.C. *followed by* LADY HUNSTANTON *and* MRS. ALLONBY.

ALICE. Lady Hunstanton and Mrs. Allonby. (*Exit L.C.*)

LADY HUNSTANTON. Good-morning, Gerald.

GERALD (*rising*). Good-morning, Lady Hunstanton. Good-morning, Mrs. Allonby.

LADY HUNSTANTON (*sitting down*). We came to inquire for your dear mother, Gerald. I hope she is better?

GERALD. My mother has not come down yet, Lady Hunstanton.

LADY HUNSTANTON. Ah, I am afraid the heat was too much for her last night. I think there must have been thunder in the air. Or perhaps it was

the music. Music makes one feel so romantic—
at least it always gets on one's nerves.

MRS. ALLONBY. It's the same thing, nowadays.

LADY HUNSTANTON. I am so glad I don't know what
you mean, dear. I am afraid you mean something wrong. Ah, I see you're examining Mrs.
Arbuthnot's pretty room. Isn't it nice and old-
fashioned?

MRS. ALLONBY (*surveying the room through her lorgnette*). It looks quite the happy English home.

LADY HUNSTANTON. That's just the word, dear; that
just describes it. One feels your mother's good
influence in everything she has about her,
Gerald.

MRS. ALLONBY. Lord Illingworth says that all influence is bad, but that a good influence is the
worst in the world.

LADY HUNSTANTON. When Lord Illingworth knows
Mrs. Arbuthnot better he will change his mind.
I must certainly bring him here.

MRS. ALLONBY. I should like to see Lord Illingworth
in a happy English home.

LADY HUNSTANTON. It would do him a great deal of
good, dear. Most women in London, nowadays,
seem to furnish their rooms with nothing but
orchids, foreigners, and French novels. But here
we have the room of a sweet saint. Fresh natural
flowers, books that don't shock one, pictures
that one can look at without blushing.

MRS. ALLONBY. But I like blushing.

LADY HUNSTANTON. Well, there is a good deal to be
said for blushing, if one can do it at the proper

moment. Poor dear Hunstanton used to tell me I didn't blush nearly often enough. But then he was so very particular. He wouldn't let me know any of his men friends, except those who were over seventy, like poor Lord Ashton; who afterwards, by the way, was brought into the Divorce Court. A most unfortunate case.

MRS. ALLONBY. I delight in men over seventy. They always offer one the devotion of a lifetime. I think seventy an ideal age for a man.

LADY HUNSTANTON. She is quite incorrigible, Gerald, isn't she? By-the-by, Gerald, I hope your dear mother will come and see me more often now. You and Lord Illingworth start almost immediately, don't you?

GERALD. I have given up my intention of being Lord Illingworth's secretary.

LADY HUNSTANTON. Surely not, Gerald! It would be most unwise of you. What reason can you have?

GERALD. I don't think I should be suitable for the post.

MRS. ALLONBY. I wish Lord Illingworth would ask me to be his secretary. But he says I am not serious enough.

LADY HUNSTANTON. My dear, you really mustn't talk like that in this house. Mrs. Arbuthnot doesn't know anything about the wicked society in which we all live. She won't go into it. She is far too good. I consider it was a great honour her coming to me last night. It gave quite an atmosphere of respectability to the party.

MRS. ALLONBY. Ah, that must have been what you thought was thunder in the air.

LADY HUNSTANTON. My dear, how can you say that? There is no resemblance between the two things at all. But really, Gerald, what do you mean by not being suitable?

GERALD. Lord Illingworth's views of life and mine are too different.

LADY HUNSTANTON. But, my dear Gerald, at your age you shouldn't have any views of life. They are quite out of place. You must be guided by others in this matter. Lord Illingworth has made you the most flattering offer, and travelling with him you would see the world—as much of it, at least, as one should look at—under the best auspices possible, and stay with all the right people, which is so important at this solemn moment in your career.

GERALD. I don't want to see the world; I've seen enough of it.

MRS. ALLONBY. I hope you don't think you have exhausted life, Mr. Arbuthnot. When a man says that, one knows that life has exhausted him.

GERALD. I don't wish to leave my mother.

LADY HUNSTANTON. Now, Gerald, that is pure laziness on your part. Not leave your mother! If I were your mother I would insist on your going.

Enter ALICE *L.C.*

ALICE. Mrs. Arbuthnot's compliments, my lady, but she has a bad headache, and cannot see any one this morning. (*Exit R.C.*)

LADY HUNSTANTON (*rising*). A bad headache! I am so sorry! Perhaps you'll bring her up to Hunstanton this afternoon, if she is better, Gerald.

GERALD. I am afraid not this afternoon, Lady Hunstanton.

LADY HUNSTANTON. Well, to-morrow, then. Ah, if you had a father, Gerald, he wouldn't let you waste your life here. He would send you with Lord Illingworth at once. But mothers are so weak. They give up to their sons in everything. We are all heart, all heart. Come, dear, I must call at the rectory and inquire for Mrs. Daubeny, who, I am afraid, is far from well. It is wonderful how the Archdeacon bears up, quite wonderful. He is the most sympathetic of husbands. Quite a model. Good-bye, Gerald; give my fondest love to your mother.

MRS. ALLONBY. Good-bye, Mr. Arbuthnot.

GERALD. Good-bye.

Exit LADY HUNSTANTON *and* MRS. ALLONBY. GERALD *sits down and reads over his letter.*

GERALD. What name can I sign? I, who have no right to any name. (*Signs name, puts letter into envelope, addresses it, and is about to seal it, when door L.C. opens and* MRS. ARBUTHNOT *enters.* GERALD *lays down sealing-wax. Mother and son look at each other.*)

LADY HUNSTANTON (*through French window at the back*). Good-bye again, Gerald. We are taking the short cut across your pretty garden. Now, remember my advice to you—start at once with Lord Illingworth.

MRS. ALLONBY. *Au revoir*, Mr. Arbuthnot. Mind you bring me back something nice from your travels—not an Indian shawl—on no account an Indian shawl. (*Exeunt.*)

GERALD. Mother, I have just written to him.

MRS. ARBUTHNOT. To whom?

GERALD. To my father. I have written to tell him to come here at four o'clock this afternoon.

MRS. ARBUTHNOT. He shall not come here. He shall not cross the threshold of my house.

GERALD. He must come.

MRS. ARBUTHNOT. Gerald, if you are going away with Lord Illingworth, go at once. Go before it kills me; but don't ask me to meet him.

GERALD. Mother, you don't understand. Nothing in the world would induce me to go away with Lord Illingworth, or to leave you. Surely you know me well enough for that. No; I have written to him to say—

MRS. ARBUTHNOT. What can you have to say to him?

GERALD. Can't you guess, mother, what I have written in this letter?

MRS. ARBUTHNOT. No.

GERALD. Mother, surely you can. Think, think what must be done, now, at once, within the next few days.

MRS. ARBUTHNOT. There is nothing to be done.

GERALD. I have written to Lord Illingworth to tell him that he must marry you.

MRS. ARBUTHNOT. Marry me?

GERALD. Mother, I will force him to do it. The wrong that has been done you must be repaired. Atonement must be made. Justice may be slow, mother, but it comes in the end. In a few days you shall be Lord Illingworth's lawful wife.

MRS. ARBUTHNOT. But, Gerald—

GERALD. I will insist upon his doing it. I will make him do it; he will not dare to refuse.

MRS. ARBUTHNOT. But, Gerald, it is I who refuse. I will not marry Lord Illingworth.

GERALD. Not marry him? Mother!

MRS. ARBUTHNOT. I will not marry him.

GERALD. But you don't understand: it is for your sake I am talking, not for mine. This marriage, this necessary marriage, this marriage which for obvious reasons must inevitably take place, will not help me, will not give me a name that will be really, rightly mine to bear. But surely it will be something for you, that you, my mother, should, however late, become the wife of the man who is my father. Will not that be something?

MRS. ARBUTHNOT. I will not marry him.

GERALD. Mother, you must.

MRS. ARBUTHNOT. I will not. You talk of atonement for a wrong done. What atonement can be made to me? There is no atonement possible. I am disgraced; he is not. That is all. It is the usual history of a man and a woman as it usually happens, as it always happens. And the ending

237

is the ordinary ending. The woman suffers. The man goes free.

GERALD. I don't know if that is the ordinary ending, mother; I hope it is not. But your life, at any rate, shall not end like that. The man shall make whatever reparation is possible. It is not enough. It does not wipe out the past, I know that. But at least it makes the future better, better for you, mother.

MRS. ARBUTHNOT. I refuse to marry Lord Illingworth.

GERALD. If he came to you himself and asked you to be his wife you would give him a different answer. Remember, he is my father.

MRS. ARBUTHNOT. If he came himself, which he will not do, my answer would be the same. Remember, I am your mother.

GERALD. Mother, you make it terribly difficult for me by talking like that; and I can't understand why you won't look at this matter from the right, from the only proper standpoint. It is to take away the bitterness out of your life, to take away the shadow that lies on your name, that this marriage must take place. There is no alternative; and after the marriage you and I can go away together. But the marriage must take place first. It is a duty that you owe, not merely to yourself, but to all other women—yes; to all the other women in the world, lest he betray more.

MRS. ARBUTHNOT. I owe nothing to other women. There is not one of them to help me. There is not one woman in the world to whom I could go for pity, if I would take it, or for sympathy, if I could win it. Women are hard on each other. That girl, last night, good though she is, fled from the room as though I were a tainted thing. She was right. I am a tainted thing. But my wrongs are my own, and I will bear them alone. I must bear them alone. What have women who have not sinned to do with me, or I with them? We do not understand each other.

Enter HESTER *behind.*

GERALD. I implore you to do what I ask you.

MRS. ARBUTHNOT. What son has ever asked of his mother to make so hideous a sacrifice? None.

GERALD. What mother has ever refused to marry the father of her own child? None.

MRS. ARBUTHNOT. Let me be the first, then. I will not do it.

GERALD. Mother, you believe in religion, and you brought me up to believe in it also. Well, surely your religion, the religion that you taught me when I was a boy, mother, must tell you that I am right. You know it, you feel it.

MRS. ARBUTHNOT. I do not know it. I do not feel it, nor will I ever stand before God's altar and ask God's blessing on so hideous a mockery as a marriage between me and George Harford. I will not say the words the Church bids us to say. I will not say them. I dare not. How could I swear to love the man I loathe, to honour him who wrought you dishonour, to obey him who,

239

in his mastery, made me to sin? No; marriage is a sacrament for those who love each other. It is not for such as him, or such as me. Gerald, to save you from the world's sneers and taunts I have lied to the world. For twenty years I have lied to the world. I could not tell the world the truth. Who can ever? But not for my own sake will I lie to God, and in God's presence. No, Gerald, no ceremony, church-hallowed or State-made, shall ever bind me to George Harford. It may be that I am too bound to him already, who, robbing me, yet left me richer, so that in the mire of my life I found the pearl of price, or what I thought would be so.

GERALD. I don't understand you now.

MRS. ARBUTHNOT. Men don't understand what mothers are. I am no different from other women except in the wrong done me and the wrong I did, and my very heavy punishments and great disgrace. And yet, to bear you I had to look on death. To nurture you I had to wrestle with it. Death fought with me for you. All women have to fight with death to keep their children. Death, being childless, wants our children from us. Gerald, when you were naked I clothed you, when you were hungry I gave you food. Night and day all that long winter I tended you. No office is too mean, no care too lowly for the thing we women love—and oh! how *I* loved *you*. Not Hannah, Samuel more. And you needed love, for you were weakly, and only love could have kept you alive. Only love can keep any one alive. And boys are careless often, and without thinking give pain, and we always fancy that when they come to man's estate and know us better they will repay us. But it is not so. The world draws them from our side, and they make friends with whom they are happier than they are with us, and have amusements from which we are barred, and interests that are not ours; and they are unjust to us often, for when they find life bitter they blame us for it, and when they find it sweet we do not taste its sweetness with them. . . . You made many friends and went into their houses and were glad with them, and I, knowing my secret, did not dare to follow, but stayed at home and closed the door, shut out the sun and sat in darkness. My past was ever with me. . . . And you thought I didn't care for the pleasant things of life. I tell you I longed for them, but did not dare to touch them, feeling I had no right. You thought I was happier working amongst the poor. That was my mission, you imagined. It was not, but where else was I to go? The sick do not ask if the hand that smooths their pillow is pure, nor the dying care if the lips that touch their brow have known the kiss of sin. It was you I thought of all the time; I gave to them the love you did not need; lavished on them a love that was not theirs. . . . And you thought I spent too much of my time in going to Church, and in Church duties. But where else could I turn? God's house is the only house where sinners are made welcome, and you were always in my heart, Gerald, too much in my heart. For, though day after day, at morn or evensong, I have knelt in God's house, I have never repented of my sin. How could I repent of my sin when you, my love, were its fruit. Even now that you are bitter to me I cannot repent. I do not. You are more to me than innocence. I would rather be your mother—oh! much rather!—than have been always pure. . . . Oh, don't you see? don't you understand! It is my dishonour that has made you so dear to me. It is my disgrace that has bound you so closely to me. It is the price I paid for you—the price of soul and body—that makes me love you as I do. Oh, don't ask me to do this horrible thing. Child of my shame, be still the child of my shame!

GERALD. Mother, I didn't know you loved me so much as that. And I will be a better son to you than I have been. And you and I must never leave each other . . . but, mother . . . I can't help it . . . you must become my father's wife. You must marry him. It is your duty.

HESTER (*running forward and embracing* MRS. ARBUTH-NOT). No, no; you shall not. That would be real dishonour, the first you have ever known. That would be real disgrace: the first to touch you. Leave him and come with me. There are other countries than England. . . . Oh! other countries over sea, better, wiser, and less unjust lands. The world is very wide and very big.

MRS. ARBUTHNOT. No, not for me. For me the world is shrivelled to a palm's breadth, and where I walk there are thorns.

HESTER. It shall not be so. We shall somewhere find green valleys and fresh waters, and if we weep, well, we shall weep together. Have we not both loved him?

GERALD. Hester!

HESTER (*waving him back*). Don't, don't! You cannot love me at all unless you love her also. You cannot honour me, unless she's holier to you. In her all womanhood is martyred. Not she alone, but all of us are stricken in her house.

GERALD. Hester, Hester, what shall I do?

HESTER. Do you respect the man who is your father?

GERALD. Respect him? I despise him! He is infamous.

HESTER. I thank you for saving me from him last night.

GERALD. Ah, that is nothing. I would die to save you. But you don't tell me what to do now!

HESTER. Have I not thanked you for saving *me*?

GERALD. But what should I do?

HESTER. Ask your own heart, not mine. I never had a mother to save, or shame.

MRS. ARBUTHNOT. He is hard—he is hard. Let me go away.

GERALD (*rushes over and kneels down beside his mother*). Mother, forgive me; I have been to blame.

243

MRS. ARBUTHNOT. Don't kiss my hands; they are cold. My heart is cold: something has broken it.

HESTER. Ah, don't say that. Hearts live by being wounded. Pleasure may turn a heart to stone, riches may make it callous, but sorrow—oh, sorrow, cannot break it. Besides, what sorrows have you now? Why, at this moment you are more dear to him than ever, *dear* though you have *been*, and oh! how dear you *have* been always. Ah! be kind to him.

GERALD. You are my mother and my father all in one. I need no second parent. It was for you I spoke, for you alone. Oh, say something, mother. Have I but found one love to lose another? Don't tell me that. Oh, mother, you are cruel. (*Gets up and flings himself sobbing on a sofa.*)

MRS. ARBUTHNOT (*to* HESTER). But has he found indeed another love?

HESTER. You know I have loved him always.

MRS. ARBUTHNOT. But we are very poor.

HESTER. Who, being loved, is poor? Oh, no one. I hate my riches. They are a burden. Let him share it with me.

MRS. ARBUTHNOT. But we are disgraced. We rank among the outcasts. Gerald is nameless. The sins of the parents should be visited on the children. It is God's law.

HESTER. I was wrong. God's law is only Love.

MRS. ARBUTHNOT (*rises, and taking* HESTER *by the hand, goes slowly over to where* GERALD *is lying on the sofa with his head buried in his hands. She touches him and he looks up*). Gerald, I cannot give you a father, but I have brought you a wife.

GERALD. Mother, I am not worthy either of her or you.

MRS. ARBUTHNOT. So she comes first, you are worthy. And when you are away, Gerald . . . with . . . her—oh, think of me sometimes. Don't forget me. And when you pray, pray for me. We should pray when we are happiest, and you will be happy, Gerald.

HESTER. Oh, you don't think of leaving us?

GERALD. Mother, you won't leave us?

MRS. ARBUTHNOT. I might bring shame upon you!

GERALD. Mother!

MRS. ARBUTHNOT. For a little then; and if you let me, near you always.

HESTER (*to* MRS. ARBUTHNOT). Come out with us to the garden.

MRS. ARBUTHNOT. Later on, later on.

Exeunt HESTER *and* GERALD.

MRS. ARBUTHNOT *goes towards door L.C. Stops at looking-glass over mantelpiece and looks into it. Enter* ALICE R.C.

ALICE. A gentleman to see you, ma'am.

MRS. ARBUTHNOT. Say I am not at home. Show me the card. (*Takes card from salver and looks at it.*) Say I will not see him.

LORD ILLINGWORTH *enters.* MRS. ARBUTHNOT *sees*

*him in the glass and starts, but does not turn round.
Exit* ALICE.

What can you have to say to me to-day, George
Harford? You can have nothing to say to me.
You must leave this house.

LORD ILLINGWORTH. Rachel, Gerald knows everything about you and me now, so some arrangement must be come to that will suit us all three.
I assure you, he will find in me the most charming and generous of fathers.

MRS. ARBUTHNOT. My son may come in at any moment. I saved you last night. I may not be able
to save you again. My son feels my dishonour
strongly, terribly strongly. I beg you to go.

LORD ILLINGWORTH (*sitting down*). Last night was
excessively unfortunate. That silly Puritan girl
making a scene merely because I wanted to kiss
her. What harm is there in a kiss?

MRS. ARBUTHNOT (*turning round*). A kiss may ruin
a human life, George Harford. *I* know that. *I*
know that too well.

LORD ILLINGWORTH. We won't discuss that at present. What is of importance to-day, as yesterday,
is still our son. I am extremely fond of him, as
you know, and odd though it may seem to you,
I admired his conduct last night immensely. He
took up the cudgels for that pretty prude with
wonderful promptitude. He is just what I
should have liked a son of mine to be. Except
that no son of mine should ever take the side

of the Puritans; that is always an error. Now, what I propose is this.

MRS. ARBUTHNOT. Lord Illingworth, no proposition of yours interests me.

LORD ILLINGWORTH. According to our ridiculous English laws, I can't legitimise Gerald. But I can leave him my property. Illingworth is entailed, of course, but it is a tedious barrack of a place. He can have Ashby, which is much prettier, Harborough, which has the best shooting in the north of England, and the house in St. James's Square. What more can a gentleman desire in this world?

MRS. ARBUTHNOT. Nothing more, I am quite sure.

LORD ILLINGWORTH. As for a title, a title is really rather a nuisance in these democratic days. As George Harford I had everything I wanted. Now I have merely everything that other people want, which isn't nearly so pleasant. Well, my proposal is this.

MRS. ARBUTHNOT. I told you I was not interested, and I beg you to go.

LORD ILLINGWORTH. The boy is to be with you for six months in the year, and with me for the other six. That is perfectly fair, is it not? You can have whatever allowance you like, and live where you choose. As for your past, no one knows anything about it except myself and Gerald. There is the Puritan, of course, the Puritan in white muslin, but she doesn't count. She couldn't tell the story without explaining that she objected to being kissed, could she? And all the women would think her a fool and the men think her a bore. And you need not be afraid that Gerald won't be my heir. I needn't tell you I have not the slightest intention of marrying.

MRS. ARBUTHNOT. You come too late. My son has no need of you. You are not necessary.

LORD ILLINGWORTH. What do you mean, Rachel?

MRS. ARBUTHNOT. That you are not necessary to Gerald's career. He does not require you.

LORD ILLINGWORTH. I do not understand you.

MRS. ARBUTHNOT. Look into the garden. (LORD ILLINGWORTH *rises and goes towards window.*) You had better not let them see you; you bring unpleasant memories. (LORD ILLINGWORTH *looks out and starts.*) She loves him. They love each other. We are safe from you, and we are going away.

LORD ILLINGWORTH. Where?

MRS. ARBUTHNOT. We will not tell you, and if you find us we will not know you. You seem surprised. What welcome would you get from the girl whose lips you tried to soil, from the boy whose life you have shamed, from the mother whose dishonour comes from you?

LORD ILLINGWORTH. You have grown hard, Rachel.

MRS. ARBUTHNOT. I was too weak once. It is well for me that I have changed.

LORD ILLINGWORTH. I was very young at the time. We men know life too early.

MRS. ARBUTHNOT. And we women know life too late. That is the difference between men and women. (*A pause.*)

LORD ILLINGWORTH. Rachel, I want my son. My

money may be of no use to him now. I may be of no use to him, but I want my son. Bring us together, Rachel. You can do it if you choose. (*Sees letter on table.*)

MRS. ARBUTHNOT. There is no room in my boy's life for *you*. He is not interested in *you*.

LORD ILLINGWORTH. Then why does he write to me?

MRS. ARBUTHNOT. What do you mean?

LORD ILLINGWORTH. What letter is this? (*Takes up letter.*)

MRS. ARBUTHNOT. That—is nothing. Give it to me.

LORD ILLINGWORTH. It is addressed to *me*.

MRS. ARBUTHNOT. You are not to open it. I forbid you to open it.

LORD ILLINGWORTH. And in Gerald's handwriting.

MRS. ARBUTHNOT. It was not to have been sent. It is a letter he wrote to you this morning, before he saw me. But he is sorry now he wrote it, very sorry. You are not to open it. Give it to me.

LORD ILLINGWORTH. It belongs to me. (*Opens it, sits down and reads it slowly.* MRS. ARBUTHNOT *watches him all the time.*) You have read this letter, I suppose, Rachel?

MRS. ARBUTHNOT. No.

LORD ILLINGWORTH. You know what is in it?

MRS. ARBUTHNOT. Yes!

LORD ILLINGWORTH. I don't admit for a moment that the boy is right in what he says. I don't admit that it is any duty of mine to marry you. I deny it entirely. But to get my son back I am ready— yes, I am ready to marry you, Rachel—and to treat you always with the deference and respect due to my wife. I will marry you as soon as you choose. I give you my word of honour.

MRS. ARBUTHNOT. You made that promise to me once before and broke it.

LORD ILLINGWORTH. I will keep it now. And that will show you that I love my son, at least as much as you love him. For when I marry you, Rachel, there are some ambitions I shall have to surrender. High ambitions, too, if any ambition is high.

MRS. ARBUTHNOT. I decline to marry you, Lord Illingworth.

LORD ILLINGWORTH. Are you serious?

MRS. ARBUTHNOT. Yes.

LORD ILLINGWORTH. Do tell me your reasons. They would interest me enormously.

MRS. ARBUTHNOT. I have already explained them to my son.

LORD ILLINGWORTH. I suppose they were intensely sentimental, weren't they? You women live by your emotions and for them. You have no philosophy of life.

MRS. ARBUTHNOT. You are right. We women live by our emotions and for them. By our passions, and for them, if you will. I have two passions, Lord Illingworth: my love of him, my hate of you. You cannot kill those. They feed each other.

LORD ILLINGWORTH. What sort of love is that which needs to have hate as its brother?

MRS. ARBUTHNOT. It is the sort of love I have for Gerald. Do you think that terrible? Well, it is terrible. All love is terrible. All love is a tragedy. I loved you once, Lord Illingworth. Oh, what a tragedy for a woman to have loved you!

LORD ILLINGWORTH. So you really refuse to marry me?

MRS. ARBUTHNOT. Yes.

LORD ILLINGWORTH. Because you hate me?

MRS. ARBUTHNOT. Yes.

LORD ILLINGWORTH. And does my son hate me as you do?

MRS. ARBUTHNOT. No.

LORD ILLINGWORTH. I am glad of that, Rachel.

MRS. ARBUTHNOT. He merely despises you.

LORD ILLINGWORTH. What a pity! What a pity for him, I mean.

MRS. ARBUTHNOT. Don't be deceived, George. Children begin by loving their parents. After a time they judge them. Rarely if ever do they forgive them.

LORD ILLINGWORTH (*reads letter over again, very slowly*). May I ask by what arguments you made the boy who wrote this letter, this beautiful, passionate letter, believe that you should not marry his father, the father of your own child!

MRS. ARBUTHNOT. It was not I who made him see it. It was another.

LORD ILLINGWORTH. What *fin-de-siècle* person?

MRS. ARBUTHNOT. The Puritan, Lord Illingworth. (*A pause.*)

LORD ILLINGWORTH (*winces, then rises slowly and goes over to table where his hat and gloves are.* MRS. ARBUTHNOT *is standing close to the table. He picks up*

251

one of the gloves, and begins putting it on). There is not much then for me to do here, Rachel?

MRS. ARBUTHNOT. Nothing.

LORD ILLINGWORTH. It is good-bye, is it?

MRS. ARBUTHNOT. For ever, I hope, this time, Lord Illingworth.

LORD ILLINGWORTH. How curious! At this moment you look exactly as you looked the night you left me twenty years ago. You have just the same expression in your mouth. Upon my word, Rachel, no woman ever loved me as you did. Why, you gave yourself to me like a flower, to do anything I liked with. You were the prettiest of playthings, the most fascinating of small romances. . . . (*Pulls out watch.*) Quarter to two! Must be strolling back to Hunstanton. Don't suppose I shall see you there again. I'm sorry, I am, really. It's been an amusing experience to have met amongst people of one's own rank, and treated quite seriously too, one's mistress and one's—

MRS. ARBUTHNOT *snatches up glove and strikes* LORD ILLINGWORTH *across the face with it.* LORD ILLINGWORTH *starts. He is dazed by the insult of his punishment. Then he controls himself and goes to window and looks out at his son. Sighs and leaves the room.*

MRS. ARBUTHNOT (*falls sobbing on the sofa*). He would have said it. He would have said it.

Enter GERALD *and* HESTER *from the garden.*

GERALD. Well, dear mother. You never came out after all. So we have come in to fetch you. Mother, you have not been crying? (*Kneels down beside her.*)

MRS. ARBUTHNOT. My boy! My boy! My boy! (*Running her fingers through his hair.*)

HESTER (*coming over*). But you have two children now. You'll let me be your daughter?

MRS. ARBUTHNOT (*looking up*). Would you choose me for a mother?

HESTER. You of all women I have ever known.

They move towards the door leading into garden with their arms round each other's waists. GERALD *goes to table L.C. for his hat. On turning round he sees* LORD ILLINGWORTH'S *glove lying on the floor, and picks it up.*

GERALD. Hallo, mother, whose glove is this? You have had a visitor. Who was it?

MRS. ARBUTHNOT (*turning round*). Oh! no one. No one in particular. A man of no importance.

Curtain.

An Ideal Husband at the Haymarket Theatre: A Talk with Mr. Oscar Wilde

BY GILBERT BURGESS

On the morning following the production of An Ideal Husband, *I met Oscar Wilde as he came down the steps of a club at the top of St. James's Street and I took advantage of the occasion to ask him what he thought of the attitude of the critics towards his play.*

"Well," *he replied as he walked slowly down the street,* "for a man to be a dramatic critic is as foolish and as inartistic as it would be for a man to be a critic of epics or a pastoral critic, or a critic of lyrics. All modes of art are one, and the modes of the art that employs words as its medium are quite indivisible. The result of the vulgar specialization of criticism is an elaborate scientific knowledge of the stage—almost as elaborate as that of the stage-carpenter and quite on a par with that of the call-boy—combined with an entire incapacity to realize that a play is a work of art, or to receive any artistic impressions at all."

From *The Sketch* (London), January 9, 1895

"You are rather severe upon dramatic criticism, Mr. Wilde."

"English dramatic criticism of our own day has never had a single success, in spite of the fact that it goes to all the first nights."

"But," I suggested, *"it is influential."*

"Certainly, that is why it is so bad."

"I don't think I quite—"

"The moment criticism exercises any influence, it ceases to be criticism. The aim of the true critic is to try and chronicle his own moods, not to try and correct the masterpieces of others."

"Real critics would be charming in your eyes, then?"

"Real critics? Ah! how perfectly charming they would be. I am always waiting for their arrival. An inaudible school would be nice. Why do you not found it?"

I was momentarily dazed at the broad vista that had been opened for me, but I retained my presence of mind, and asked:

"Are there absolutely no real critics in London?"

"There are just two."

"Who are they?" I asked eagerly.

Mr. Wilde, with the elaborate courtesy for which he has always been famous, replied, "I think I had better not mention their names; it might make the others so jealous."

"What do the literary cliques think of your plays?"

"I don't write to please cliques; I write to please myself. Besides, I have always had grave suspicions that the basis of all literary cliques is a morbid love of meat-teas. That makes them sadly uncivilized."

"Still, if your critics offend you, why don't you reply to them?"

"I have far too much time. But I think some day I will give a general answer in the form of a lecture in a public hall which I shall call *Straight Talks to Old Men*."

"What is your feeling towards your audiences—towards the public?"

"Which public? There are as many publics as there are personalities."

"Are you nervous on the night that you are producing a new play?"

"Oh, no; I am exquisitely indifferent. My nervousness ends at the last dress rehearsal; I know then what effect my play, as presented upon the stage, has produced upon me. My interest in the play ends there, and I feel curiously envious of the public— they have such wonderful fresh emotions in store for them."

I laughed, but Mr. Wilde rebuked me with a look of surprise.

"It is the public, not the play, that I desire to make a success."

"But I'm afraid I don't quite understand—"

"The public makes a success when it realizes that a play is a work of art. On the three first nights I have had in London, the public has been most successful, and, had the dimensions of the stage admitted of it, I would have called them before the curtain. Most managers, I believe, call them behind."

"I imagine, then, that you don't hold with the opinion that the public is the patron of the dramatist?"

"The artist is always the munificent patron of the public. I am very fond of the public, and, personally, I always patronize the public very much."

"What are your views upon the much vexed question of subject matter in art?"

"Everything matters in art except the subject."

When I recovered, I said, "Several plays have been written lately that deal with the monstrous injustice of the social code of morality at the present time."

"Oh," *answered Mr. Wilde with an air of earnest conviction,* "it is indeed a burning shame that there should be one law for men and another law for women. I think—" *he hesitated, and a smile as swift as Sterne's "hectic of a moment" flitted across his face*—"I think that there should be no law for anybody."

"In writing, do you think that real life or real people should ever give one inspiration?"

"The colour of a flower may suggest to one the plot of a tragedy; a passage in music may give one the sestet of a sonnet; but whatever actually occurs gives the artist no suggestion.

"Every romance that one has in one's life is a romance lost to one's art. To introduce real people into a novel or a play is a sign of an unimaginative mind, a coarse, untutored observation and an entire absence of style."

"I am afraid I can't agree with you, Mr. Wilde; I frequently see types and people who suggest ideas to me."

"Everything is of use to the artist except an idea."

After that I was silent, until Mr. Wilde pointed to the bottom of the street and drew my attention to the "apricot-coloured palace" which we were approaching. So I continued my questioning.

"The enemy has said that your plays lack action."

"Yes, English critics always confuse the action of a play with the incidents of a melodrama. I wrote the first act of *A Woman of No Importance* in answer to the critics who said that *Lady Windermere's Fan* lacked action. In the act in question, there was absolutely no action at all. It was a perfect act."

"What do you think is the chief point that critics have missed in your new play?"

"Its entire psychology—the difference in the way in which a man loves a woman from that in which a woman loves a man; the passion that women have for making ideals (which is their weakness) and the weakness of a man who dares not show his imperfections to the thing he loves. The end of Act I, and the end of Act II, and the scene in the last act, when Lord Goring points out the higher importance of a man's life over a woman's—to take three prominent instances—seem to have been missed by most of the critics. They failed to see their meaning; they really thought it was a play about a bracelet. We must educate our critics—we must really educate them," *said Mr. Wilde half to himself.*

"The critics subordinate the psychological interest of a play to its mere technique. As soon as a dramatist invents an ingenious situation, they compare him with Sardou, but Sardou is an artist not because of his marvellous instinct of stagecraft, but in spite of it. In the third act of *La Tosca*, the scene of torture, he moved us by a terrible human tragedy, not by his knowledge of stage methods. Sardou is not understood in England because he is only known through a rather ordinary travesty of his play *Dora*, which was brought out here under the title of *Diplomacy*. I have been considerably amused by so many of the critics suggesting that the incident of the diamond bracelet in Act III of my new play was suggested by Sardou. It does not occur in any of Sardou's plays, and it was not in my play until less than ten days before production. Nobody else's work gives me any suggestion. It is only by entire isolation from everything that one can do any work. Idleness gives one the mood in which to write, isolation the conditions. Concentration on one's self recalls the new and wonderful world that one presents in the colour and cadence of words in movement."

"And yet we want something more than literature in a play," said I.

"That is merely because the critics have always propounded the degrading dogma that the duty of the dramatist is to please the public. Rossetti did not weave words into sonnets to please the public, and

Corot did not paint silver and grey twilights to please the public. The mere fact of telling an artist to adopt any particular form of art in order to please the public makes him shun it. We shall never have a real drama in England until it is recognized that a play is as personal and individual a form of self-expression as a poem or a picture."

"I'm afraid you don't like journalists?" I remarked nervously.

"The journalist is always reminding the public of the existence of the artist. That is unnecessary of him. He is always reminding the artist of the existence of the public. That is indecent of him."

"But we must have journalists, Mr. Wilde."

"Why? They only record what happens. What does it matter what happens? It is only the abiding things that are interesting, not the horrid incidents of everyday life. Creation for the joy of creation is the aim of the artist, and that is why the artist is a more divine type than the saint. The artist arrives at his moment with his own mood. He may come with terrible purple tragedies; he may come with dainty rose-coloured comedies—what a charming title!" *added Mr. Wilde with a smile.* "I must write a play and call it *A Rose-Coloured Comedy.*"

"What are the exact relations between literature and the drama?"

"Exquisitely accidental. That is why I think them so necessary."

"And the exact relations between the actor and the dramatist?"

Mr. Wilde looked at me with a serious expression which changed almost immediately into a smile, as he replied, "Usually a little strained."

"But surely you regard the actor as a creative artist?"

"Yes," replied Mr. Wilde with a touch of pathos in his voice, "terribly creative—terribly creative!"

"Do you consider that the future outlook of the English stage is hopeful?"

"I think it must be. The critics have ceased to prophesy. That is something. It is in silence that the artist arrives. What is waited for never succeeds; what is heralded is hopeless."

We were nearing the sentries at Marlborough House, and I said: "Won't you tell me a little more, please? Let us walk down Pall Mall—exercise is such a good thing."

"Exercise!" he ejaculated with an emphasis which almost warrants italics. "The only possible form of exercise is to talk, not walk."

And as he spoke, he motioned to a passing hansom. We shook hands, and Mr. Wilde, giving me a glance of approval, said: "I am sure that you must have a great future in literature before you."

"What makes you think so?" I asked as I flushed with pleasure at the prediction.

"Because you seem to be such a very bad interviewer. I feel sure that you must write poetry. I certainly like the colour of your necktie very much. Good-bye."

Mr. Oscar Wilde on
Mr. Oscar Wilde

I found Mr. Oscar Wilde (writes a Representative) making ready to depart on a short visit to Algiers, and reading—of course, nothing so obvious as a time-table, but a French newspaper which contained an account of the first night of the *Ideal Husband* and its author's appearance after the play.

"How well the French appreciate these brilliant wilful moments in an artist's life," remarked Mr. Wilde, handing me the article as if he considered the interview already at an end.

"Does it give you any pleasure," I inquired, "to appear before the curtain after the production of your plays?"

"None whatsoever. No artist finds any interest in seeing the public. The public is very much interested in seeing an artist. Personally, I prefer the French custom, according to which the name of the dramatist is announced to the public by the oldest actor in the piece."

"Would you advocate," I asked, "this custom in England?"

From *St. James's Gazette* (London), January 18, 1895

"Certainly. The more the public is interested in artists, the less it is interested in art. The personality of the artist is not a thing the public should know anything about. It is too accidental." Then, after a pause—"It might be more interesting if the name of the author were announced by the *youngest* actor present."

"It is only in deference, then, to the imperious mandate of the public that you have appeared before the curtain?"

"Yes; I have always been very good-natured about that. The public has always been so appreciative of my work I felt it would be a pity to spoil its evening."

"I notice some people have found fault with the character of your speeches."

"Yes, the old-fashioned idea was that the dramatist should appear and merely thank his kind friends for their patronage and presence. I am glad to say I have altered all that. The artist cannot be degraded into the servant of the public. While I have always recognized the cultured appreciation that actors and audience have shown for my work, I have equally recognized that humility is for the hypocrite, modesty for the incompetent. Assertion is at once the duty and privilege of the artist."

"To what do you attribute, Mr. Wilde, the fact that so few men of letters besides yourself have written plays for public presentation?"

"Primarily the existence of an irresponsible censorship. The fact that my 'Salomé' cannot be performed is sufficient to show the folly of such an institution. If painters were obliged to show their pictures to clerks at Somerset House, those who think in form and colour would adopt some other mode of expression. If every novel had to be submitted to a police magistrate, those whose passion is fiction would seek some new mode of realization. No art ever survived censorship; no art ever will."

"And secondly?"

"Secondly to the rumour persistently spread abroad by journalists for the last thirty years, that the duty of the dramatist was to please the public. The aim of art is no more to give pleasure than to give pain. The aim of art is to be art. As I said once before, the work of art is to dominate the spectator— the spectator is not to dominate art."

"You admit no exceptions?"

"Yes. Circuses, where it seems the wishes of the public might be reasonably carried out."

"Do you think," I inquired, "that French dramatic criticism is superior to our own?"

"It would be unfair to confuse French dramatic criticism with English theatrical criticism. The French dramatic critic is always a man of culture and generally a man of letters. In France poets like Gautier have been dramatic critics. In England they are drawn from a less distinguished class. They have neither the same capacities nor the same opportunities. They have all the moral qualities, but none of the artistic qualifications. For the criticism of such a complex mode of art as the drama, the highest culture is necessary. No one can criticise drama who is not capable of receiving impressions from the other arts also."

"You admit they are sincere?"

"Yes; but their sincerity is little more than stereotyped stupidity. The critic of the drama should be versatile as the actor. He should be able to change his mood at will and should catch the colour of the moment."

"At least they are honest?"

"Absolutely. I don't believe there is a single dramatic critic in London who would deliberately set himself to misrepresent the work of any dramatist—unless, of course, he personally disliked the dramatist, or had some play of his own he wished to produce at the same theatre, or had an old friend among the actors, or some natural reasons of that kind. I am speaking, however, of London dramatic critics. In the provinces both audience and critics are cultured. In London it is only the audience who are cultured."

"I fear you do not rate our dramatic critics very highly, Mr. Wilde; but, at all events, they are incorruptible?"

"In a market where there are no bidders."

"Still, their memories stand them in good stead," I pleaded.

"The old talk of having seen Macready: that must be a very painful memory. The middle-aged boast that they can recall *Diplomacy*: hardly a pleasant reminiscence."

"You deny them, then, even a creditable past?"

"They have no past and no future, and are incapable of realizing the colour of the moment that finds them at the play."

"What do you propose should be done?"

"They should be pensioned off, and only allowed to write on politics or theology or bimetallism, or some subject easier than art."

"In fact," I said, carried away by Mr. Wilde's aphorisms, "they should be seen and not heard."

"The old should neither be seen nor heard," said Mr. Wilde, with some emphasis.

"You said the other day there were only two dramatic critics in London. May I ask—"

"They must have been greatly gratified by such an admission from me; but I am bound to say that since last week I have struck one of them from the list."

"Whom have you left in?"

"I think I had better not mention his name. It might make him too conceited. Conceit is the privilege of the creative."

"How would you define ideal dramatic criticism?"

"As far as my work is concerned, unqualified appreciation."

"And whom have you omitted?"

"Mr. William Archer, of the *World*."

"What do you chiefly object to in his article?"

"I object to nothing in the article, but I grieve at everything in it. It is in bad taste in him to write of me by my Christian name, and he need not have stolen his vulgarisms from the *National Observer* in its most impudent and impotent days."

"Mr. Archer asked whether it was agreeable to you to be hailed by your Christian name when the enthusiastic spectators called you before the curtain."

"To be so addressed by enthusiastic spectators is as great a compliment as to be written of by one's Christian name is in a journalist bad manners. Bad manners make a journalist."

"Do you think French actors, like French criticism, superior to our own?"

"The English actors act quite as well; but they act best between the lines. They lack the superb elocution of the French—so clear, so cadenced, and so musical. A long, sustained speech seems to exhaust them. At the Théâtre Français we go to listen; to an English theatre we go to look. There are, of course, exceptions. Mr. George Alexander, Mr. Lewis Waller, Mr. Forbes Robertson, and others I might mention, have superb voices and know how to use them. I wish I could say the same of the critics; but in the case of the literary drama in England there is too much of what is technically known as "business." Yet there is more than one of our English actors who is capable of producing a wonderful dramatic effect by aid of a monosyllable and two cigarettes."

For a moment Mr. Wilde was silent, and then added, "Perhaps, after all, that is acting."

"But are you satisfied with the interpreters of the *Ideal Husband*?"

"I am charmed with all of them. Perhaps they are a little too fascinating. The stage is the refuge of the too fascinating."

"Have you heard it said that all the characters in your play talk as you do?"

"Rumours of that kind have reached me from time to time," said Mr. Wilde, lighting a cigarette, "and I should fancy that some such criticism has been made. The fact is that it is only in the last few years that the dramatic critic has had the opportunity of seeing plays written by any one who has a mastery of style. In the case of a dramatist also an artist it is impossible not to feel that the work of art, to be a work of art, must be dominated by the artist. Every play of Shakespeare is dominated by Shakespeare. Ibsen and Dumas dominate their works. My works are dominated by myself."

"Have you ever been influenced by any of your predecessors?"

"It is enough for me to state definitely, and I hope once for all, that not a single dramatist in this century has ever in the smallest degree influenced me. Only two have interested me."

"And they are?"

"Victor Hugo and Maeterlink."

"Other writers surely have influenced your other works?"

"Setting aside the prose and poetry of Greek and Latin authors, the only writers who have influenced me are Keats, Flaubert, and Walter Pater; and before I came across them I had already gone more than halfway to meet them. Style must be in one's soul before one can recognize it in others."

"And do you consider the *Ideal Husband* the best of your plays?"

A charming smile crossed Mr. Wilde's face.

"Have you forgotten my classical expression—that only mediocrities improve? My three plays are to each other, as a wonderful young poet has beautifully said,

> as one white rose
> On one green stalk to another one.

They form a perfect cycle, and in their delicate sphere complete both life and art."

"Do you think that the critics will understand your new play [*The Importance of Being Earnest*], which Mr. George Alexander has secured?"

"I hope not."

"I dare not ask, I suppose, if it will please the public?"

"When a play that is a work of art is produced on the stage, what is being tested is not the play, but the stage; when a play that is *not* a work of art is produced on the stage, what is being tested is not the play, but the public."

"What sort of play are we to expect?"

"It is exquisitely trivial, a delicate bubble of fancy, and it has its philosophy."

"Its philosophy!"

"That we should treat all the trivial things of life very seriously, and all the serious things of life with sincere and studied triviality."

"You have no leanings towards realism?"

"None whatever. Realism is only a background; it cannot form an artistic motive for a play that is to be a work of art."

"Still, I have heard you congratulated on your pictures of London society."

"If Robert Chiltern, the Ideal Husband, were a common clerk, the humanity of his tragedy would be none the less poignant. I have placed him in the higher ranks of life merely because that is the side of social life with which I am best acquainted. In a play dealing with actualities, to write with ease one must write with knowledge."

"Then you see nothing suggestive of treatment in the tragedies of everyday existence?"

"If a journalist is run over by a four-wheeler in the Strand, an incident I regret to say I have never witnessed, it suggests nothing to me from a dramatic point of view. Perhaps I am wrong; but the artist must have his limitations."

"Well," I said, rising to go, "I have enjoyed myself immensely."

"I was sure you would," said Mr. Wilde. "But tell me how you manage your interviews."

"Oh, Pitman," I said carelessly.

"Is that your name? It's not a very *nice* name."
Then I left.

SELECTED BIBLIOGRAPHY

Works by Oscar Wilde

Ravenna, 1878   Poem
Poems, 1881
Vera, 1883   Play
The Happy Prince and Other Tales, 1888   Fairy Tales
Duchess of Padua, 1891   Play
The House of Pomegranates, 1891   Fairy Tales
Intentions, 1891   Critical Essays
Lord Arthur Savile's Crime and Other Stories, 1891
The Picture of Dorian Gray, 1891   Novel
The Soul of Man Under Socialism, 1891   Essay
Lady Windermere's Fan, 1892   Play
Salome, 1893   Play
A Woman of No Importance, 1893   Play
The Sphinx, 1894   Poem
An Ideal Husband, 1895   Play
The Importance of Being Earnest, 1895   Play
The Ballad of Reading Gaol, 1898   Poem
De Profundis, 1905   Apologia
The Artist as Critic: Critical Writings of Oscar Wilde,
   ed. Richard Ellmann (1970)
The Complete Works of Oscar Wilde. Intro. Vyvyan
   Holland. New York: HarperCollins, 1966; 1989
   rpt.
The Letters of Oscar Wilde, ed. Rupert Hart-Davis.
   New York: Harcourt, Brace & World, 1962.

More Letters of Oscar Wilde, ed. Rupert Hart-Davis. London: John Murray, 1985.

General Works on Oscar Wilde

Beckson, Karl, ed., *Oscar Wilde: The Critical Heritage* (1970).

Ellmann, Richard, *Oscar Wilde* (1987).

Croft-Cooke, Rupert, *Feasting with Panthers* (1967).

Gagnier, Regenia, ed., *Critical Essays on Oscar Wilde* (1991).

Harris, Frank, *Oscar Wilde: His Life and Confessions* (1916; 1959 rpt).

Hyde, H. Montgomery, *The Annotated Oscar* (1982).

————, *Oscar Wilde: A Biography* (1975).

————, *The Trials of Oscar Wilde* (1948; 1962 rev. ed.).

Jullian, Philippe, *Oscar Wilde* (1968).

Lewis, Lloyd, and Henry Justin Smith, *Oscar Wilde Discovers America* (1936).

Mason, Stuart, *Oscar Wilde: Art and Morality* (1912; rpt. 1971).

Mikhail, E. H., *An Annotated Bibliography* (1978).

————, *Oscar Wilde: Interviews and Recollections* (1979).

Page, Norman, *An Oscar Wilde Chronology* (1991).

Pearson, Hesketh, *The Life of Oscar Wilde* (1946).

Schmidgall, Gary, *The Stranger Wilde: Interpreting Oscar* (1994).

Small, Ian, *Oscar Wilde Revalued: An Essay on New Materials and Methods of Research* (1993).

AMERICAN CLASSICS

☐ **THIS SIDE OF PARADISE by F. Scott Fitzgerald.** Considered scandalous (and brilliant) when it was published in 1920, this timeless autobiographical novel of youth and alienation describes the intellecutal, spiritual, and sexual education of young Amory Blaine in the tumultuous America of the early 1900s.
(526104—$5.95)

☐ **BERNICE BOBS HER HAIR and Other Stories by F. Scott Fitzgerald.** Set amid golf courses, country clubs, and big houses where flappers dance at cotillions, the short stories of F. Scott Fitzgerald brilliantly portray the Jazz Age as seen by the "smart set." All the works in this new collection come from his first year as a professional writer.
(526112—$5.95)

☐ **DODSWORTH by Sinclair Lewis.** Fifty-year-old millionaire Sam Dodsworth is off on a tour of Europe with his wife, Fran, a beautiful, but spoiled woman modeled on Sinclair's ex-wife. The result is a devastating, surprisingly contemporary portrait of a marriage falling apart.
(525981—$4.95)

☐ **SHOWBOAT by Edna Ferber.** Now, this new edition brings you Ferber's authentic, breathtaking story—rich, complex, and more entertaining than ever. Provocative when it first appeared and still a tour de force that becomes, in fact, a portrayal of women of astonishing strength, *Show Boat* is wonderful reading—a river journey into the depths and eddies of our heritage and our dreams.
(526007—$5.95)

☐ **PLUNKITT OF TAMMANY HALL A Series of Very Plain Talks on Very Practical Politics by William L. Riordon. With a New Introduction by Peter Quinn.** This classic work offers the unblushing, unvarnished wit and wisdom of one of the most fascinating figures ever to play the American political game and win. George Washington Plunkitt rose from humble beginnings to become ward boss of the Fifteenth Assembly District in New York, a key player in the powerhouse political team of Tammany Hall.
(526201—$5.95)

Prices slightly higher in Canada.

Buy them at your local bookstore or use this convenient coupon for ordering.

PENGUIN USA
P.O. Box 999 — Dept. #17109
Bergenfield, New Jersey 07621

Please send me the books I have checked above.
I am enclosing $_____ (please add $2.00 to cover postage and handling). Send check or money order (no cash or C.O.D.'s) or charge by Mastercard or VISA (with a $15.00 minimum). Prices and numbers are subject to change without notice.

Card #_____ Exp. Date _____
Signature_____
Name_____
Address_____
City _____ State _____ Zip Code _____

For faster service when ordering by credit card call **1-800-253-6476**

Allow a minimum of 4-6 weeks for delivery. This offer is subject to change without notice.